Beyond Bullying

BEYOND BULLYING

Breaking the Cycle of Shame,
Bullying, and Violence

Jonathan Fast

OXFORD
UNIVERSITY PRESS

OXFORD
UNIVERSITY PRESS

Oxford University Press is a department of the University of
Oxford. It furthers the University's objective of excellence in research,
scholarship, and education by publishing worldwide.

Oxford   New York
Auckland   Cape Town   Dar es Salaam   Hong Kong   Karachi
Kuala Lumpur   Madrid   Melbourne   Mexico City   Nairobi
New Delhi   Shanghai   Taipei   Toronto

With offices in
Argentina   Austria   Brazil   Chile   Czech Republic   France   Greece
Guatemala   Hungary   Italy   Japan   Poland   Portugal   Singapore
South Korea   Switzerland   Thailand   Turkey   Ukraine   Vietnam

Oxford is a registered trademark of Oxford University Press
in the UK and certain other countries.

Published in the United States of America by
Oxford University Press
198 Madison Avenue, New York, NY 10016

Library of Congress Cataloging-in-Publication Data
Fast, Jonathan.
Beyond bullying : breaking the cycle of shame, bullying, and violence /
Jonathan Fast.
    pages cm
Includes bibliographical references and index.
ISBN 978–0–19–938364–1 (alk. paper)
1. Shame.   2. Bullying.   3. Bullying—Prevention.   I. Title.
BF575.S45F27 2016
152.4'4—dc23
2015011398

9 8 7 6 5 4 3 2 1
Printed in the United States of America
on acid-free paper

This book is dedicated to my children, Molly Jong-Fast Greenfield, Benjamin Fast, and Daniel Fast, with great love and respect.

CONTENTS

INTRODUCTION

In the 1990s a rash of school rampage shootings changed the landscape of American childhood. While the victims were relatively few, their tragic deaths made the public feel as though school was no longer a safe place. The public demanded immediate action: *Stop the killings! Make schools safe again!* Investigators sifted through the debris searching for characteristics shared by the shooters in the hopes of creating a profile that might help them find the next shooter before he or she did any harm. Some similarities were obvious and unsurprising. Nearly all the shooters were boys, and all were between the ages of 11 and 21. All lived in rural or suburban neighborhoods. All were unpopular. Most of them loved guns and violent video games. But that was where the similarities ended. Some were from dirt-poor homes; others were well-to-do middle-class kids, the children of teachers, lawyers, and engineers. Some were good-looking; others were skinny or chubby, with thick glasses or bangs. Some lied like conmen, but others were socially inept. Some were brilliant, and others had learning disabilities. Some suffered from serious psychiatric problems while others seemed relatively sane. Eventually, from this sea of randomness, one single factor began to overshadow all others:

They had all been bullied.

Suddenly bullying, an activity that had been more or less ignored for centuries, or praised as a way of toughening up the next generation, took the spotlight as a source of personal misery and potential public menace. Further research suggested that the problems created by being bullied did not necessarily vanish after graduation but often foreshadowed lifelong depression, anxiety, and low self-esteem.[1] Nor did the bullies fare well in adulthood. Statistical data showed them committing crimes four or five times as frequently as their non-bullying peers.[2]

Countless books and articles about bullying have appeared in recent years. Despite myriad solutions developed by "experts in the field," bullying has become more common and more vicious. Cyberbullying, the spreading of malicious gossip on Facebook, Twitter, and other social media, has created opportunities for emotional injury undreamed of in ages past.

This book differs from its shelf-mates in that it explores bullying as a problem of shame, shame management, and social status. The first chapter explores the evolutionary importance of shame, how shame shapes culture, why it remains "hidden in plain sight," and how it is managed and mismanaged. I draw on research from a number of sources, including writings in psychology, psychiatry, sociology, and anthropology, to lay the foundation for subsequent chapters. Chapter 2 focuses on bullying in schools. The third chapter explores homophobia, a problem that leads to the bullying of lesbian, gay, bisexual, and transgender students and students with nontraditional gender presentation. The fourth chapter is a case study of a suicide cluster that occurred in Anoka, Minnesota, in 2011 and whether it was actually caused by a school board policy prohibiting the discussion of homosexuality in the classroom, as some members of the liberal media have claimed. Chapters 5 and 6 address the role of shame and scapegoating in domestic violence and racism. Chapter 7 suggests that excessive shame coupled with a lack of healthy shame management strategies are two of the factors that have led to an escalating number of school rampage shootings and other acts of domestic terrorism. In the final chapter, I discuss "restorative practices" as an antidote for bullying and acts of shame/rage that are harmful to the community.

While some authorities consider shame the "master emotion,"[3] its existence is rarely acknowledged. Many people remain unaware of it even when they are experiencing it. It is truly the secret agent of emotions, its presence revealed only at the moment of shaming by a wave of queasiness, a confusion of thoughts, and a rush of blood to the face. If the shaming event is powerful enough, memories of it may haunt the person for years to come, reshaping his or her life for better or worse. The shame may be transformed into shame/rage and lead children and adults to acts of violence that mystify friends and family. Some scholars believe that all criminal violence is fueled by shame.[4]

The centrality of shame in understanding human behavior is a paradigm shift that began some 45 years ago with the work of Helen B. Lewis[5] and has gained many followers since that time, some of them well known to students of psychology and sociology, including John Bradshaw,

June Tangney, Thomas Scheff, James Gilligan, Paul Ekman, and Sylvan Tomkins, among others.

The reader should be aware that this book does not represent the mainstream of psychological thinking about human behavior. Even in the field of psychology, where patients are encouraged to explore their innermost feelings, shame is rarely spoken of. Textbooks are thought to present the current paradigm of a subject at the time when they are published. A popular introductory text in psychology[6] of 768 pages mentions "shame" 6 times, "emotion" 60 times, and "cognitive" (pertaining to thoughts, memories, problem-solving, and other essentially nonemotional mental processes) 90 times. Another introductory text[7] of 640 pages, lists "shame" 5 times, "emotions" 61 times, and "cognitive" 94 times. Obviously the authors of these books present psychology as a field that features thinking over feeling.

People often associate shame with childhood[8] because of accidents that occur during toilet training. They convince themselves that because we master our bowels, we master our shame. The deception appears to be validated because as adults we can avoid many of the shameful situations that plagued us as children. We are no longer prisoners of the classroom, the schoolyard, or the abusive or alcoholic home where we grew up, were it our misfortune to be born under such circumstances. In fact, if we so choose, we can as adults avoid human contact altogether and refuse to leave the house.

We avoid naming shame and retreat from discussing it, as Harry Potter's friends avoid mentioning Voldemort. Instead we are *mortified* or *humiliated, embarrassed* or *crushed*. Teens are *diss'ed* or consider an experience *awkward* or *creepy*. Bullying, a method of shaming, is replaced among grown-ups by labels such as *workplace harassment, domestic violence, racism,* and *assault*. While the labels change, the bullying continues throughout our lives in ways both subtle and overt. We are refused entrance into groups or communities. We are made to feel unworthy of what we have worked for or been given. We are swaddled in advertising that tries to convince us that our pores are too large, our teeth too yellow, our bodies too soft, our homes too small, our children deprived of toys and books that will give them the head start they need to beat out the competition, and so on.

Those whose self-image has been ravaged by shame and who have no healthy way to manage it may turn to crime and violence for self-validation. Crimes are prosecuted without much attention to the shame experienced by the victims or the offender. Prisons dispense more shame and confine the offender alongside experienced criminals, who can provide him or her with graduate training in the fine points of predatory behavior.

In other words, I believe that the lion's share of human misery is the result of shame that is misdirected, unidentified, or unacknowledged. While I cannot in good conscience offer a "cure" for bullying (I strongly believe that there is no such thing), I have tried to provide the reader with a wealth of information about how shame informs bullying, healthy and unhealthy ways of managing shame, the utility of restorative processes in creating civil schools, and the value of restorative justice in repairing the social damage of crime. I would like to think that, with this information, the reader will be better equipped to deal with bullying of every sort and that we will be moved, if only by a single degree, closer toward a destination where all people are equally valued and respected.

Many people helped me find the time and sustain the energy to write this book. Above all, I would like to thank my wife, the Reverend Barbara Fast, for her encouragement, her suggestions, and her patience in listening while I unraveled aloud tangled skeins of ideas; Daniel Fast and Ben Fast for talking through ideas with me; Molly and Matt Greenfield for their endless hospitality and stimulating company; Carmen Hendricks, the dean of the Wurzweiler School of Social Work at Yeshiva University, who facilitated the sabbatical during which most of the book was written; Bene Reiter, my resourceful research assistant on this and other projects; Dana Bliss, my editor at Oxford University Press, who encouraged me to undertake this project; Scott McClanahan, for his wonderful illustrations; Jefferson Fietek and Melissa Thompson, for helping me understand the politics and economics of the Anoka Hennepin School District; Marc Maron, who gave up several hours of a busy day to talk to me about comedy and shame; Harriet Lerner, Emily Kofron, Atte Oksanen, Eliza Ahmed, John Bailie, and Marji Lipshez-Shapiro for reviewing early versions of this manuscript, or sections of it, and making many helpful suggestions.

NOTES

1. Dan Olweus, *Bullying at School* (Oxford: Blackwell, 1993).
2. Ibid.
3. Thomas Scheff, *Bloody Revenge: Emotions, Nationalism and War* (Lincoln, NE: iUniverse, 2000); C. Poulson, "Shame: The Master Emotion?" University of Tasmania, School of Management Working Paper Series (Hobart: University of Tasmania, 2000).

4. James Gilligan, *Preventing Violence: Prospects for Tomorrow* (New York: Thames & Hudson, 2001); James Gilligan, *Violence: Our Deadly Epidemic and Its Causes* (New York: Putnam, 1996).

5. Helen B. Lewis, *Shame and Guilt in Neurosis* (Madison, CT: International Universities Press, 1971).

6. Rod Plotnik and Haig Kouyoumdjian, *Introduction to Psychology*, 9th ed. (Belmont, CA: Cengage Learning, 2010).

7. James W. Kalat, *Introduction to Psychology*, 10th ed. (Belmont, CA: Cengage Learning, 2013).

8. For example, see Eric H. Erikson, *Childhood and Society* (New York: W.W. Norton, 1950).

Beyond Bullying

CHAPTER 1
About Shame

SHAME'S EVOLUTIONARY FUNCTION

In 1859, after years of cautious reflection and endless re-examination of the evidence, Charles Darwin published *The Origin of the Species,*[1] creating a controversy that continues to this day. Darwin wrote that the diversity of life on Earth, of lizards and apes and human beings, is the result of our evolutionary descent from common ancestors, rather than the hierarchical scheme of creation described in the Bible. Thirteen years later, hoping to buttress his theory with evidence that even those emotions that were considered innately human were shared with other species, he published *The Expression of the Emotions in Man and Animals.*[2] Collected within its pages were illustrations and photographs of people around the world, including aboriginal peoples and animals of various kinds, expressing pleasure, disgust, rage, shame, and other emotions in such a way that similarities in their facial expressions and behavioral gestures were immediately apparent.

Paul Ekman,[3] a renowned American psychologist with an interest in the emotions, confirmed Darwin's hypothesis by showing photographs of human faces to people of different Eastern and Western cultures.[4] Each subject was told a one-sentence story suggesting one of the emotions being studied: "His (her) friends have come and he (she) is happy." The subject was then shown three pictures depicting three different emotions and asked to identify the picture that best illustrated the emotion. The rates of similar responses among citizens of Brazil, Argentina, Japan, and the United States were highly consistent. Determined to put the controversy to rest once and for all, Ekman and his colleague W. V. Friesen travelled to Papua New Guinea, and conducted the same experiment with members of the Fore tribe, an "isolated, Neolithic material culture."[5] The Fore people were illiterate and had no exposure to television, radio, magazines, or newspapers. Ekman and Friesen found that the results were totally consistent with those obtained from contemporary cultures. The basic emotions did not need to be learned; people were born knowing them. They made a second intriguing discovery that we will return to later in this chapter: that the Fore had very specific "display rules," culture-specific prescriptions about who can show emotions to whom and when.

SHAME IS A PROTOTYPE EMOTION

Robert Plutchik, a contemporary of Ekman's and a psychologist long associated with Einstein College of Medicine, agreed that certain basic emotions were inborn. He referred to the most basic emotions as "prototype emotions" (sadness, happiness) to distinguish them from the more complex emotions (remorse, nostalgia), which he believed were the results of the blending of prototype emotions. He used the metaphor of the color wheel, whose primary colors can be blended to create a universe of tints and hues. A layer of cognitions is then added to clarify the meaning and use of the new emotion. For example, Plutchik considered contempt, which is *not* a prototype emotion, the result of a blending of two prototype emotions, anger and disgust. The learned, cognitive part of contempt involves its application, when, where, and upon whom to use it.[6]

Plutchik posed a series of statements or "postulates" to be considered by anyone investigating an emotion. First, he agreed with Darwin and Ekman that all creatures, man and animal alike, have a repertoire of inborn emotions and that emotions themselves have evolved along with different species, according to the needs of that species. For example, as any dog owner knows, pets, when shamed, behave in much the same way as humans. If we return home to find our pet gnawing on what remains of the roast chicken we left on the counter to cool off and we point out to him the error of his ways, he will avoid our gaze, perhaps cover his nose with his paws, slouch into the next room, or hide under the bed. We could hypothesize that shame has been useful to dogs, in an evolutionary sense, because it makes them seem more human and repentant and thus easier to forgive. A heightened sense of shame assures us that dogs have incorporated the code of behaviors that are permitted or forbidden in our home. This is particularly important since a large dog is capable of maiming or killing a human being. Cats, on the other hand, do not seem to display shame but are capable of displaying contentment by purring, a trait that endears them to humans, who in turn will feed them and care for them. In other words, any of the prototype emotions that has survived to this day in man or animal does so because it continues to fulfill some important evolutionary function.

SHAME KEEPS PEOPLE IN GROUPS

What then is the function of shame that has made it endure as a prototype emotion for the 250,000 years that man has walked the earth?[7] People yearn to be in relationships, in couples and in groups. Gershen Kaufman, who frequently writes on shame, has this to say:

> Few strivings are as compelling as is our need to identify with someone, to feel a part of something, to belong somewhere. Whether it is in relation to one significant other, or the family, or one's own peer group, we experience some vital need to belong. And it is precisely the identification need which most assuredly confers that special sense of belonging. So powerful is that striving that we might feel obliged to do most anything in order to secure our place.[8]

Judith Herman, a professor of psychiatry at Harvard Medical School, agrees that shame is one of the primary regulators of "attachment, care-giving, mating, and social ranking, inclusion, exclusion and cooperation"[9] among primates. She adds the caveat that while this is so during peacetime, during war, when society inches toward chaos, fear takes over the task of social regulation and violence enforces it.

We all want to be members of a group, be it a dyad consisting of ourselves and that someone with whom we choose to spend the rest of our lives or an extended family who celebrates each others' successes and helps one another through hard times. It may be an explicit group, with a name and a charter of detailed requirements, such as the school honor role, varsity football team, or all-state orchestra, or it may be a more abstract and implicit group, a group without a name or a charter, a group signified by nothing more than the fact that its members share a social situation or experience:[10] Kids Who Can Tie Their Own Shoes, Teens With Prom Dates, or Seniors Headed for Ivy League Schools.

Lest any confusion remain, shame is *not* the force that brings us into a group. One marries, as the old proverb goes, for love in youth, security in midlife, and companionship in old age. People join families by the will of nature and circumstance. They choose colleges by trying to predict what preparation will serve them well in later life, and they join communities with the hope that they will contain people who are well-behaved, and have similar interests and intentions.

Shame occurs in two types of situations. It occurs when our membership in an existing group is threatened by our inappropriate behavior. If we commit a serious crime, our family may disown us. If we cause trouble in school, we risk getting expelled. While a new hire may not lose her job for spilling coffee on her white sweater on the way to a meeting with the boss, she certainly feels as though she will. In examples like this, we shame ourselves (Figure 1.1).

Shame also occurs in a second type of situation when ambition for wealth, status, or personal or professional satisfaction drives us to seek entry in a group of higher status. We apply to an Ivy League college only to discover that we do not meet its academic standards. We audition for a chamber music group but our musicianship is under par. In situations such as this, we are shamed by the person who rejects us from the group, someone we might consider the "gatekeeper." Some might add a third type of situation, the experience of empathic shame over the humiliation of another human being, just as we might share their happiness or grief.

All shame experiences involve a group, or at least one other person, because shame needs a referent. One can only feel shame if one is incapable of meeting the cultural, behavioral, intellectual, or ideological standards of others. For someone who has been isolated from birth, there is no shame. To paraphrase Karl Marx,[11] a man who lives in a middle-class community might be perfectly content with his social status, but if a rich man moves in next door and builds a mansion, feelings of financial inadequacy will begin to disturb his sleep. The new neighbor is a representative of a group that might be called The Rich.

Fortunately, most of us maintain membership in many groups, both explicit and implicit, at the same time. If we are shamed, and our membership in a group seems tenuous, we can still seek solace and support from our secure membership in other groups. A child who is bullied at school still has (we hope) some family member or close friends to comfort him by helping him process the shame, and by this I mean talk about it, analyze it, test its validity, plan a way to make amends, and so forth until the memory of it loses its sting. It is the child who feels as though he he is exiled from *all* groups and has no way to manage his shame who is our greatest concern; he is most likely to harbor violent, destructive impulses and runs the greatest risk of turning them against himself or another.

Sometimes We Shame Ourselves

Figure 1.1:
Sometimes we shame ourselves.

Shame can be a powerful constructive force for helping children master the skills required to move into an adult role. When five-year-old Sam finger-paints on his plate with his mashed peas, his mother says, "You can't eat at the grownup table until you stop sticking your fingers in your food." She is letting him know how this particular behavior prevents him from joining The Grownups, a high-status group. We call this "healthy shaming" because it encourages children (and adults) to master skills that will make them more autonomous and socially appealing in the Grownups' world.

When James is suspended for spray-painting his name across the dumpster in the middle-school parking lot, he is briefly exiled from his group, Kids Who Attend School, and sentenced to a different group, Boys Who Have Been Suspended. To his parents, who discuss the incident in hushed and worried tones, the group has a scarier name: Would-Be Juvenile Delinquents. But they have nothing to worry about. James is sufficiently ashamed and angry with himself that he will not vandalize property again.

Janice, a freshman at college, drives down to Fort Lauderdale for spring break. At a party the first night she drinks more than she had planned—much more—and on her way back to the motel the erratic course of her car attracts the attention of the highway patrol. After failing a breathalyzer test, she spends the rest of the night in a holding cell with a drunk, an old man with a drool-caked beard, and three prostitutes. Janice realizes, with shock and horror, that she has left the group of College Freshman With Wonderful Prospects and joined a group we might call Petty Criminals and Lowlifes. After her night in the cell, she becomes meticulous about designating a sober driver (sometimes herself) before attending a party.

While the first case illustrates healthy shaming, a more accurate term for the second and third case would be "reintegrative shaming,"[12] because the punishment reminds the offender what behavior is necessary to be reintegrated into a high-status group. Consider the difference between Janice's one night in jail and the dehumanizing effects of long-term prison sentences, where shame that could be reintegrative instead becomes toxic.

Parents, teachers, police, and other authorities help people learn to adhere to behaviors that have been recognized as safe, respectful, and appropriate within the dominant culture. To answer a question posed earlier, this is the key to shame's evolutionary importance: it helps the human race behave acceptably in groups, where there are always rules of what is acceptable and what is not. A human being will not survive in isolation. Healthy shame enables companionship, collaboration, religion, and nationalism, to name only a few of the benefits groups provide.

But shame is a double-edged sword. The same power that makes shame an unparalleled disciplinary and didactic force makes it a formidable and sometimes lethal weapon in the hands of bullies and bigots. Shame that criticizes what one *is* rather than what one *does* is considered "toxic shame"[13] because it poisons one's self-concept. What one does can be changed, but what one is cannot.

Consider a child who constantly forgets to complete his homework. The parent who says "Your father and I expect you to study and get good grades" is using healthy shame by reminding the child that academic success is part of the family culture. If the child wishes to remain a member in good standing, he or she needs to be attentive, study hard, and go to college. However, if a parent, driven by frustration and anger, exclaims "You're so lazy, you'll never amount to anything!" the shame becomes toxic. The locution offers no escape; the allegation of laziness cuts to the core of a person's self-concept (Figure 1.2).

If shame is used intentionally to injure a person's self-concept, then it should be considered "weaponized shame." Bullying, bigotry, workplace harassment, domestic violence, physical and sexual abuse, and hate crimes are all forms of weaponized shame. It makes no difference that the perpetrator mistakenly believes that battering his child will teach him to show some respect, or punishing a spouse for burning dinner will change her cooking habits. He may say "I'm doing this for your own good" or "I'm doing this to teach you a lesson" to hide his aggression from the victim or even himself, but such excuses only breed more anger and shame (Figure 1.3).

THE ACKNOWLEDGEMENT OF SHAME IS TABOO

Now you may be asking yourself, if Dr. Fast is right, if shame is so important, so central to human behavior, then how come it is so seldom discussed, examined, or even mentioned?

First, while shame is often present, it is easily overlooked. Ekman did not include shame in his list of prototype emotions until 1990,[14] some 20 years after his trip to New Guinea, because he had been studying emotions as they were expressed by the facial muscles, and shame is one of the only emotions that is *not* expressed by the facial muscles.[15]

Although shame is not expressed by the face, it manifests itself in other ways, which vary from one person to the next. The thought process may

Sometimes Others Shame Us

Figure 1.2:
Sometimes others shame us.

become confused, or labored. Some feel the sensation of heat in the face or the chest, or a tingling in the palms. Some blush—but others do not. An emblematic gesture involves covering the eyes or the face and lowering the head (Donald Nathanson ascribes this to a loss of muscle tone in the neck and shoulders).[16]

The word itself, *shame*, has a pre-Germanic root, *skem* or *kem*, meaning "to cover one's self."[17] Masaccio's painting of the Expulsion from Paradise

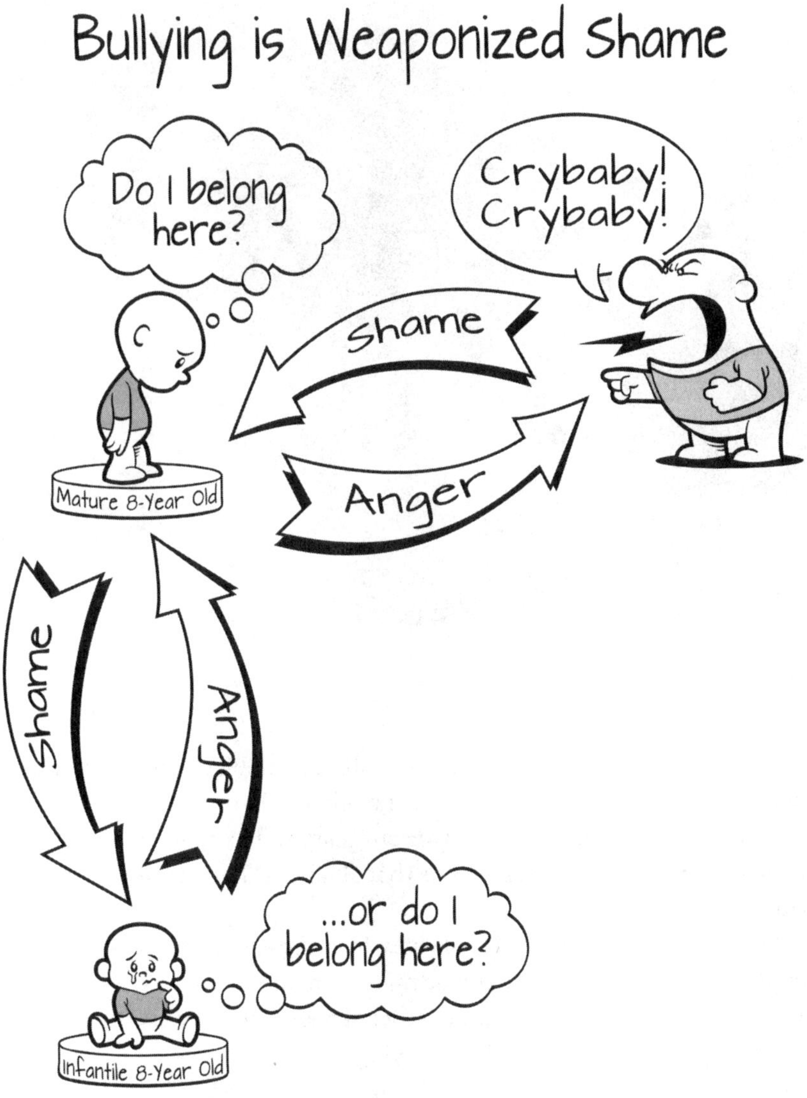

Figure 1.3:
Bullying is weaponized shame.

(Figure 1.4) shows Adam hiding his face in his hands and Eve covering her breasts and genitals. ("And the LORD God called unto Adam, and said unto him, Where are you? And he said, I heard thy voice in the garden, and I was afraid, because I was naked; and I hid myself."[18]

Sophocles has Oedipus blind himself on discovering that he had had intercourse with his mother. A classic poster, "Shame May Be Fatal," warning of the dangers of venereal disease, depicts a stylized head, face hidden

Figure 1.4:
Expulsion from Paradise by Masaccio (1401–1428) Detail.

in hands. A colleague of mine who was blind from birth told me that she hides her face when ashamed even though she has never seen another person engage in this behavior; this suggests to her that the reaction is inborn and supports the hypothesis that shame is "hard-wired" in human beings.

Because shame leaves few facial clues, it can be easily concealed by those intent on doing so. Likewise, shame management strategies are easily disguised as quotidian behaviors, unassociated with the depths of emotionality they address. Consider the following.

Mrs. Smith had recently died, leaving her 60-year-old daughter a gold bracelet of considerable value. This was a wealthy family where love was often confused with the possession of valuables. At a dinner party attended by family, her 55-year-old sister noticed the bracelet for the first time.

"How did you get that?" she asked.

"Mother gave it to me before she died," The older sister replied.

"You were always her favorite."

"It means nothing to me. I would give it to you in an instant."

"I'll take it," the younger sister said, unexpectedly.

The table grew silent waiting to see how the older daughter would respond. With the bracelet still encircling her wrist, the older daughter rose and, as if just recalling a matter of some importance, disappeared down the hall. After a few minutes the host went to see what had become of her. She was in the bedroom, lying on the bed, watching TV with assorted nieces and nephews. She claimed that she had come in "to check on them" and had gotten engrossed in the movie they were watching. Although a deep sibling rivalry had resurfaced, and the elder daughter had revealed her own hypocrisy to an audience of intimate friends, the sisters and the other guests continued as though nothing emotional had taken place. Had the older sister's response involved anger, sadness, amazement, or disgust, other guests would have recognized the signs, but shame, like a secret agent, can travel through hostile territories unnoticed.

A second reason involves the "display rules" that Ekman and Friesen discovered while working with the Fore people in New Guinea, rules determining the circumstances under which individuals could express one emotion or another. Our own culture has display rules too: little girls should smile; men should not cry. Adults, if they wish to be popular, should not appear too depressed or angry. The display rule for shame is this: because it is associated with little children, weakness, failure, and social exclusion, its display is forbidden for those who wish to appear mature, powerful, successful, and a welcome addition to social gatherings.

The discussion of shame is even avoided in therapeutic sessions, where the most sensitive topics are supposedly fair game. Helen B. Lewis, a psychoanalyst and researcher whose work is probably responsible for the current interest in this topic, discovered by analyzing hundreds of hours of psychotherapy sessions that patients were often in a state of shame and that this condition was "virtually always" unacknowledged by the patient and the therapist.[19] "Lewis's work suggests that shame is a haunting presence in psychotherapy, a presence that is usually hidden, disguised, or ignored by both patient and therapist."[20] In her own clinical practice, Lewis found that by helping her patients acknowledge and work through their shame experiences, they made better progress in therapy and had fewer relapses. Lewis published her original research in 1971. A letter to the editor of *Psychiatric News* in 2001 from a young woman beginning her career as a psychoanalytically trained psychiatrist complained that shame was rarely mentioned in her coursework or in her supervision.[21] In an article from 2011, J. P. Tangney and Ronda Dearing, after polling expert clinicians about shame in therapy, stated that shame was "easily overlooked or actively avoided in therapy sessions,"[22] as it had been 40 years earlier.

What is so bad about ignoring shame?

Powerful emotions, when unacknowledged, tend to be expressed through "acting out" behavior, even by the most well-buttoned-down individuals. The body seems to have a need to express one's true feelings even if the mind has chosen to hide them and the mouth to be mute. One might better understand this by considering other ways the body "speaks," as in mime or dance, and the primeval nature of such physiological communications. "Acting out" is a label usually applied to misbehaving children. The idea is that because children have a limited vocabulary, they will physically enact emotions that they cannot identify. A child who is angry at his sister may act out by punching her, at which point a parent well-read in the literature of Raising Well-Adjusted Children will intervene saying, "Use your words, not your fists," or something like that. In fact, teenagers and adults frequently act out, not necessarily because of a limited vocabulary but because they cannot "hear" their own inner voices or identify their own feelings.

While human behavior is complex, an act as simple as being able to identify one's feelings can constitute an important step toward reducing acting out behavior. "Name it to tame it," some therapists say.

STATE SHAME AND TRAIT SHAME

We are all familiar with the anxiety one anticipates prior to speaking in front of an audience, preparing to meet the new in-laws, or embarking on a new job. Psychologists who study emotions consider this "state" anxiety because it is transient. Like a good plumber or electrician, it comes, does its work (puts your brain and body in high gear so you will do your best), and leaves. We complete our speech to the chamber of commerce, charm our new in-laws, and impress our boss, and our anxiety is replaced by a feeling of self-worth and accomplishment. In contrast, we all know people whom we think of as *anxious people*. They may be seen studying their watches, worrying about having left the stove on, or anticipating disasters, however unlikely, in their own lives or the lives of those they love. For them anxiety is a *trait*, a pretty much permanent part of their personality. Anxiety has been so much a part of their growing up that it has worn ruts in their brain through which thoughts of impending doom continually flow. (I use anxiety for this example because it is more readily visible than shame.) If shame is a secret agent, anxiety is a tightrope walker in a spangled suit. It's display is deemed acceptable because it seems to be an indicator of valued qualities such as responsibility, intensity, and caution, pushed to extremes.

Trait shame unlike trait anxiety, is rarely studied. Most of what we do know about trait shame comes from writings about people with addictions[23] and incarcerated violent criminals.[24] The alcoholic or drug-addicted family is a kind of hothouse for shame. Alcoholic and addicted parents misbehave, insult people, get into fights, lose their jobs, and wreck their cars. They may commit acts of domestic violence, cheat on their spouses, and neglect and abuse their children. In situations like these, the shame seems to take on a life of its own, to flow like a toxic effluence across the generations. Children who have given up their youth to protect the alcoholic parent, phone into work when the parent is too hungover to get out of bed, or babysit his siblings when the parent is jailed after a DUI carry on the shame themselves even though they have worked heroically to keep the family intact. In the words of the prophet Jeremiah (31:29), "The fathers have eaten a sour grape, and the children's teeth are set on edge."

Another source of information about trait shame comes from the study of violent criminals. James Gilligan, currently a professor of psychiatry at New York University Medical School and a former director of mental health for the Massachusetts prison system, writes at length about the remarkable degree of shame experienced by violent, incarcerated criminals. Shame, he writes,

> is probably the most carefully guarded secret held by violent men . . . They try so hard to conceal this secret because it is so deeply shameful to them, and of course shame further motivates the need to conceal. The secret is that they feel ashamed, deeply ashamed, chronically ashamed, acutely ashamed, over matters that are so trivial that their very triviality makes it even more shameful to feel ashamed about them, so they are ashamed even to reveal what shames them.[25]

Gilligan is saying that those who suffer from trait shame become extremely sensitive and reactive to shaming events, in particular those that directly imply disrespect.[26] In communities where poverty, violence, and a lack of services make survival a daily challenge, pride and worthiness become precious commodities. Acts of disrespect that might be ignored or laughed off in more economically robust communities become battles of honor fought with knives, razors, or guns at 2 AM in dark alleys. The word "disrespected" is used so often among this population that it has been shrunken from four syllables to one—"dissed"—to slide off the tongue more easily. During the time I worked as a clinical social worker in an urban public school, one of my clients, an underprivileged teenage girl, slashed another girl in the face with a razor because she had "rolled her eyes" while passing her in the hallway. She explained this act of violence to me as though it was the most common and sensible response one might make.

Such exaggerated reactions to inconsequential provocations are typical of individuals who live with trait shame. They are more vulnerable to episodes of state shame. They have shame experiences more frequently, experience the shame as more severe, and have more difficulty managing it. The violent criminals Gilligan observed also went to great lengths to conceal their shame, to the extent that they appeared, on superficial examination, to have suppressed their shame mechanism completely. They wanted to appear as though the opinions of others mattered not a whit to them, and they were free to ignore all of society's restrictions. But in such cases it is never clear whether shame has been truly banished or simply concealed in a very deep place in the soul.

NATHANSON'S COMPASS OF SHAME

When we experience a feeling that is deeply disturbing, we search for a way to rid ourselves of it or at least come to terms with it. How we do this varies greatly from person to person. Sometimes it is a style we have learned from a parent, or it may be the results of other circumstances of our childhood. In 1992 Donald Nathanson, attempting to create a taxonomy of shame management strategies, identified four categories that he associated with the four points of the compass. Nathanson was trained as an endocrinologist but, growing up in Brooklyn with a "family that considered grand opera a good model for the normal range of emotion," he eventually chose a psychiatric residency and became a researcher and clinician with a special interest in the emotions and shame in particular.

The four points of Nathanson's compass are withdrawal, avoidance, attack self, and attack others (Figure 1.5). He considers withdrawal and avoidance as polar opposites, as he does attack self and attack others.

Withdrawal, the northern point of the compass, refers to hiding, the behavior we have identified as emblematic of shame. In its mildest form, it may be covering the face with the hands or escaping into another room. In its more severe forms, as with trait shame, it might consist of living in isolation in the woods, as some disaffected returning Vietnam veterans chose to do in the 1970s, or refusing to leave one's home.

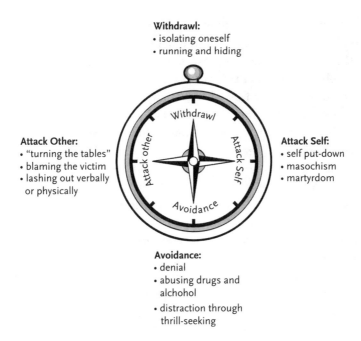

Withdrawl:
- isolating oneself
- running and hiding

Attack Other:
- "turning the tables"
- blaming the victim
- lashing out verbally or physically

Attack Self:
- self put-down
- masochism
- martyrdom

Avoidance:
- denial
- abusing drugs and alchohol
- distraction through thrill-seeking

Figure 1.5:
Nathanson's Compass of Shame.

The southern pole of the compass, avoidance, encompasses addictions and some psychological defense mechanisms. People with addictions use drugs, alcohol, and high-risk behaviors such as stealing cars and promiscuous sex to numb themselves to shame.[27] Drugs and alcohol overpower shame the way whitewashing a wall hides disturbing graffiti. The shadow of the graffiti shows through, but as long as the addict or alcoholic continues to brush paint over it, it can be ignored. The fear of facing this mass of hidden shame is one of the factors that make recovery so challenging. Avoidance also includes defense mechanisms, a form of self-deception that people use unconsciously to protect themselves from intolerable emotions. Denial is a common defense mechanism among addicts and alcoholics. The person in denial often denies having a drinking problem: "I only drink after 5 PM"; "It doesn't interfere with my work"; "I can stop anytime I want to"; "It's just a way to wind down."

Narcissism is another common defense against shame. The narcissist behaves with grandiosity and thinks he deserves special treatment because of his intelligence, good looks, or other talent or gift, real or imagined. This overblown pride, many researchers believe,[28] is an attempt to divert the individual's attention and that of others away from the shame he or she suffers as a result of what he or she perceives as grievous personal flaws. The narcissistic personality is like a stage set for a movie, a grand house of stone that on closer examination reveals itself to be nothing more than painted cardboard, braced to stand upright but fragile enough to be toppled by a word or two of criticism.

The eastern point of Nathanson's compass, attack self, describes the shame rage turned inward. In this behavior, people blame and punish themselves for the shame event, even if there was no way to prevent it. This reduces their helplessness by making them feel as though they have taken control of the shame, that they own it and that by hurting themselves they are mastering the shame. Those of us who have worked in psychiatric settings are familiar with patients who cut themselves on the thighs or arms or stomachs to relieve a pressure that they are often hard put to describe.[29] Suicide and suicide attempts are more extreme examples. In a shame-based culture, such as China during the T'ang Dynasty, court nobles who had disgraced themselves performed ritualized suicide to restore their honor. Samurai in Edo period Japan copied this practice, and it has come down to us with its Japanese name, *harakiri* (cutting the stomach) or hari-kari, as it is often transliterated.

Anger turned outward is expressed by the western point of Nathanson's compass, attack other. Here we find the bullies. The shame is resolved by being displaced onto another individual. Attacking that person and defeating him makes the shame victim feel as though he or she has defeated his or her own shame.[30] This is the basis of racism, homophobia, and domestic violence. It was most obvious in the centuries-old practice of dueling, of the gentry responding to insult by battling to first blood or death with pistol or blade.[31]

BEYOND NATHANSON'S COMPASS: MANAGING STATE SHAME

During the years that I interviewed people who had suffered from different kinds of shame, and recorded my own experiences with shame, I noticed that while unhealthy or dysfunctional shame management strategies fit neatly into Nathanson's compass, healthy strategies did not. To further investigate this, I asked 30 of my students to keep "shame diaries" for extra course credit. They provided me with descriptions of 276 shame incidents, what precisely had occurred, who was responsible, and how they had responded.

The majority of the participants, about 85 percent, used healthy strategies. The two most common strategies my students reported were talking over the incident with a trusted friend or family member and carrying out a similar kind of conversation with themselves, what psychologists refer to as "self-talk." The confidante could be a parent or sibling, a mentor, or a supervisor at work. It was never with a therapist, although many of them were in therapy. (This corresponds to Lewis's finding of 50 years ago.[32])

These discussions usually centered on reassuring the shamed person that the transgression was not so awful as he or she may have believed and would not result in the dire consequences anticipated. Sometimes it included a plan to make amends with the shamer or to commit a socially condoned act of vengeance, such as leaving a scathing online review for a vendor they believed had cheated them. (While such an act is encouraged by websites that invite us to evaluate our dentist, the company that repaired our patio, or the disappointing book we have purchased, the line between consumer protection and character assassination is a thin one, easily crossed.)

The act of confession, where a priest listens to the transgressions of a congregant nonjudgmentally, is a formalized version of this activity, as is the Jewish tradition of Yom Kippur, the Day of Atonement, and the holiest day of the Jewish year. On Yom Kippur the temple service includes a ritual called וִדּוּי or *Vidui,* in which worshipers confess their sins privately to God. Maimonides, however, a great rabbinic scholar of the twelfth century, considered confession to the victim "immensely praiseworthy."[33] He believed the proper formula was to acknowledge the transgression, express remorse, and promise not to do it again.

Alcoholics Anonymous (AA), a more modern faith-based practice, also values direct personal apology. It is a central element in the Twelve Steps.[34]

Step 8: Made a list of all persons we had harmed, and became willing to make amends to them all.
Step 9: Made direct amends to such people wherever possible, except when to do so would injure them or others.

Two more strategies tied for second place among my students in shame management. One was "ignoring" the event. In Nathanson, this falls under the category of avoidance. Lewis called this "unacknowledged shame"[35] and Gilligan, "secret shame."[36] All agree that *not* processing the shame often leads to acting-out behavior, and that this behavior, depending on the intensity of the shame and a number of other risk factors, is most likely to lead to a violent resolution. The second strategy was making a joke about it. Some authorities consider joking about shame a way of avoiding it and therefore unhealthy,[37] but others believe it is healthy or even the healthiest of shame management strategies.[38] Lewis wrote,

"Most important for the discharge of the shame state is the awareness that shame can be discharged in good-humored laughter at the self and its relation to the other. After all, shame is 'only about the self.'"[39] Both Gilligan and Lewis "assume that normal shame is resolved through verbal means and through humor."[40] Thomas T. Scheff describes a course he taught where students volunteered to share their most embarrassing experiences and invariably became "convulsed with laughter"[41] at repeating it in a safe and supportive classroom environment. Some stated that it evoked unprocessed shame incidents of their past. They felt as though the classroom "confession" had unburdened them.

Strategies practiced least frequently by the students included getting angry at, or blaming, the person perceived to be the source of the shame (Nathanson's "attack other") or making amends with the person who caused the shame. The strategies least often reported were hiding, or wanting to hide (Nathanson's "withdrawal"); getting angry at or blaming one's self (Nathanson's "attack self"); crying; meditating; journaling; fantasizing about acts of violence; or using alcohol, drugs, or other addictive behaviors to numb the shame ("avoidance.") Such behaviors may be relatively harmless. *Imagining* punching a rude bully may be a rewarding fantasy; taking a stiff drink after a day at work when one's competency has been questioned because of an accounting error may be a welcome escape. But for some people the fantasy of personalized, retaliatory violence is not unrelated to the commission of actual physical or emotional violence. Likewise, the drink that dissolves shame can lead, under certain circumstances, to a habit of excessive drinking that in turn leads to misery and destruction.

POSITIVE STRATEGIES FOR MANAGING TRAIT SHAME

Trait shame, as described earlier, is shame accumulated early on that is pervasive and enduring and often shapes a person's entire life. In some cases women with trait shame may devote their lives to good works, such as helping other women who have had similar shame-evoking experiences. The accumulation of worthiness counteracts the shame. It functions like a kind of penance. This does not mean that all women who pursue altruistic careers are similarly driven. People follow the paths of righteousness for many reasons. The desire to help others may be the highest of spiritual callings. Likewise, *some* men with trait shame are driven to achieve fame and amass a fortune to prove their worth. But again, not *all* ambitious and successful men are similarly driven. To summarize and perhaps overgeneralize, worthiness for women involves repairing and improving the social networks; for men it is the triumph over other men.[42] These are consistent with the gender roles our culture has assigned us, but as women move toward achieving social and economic equality, the strategies may become less pat.

Other ways of managing trait shame resemble more intense or enduring versions of state shame strategies. Rather than resorting to humor to discharge a specific incident, a person with trait shame who enjoys getting up on stage, and can make others laugh, might pursue a career as a stand-up comic. Many stand-up comedians seem to be motivated by the need to describe shameful experiences from their own lives in front of an audience and to have these confessions greeted with the friendly laughter of recognition and acceptance. Rodney Dangerfield mined his material from a catchphrase, "I don't get no respect!" repeated in a mournful tone and followed by an anecdote about him being badly treated and unloved.

> I asked my old man if I could go ice-skating on the lake. He told me, 'Wait 'til it gets warmer.'

The more often he repeated his catchphrase, the more respect he seemed to garner, at least as measured by fame and financial gain.

Army Staff Sergeant Bobby Henline's face was horribly disfigured as the result of a roadside explosion outside of Baghdad in April of 2007. Thirty-eight percent of his body was burned, and his head was burned to the skull. He spent six months in the hospital and endured more than 40 surgeries, including the amputation of his left hand. Returning to civilian life, he found relief in pursuing a career of stand-up comedy and motivational speaking, the source of his humor being his own disfigurement.[43] His comedy provides incalculable support to other wounded soldiers, as well as a firsthand account of the sacrifices our soldiers made during the conflict in Iraq.

Comedians who fail to elicit laughter during a performance often experience a uniquely horrible sensation they call "flop sweat," a wave of terror that produces a cold sweat across the body. I suspect that the silence of the audience is unconsciously interpreted as the rejection of a confession and constitutes shame in its most virulent form.

One shame management technique does not preclude another. Many successful stand-up comedians were alcoholics or addicts prior to discovering, or succeeding in, making crowds laugh. Some, like Lenny Bruce and Rodney Dangerfield, despite their professional success, continued abusing substances to the detriment of their professional careers and their lives.

At this point readers who have attended a 12-step meeting such as AA might reflect that such meetings resemble stand-up comedy performances in certain ways but without the specific aim of evoking laughter (although good-natured laughter may accompany the speaker's description of she-nanigans committed while drinking or using drugs). This type of laughter might be called "laughter of recognition" or "laughter of solidarity," and it has a special meaning because it comes from a place deep within the human heart. One of the features of an AA meeting or a well-facilitated therapy group is that regardless of how shameful the revelations of the speakers, other group members will accept their testimony nonjudgmen-tally. There is no possibility of being judged, failing to please, flop-sweat, or exclusion, since the "culture" of the group is non-judgemental acceptance.

DYSFUNCTIONAL WAYS OF MANAGING TRAIT SHAME

Violence may be directed inward or outward. This is why Nathanson positions attack self and attack other at opposite poles of his compass of shame. Women, because of their long-established role of peacekeepers and maintainers of the social network, tend to manage trait shame by harming themselves. This may take the form of self-deprecating remarks, self-hatred, seeking out men who will victimize them, cutting or piercing themselves (although piercing and tattoos, having become socially accept-able, may or may not represent efforts at shame management), making suicide attempts, and committing suicide. Men are more apt to commit violence that targets others.[44] While these behaviors tend to follow gen-der lines, there are many exceptions. There are men who cut themselves and women who kill. How much of the division between male and female modes of expressing violence is a result of our cultural programming and how much the influence of testosterone and other biological determinants is not yet well understood. Most likely all these factors come into play.

It has been suggested that groups of men and women, when united by the impact of a shared event, employ the same shame management tech-niques on a grand scale. A group of abused and mistreated teenage girls may imagine that they are witches and gather in the evenings to cut them-selves, a situation that occurred at a high school where I once worked. Teenage boys dealing with the shame of being poor and having few pros-pects in life may use their keys to gouge away the paint on expensive cars parked in their neighborhood that have come to symbolize the success that is out of their reach. During Reconstruction, bands of men in white hoods gathered to burn down black churches to manage the shame/rage of losing their slaves, the economic engine that drove their communities. Several writers have suggested that Hitler's rise to power was the result of Germany's shame at the terms of their defeat in World War I.[45]

Gilligan writes, "I have yet to see a serious act of violence that was not provoked by the experience of feeling shamed and humiliated, disrespected and ridiculed, and that did not represent the attempt to prevent or undo this 'loss of face'—no matter how severe the punishment, even if it includes death."[46]

NOTES

1. Charles Darwin, *On the Origin of Species by Means of Natural Selection: Or the Preservation of Favoured Races in the Struggle for Life* (New York: D. Appleton, 1869).
2. Charles Darwin, *The Expression of the Emotions in Man and Animals* (London: John Murray, 1872), http://darwin-online.org.uk/content/frameset?itemID=F1142& viewtype=text&pageseq=1
3. Ekman, incidentally, was the model for Cal Lightman, the crime-solving psychologist of Fox Network's show, *Lie to Me*. Ekman's work involved the discernment of truth from examining body language and the play of facial muscles.
4. P. Ekman and W. V. Friesen, "Constants Across Cultures in the Face and Emotion," *Journal of Personality and Social Psychology* 17, no. 2 (1971): 126.
5. Ibid., 125.
6. Robert C. Solomon, *The Passions: Emotions and the Meaning of Life* (Indianapolis: Hackett, 1976).
7. Kate Ravilious, "Humans 80,000 Years Older than Previously Thought?" *National Geographic News*, December 3, 2008, http://news.nationalgeographic.com/news /2008/12/081203-homo-sapien-missions.html.
8. Gershen Kaufman, *Shame: The Power of Caring*, 3rd ed., rev. and exp. (Rochester, VT: Schenkman Books, 1992), 33.
9. Judith Lewis Herman, "Shattered Shame States and Their Repair," paper presented at the John Bowlby Memorial Lecture, Cambridge, MA, March 10, 2007, 2.
10. See W. R. Bion, *Experiences in Groups: And Other Papers*, 1st ed. (New York: Routledge, 1991), for a more detailed explanation of this way of conceptualizing groups.
11. "A house may be large or small; as long as the neighboring houses are likewise small, it satisfies all social requirements for a residence. But let there arise next to the little house a palace, and the little house shrinks to a hut. The little house now makes it clear that its inmate has no social position at all to maintain" (Karl Marx, "Wage Labour and Capital," trans. Frederick Engels, *Neue Rheinische Zeitung*, 1849).
12. John Braithwaite, *Crime, Shame and Reintegration* (Cambridge, UK: Cambridge University Press, 1989). Braithwaite created this terminology.
13. This terminology is from John Bradshaw, *Healing the Shame That Binds You*, 1st ed. (New York: HCI, 1988).
14. Paul Ekman, "Basic Emotions," in *Handbook of Cognition and Emotion*, ed. Tim Dalgleish and Mick Power (New York: Wiley, 2000).

15. Carroll E. Izard, *Human Emotions* (New York: Plenum, 1977).
16. Donald L. Nathanson, "Affect and Hypnosis: On Paying Friendly Attention to Disturbing Thoughts," *International Journal of Clinical and Experimental Hypnosis* 57, no. 4 (August 31, 2009): 319–342.
17. C. T. Onions, ed., *The Oxford Dictionary of English Etymology* (Oxford: Oxford University Press, 1966).
18. Genesis 3:9, 3:10, in *The KJV Study Bible* (Nashville: Barbour, 2011).
19. Helen B. Lewis, *Shame and Guilt in Neurosis* (Madison, CT: International Universities Press, 1971).
20. Thomas J. Scheff and Suzanne M. Retzinger, *Emotions and Violence* (Lincoln, NE: iUniverse, 2002), 13.
21. Lisa Moran, "Shame and Violence," Letter to *Psychiatric News*, June 15, 2001.
22. J. P. Tangney and Ronda L. Dearing, "Working With Shame in the Therapy Hour: Summary and Integration," in *Shame in the Therapy Hour*, ed. Ronda L. Dearing and June Price Tangney, 1st ed. (Washington, DC: American Psychological Association, 2011), 377.
23. See, for example, Beverly J. Flanigan, "Shame and Forgiving in Alcoholism," *Alcoholism Treatment Quarterly* 4, no. 2 (March 7, 1988): 181–195, doi:10.1300/J020v04n02_11; R. T. Potter-Efron, *Shame, Guilt and Alcoholism: Treatment Issues in Clinical Practice* (New York: Haworth Press, 1989); Ronald T. Potter-Efron and Donald E. Efron, "Three Models of Shame and Their Relation to the Addictive Process," *Alcoholism Treatment Quarterly* 10, no. 1–2 (August 6, 1993): 23–48; Atte Oksanen, "Drinking to Death: Traditional Masculinity, Alcohol and Shame in Finnish Metal Lyrics," *Nordic Studies on Alcohol and Drugs* 28, no. 4 (January 1, 2011): 357–372.
24. James Gilligan. *Violence: Our Deadly Epidemic and Its Causes.* New York City, NY: G.P. Putnam, 1996.
25. Ibid., 111.
26. Ibid., 105.
27. See, for example, Potter-Efron, *Shame, Guilt and Alcoholism*; Potter-Efron and Efron, "Three Models of Shame"; Flanigan, "Shame and Forgiving"; Oksanen, "Drinking to Death"; Tim Sheehan, *Shame* (Center City, MN: Hazelden, 2002); Mic Hunter, *The Twelve Steps and Shame* (Center City, MN: Hazelden, 1988); and others.
28. L. Wurmser, "Shame: The Veiled Companion of Narcissism," in *The Many Faces of Shame*, ed. D. L. Nathanson (New York: Guilford Press, 1987); Otto F. Kernberg, "Factors in the Psychoanalytic Treatment of Narcissistic Personalities," *Journal of the American Psychoanalytic Association* 18 (1970): 51–85; Helen B. Lewis, "Shame and the Narcissistic Personality," in *The Many Faces of Shame*, ed. D. L. Nathanson (New York: Guilford Press, 1987); Heinz Kohut, *The Analysis of the Self: A Systematic Approach to the Psychoanalytic Treatment of Narcissistic Personality Disorders* (Madison, CT: International Universities Press, 1971).
29. Steven Levenkron, *Cutting: Understanding and Overcoming Self-Mutilation*, rev. ed. (New York: W. W. Norton, 1998); Judith Himber, "Blood Rituals: Self-Cutting in Female Psychiatric Inpatients," *Psychotherapy: Theory, Research, Practice, Training* 31, no. 4 (1994): 620–631, doi:10.1037/0033-3204.31.4.620; Armando R. Favazza, *Bodies Under Siege: Self-Mutilation and Body Modification in Culture and Psychiatry* (Baltimore: Johns Hopkins University Press, 1996).
30. This is similar to a defense mechanism called "displacement."

31. Ariel A. Roth, "The Dishonor of Dueling," *Origins* 16, no. 1 (1989): 3–7; Barbara Holland, *Gentlemen's Blood: A History of Dueling* (New York: Bloomsbury, 2004).
32. Lewis, *Shame and Guilt in Neurosis*.
33. Maimonides, *Mishneh Torah Hilchot Teshuvah—The Laws of Repentance*, trans. Rabbi Eliyahu Touger (New York: Moznaim, 1990).
34. *Alcoholics Anonymous: The Story of How Many Thousands of Men and Women Have Recovered from Alcoholism*, 4th ed. (New York: Alcoholics Anonymous World Services, 2001).
35. Lewis, *Shame and Guilt in Neurosis*.
36. Gilligan, *Violence: Our Deadly Epidemic and Its Causes*.
37. J. Elison, R. Lennon, and S. Pulos, "Investigating the Compass of Shame: The Development of the Compass of Shame Scale," *Social Behavior and Personality: An International Journal* 34, no. 3 (2006): 221–238.
38. Scheff and Retzinger, *Emotions and Violence*.
39. Lewis, "Shame and the Narcissistic Personality," 110.
40. "Social-Emotional Origins of Violence: A Theory of Multiple Killing," unpublished manuscript (2012), 6.
41. Ibid.
42. Carol Gilligan, *In a Different Voice: Psychological Theory and Women's Development*, 1st ed. (Cambridge, MA: Harvard University Press, 1993).
43. Scott Huddleston, "Wounded Soldier Heals With Comedy," *San Antonio Express-News*, August 13, 2010, http://www.mysanantonio.com/entertainment/stage/article/Wounded-soldier-heals-with-comedy-848017.php#src=fb; David Wood, "Bobby Henline, U.S. Soldier Saved From the Brink of Death, Pursues His Stand-Up Comedy Dreams (Video)," *Huffington Post*, October 21, 2011, http://www.huffingtonpost.com/2011/10/21/bobby-hemline-us-soldier-_n_1023916.html.
44. L Pulkkinen, "Proactive and Reactive Aggression in Early Adolescence as Precursors to Anti- and Prosocial Behavior in Young Adults," *Aggressive Behavior* 22, no. 4 (1996): 241–257.
45. Gilligan, "Violence: Our Deadly Epidemic and Its Causes." Scheff, *Bloody Revenge*.
46. Gilligan, Violence: Our Deadly Epidemic and Its Causes. 110.

CHAPTER 2

Bullying In and Out of Schools

BULLIES AND VICTIMS: MADE FOR EACH OTHER

Seventy percent of people get bullied at some point in their childhood.[1] I was bullied. I was a fat, clumsy little boy and I got teased by a slim, athletic boy named Mark at summer camp when I was eight years old. I finally lost my temper, knocked him down on the worktable in woodshop, and began to strangle him. I might have really hurt him—I was that blind with shame/rage—if the counselors had not pulled us apart. The sense of losing control scared us both and pretty much put an end to it.

Casual bullying often stops after a few incidents. Sometimes the bullies are simply jokers with a poor sense of the distinction between funny and hurtful. Once the harm they are creating is pointed out to them, they stop. Some children ingratiate themselves with the bully. Others fight back. Seven percent stay home pretending to be sick ("hiding" on Nathanson's compass of shame).[2] Sometimes adults intervene and the threat of unpleasant consequences is enough to reduce the bullying to a bearable level. Some children accumulate enough social capitol to make themselves invulnerable. Jason Segal, a popular comic actor who played the character Marshall for 11 years on *How I Met Your Mother*, recalled being bullied in middle school and high school. By the age of 12 he had reached his full adult height of six foot four, and this made him feel like a monster alongside the other "normal" children. He admitted that he still has flashbacks of an incident when bullies surrounded him and took turns jumping on his back while the others chanted, "Ride the oaf! Ride the oaf!" He increased his status by becoming increasingly funny and outrageous and putting his size to good use as a star basketball player.[3] He has talked about his bullying publically on a number of occasions, suggesting that talk-show confession may offer a similar release to confiding in a friend or sharing with a trusted group.

The serious problems occur when a bully who manages trait shame by an "attack other" strategy finds a victim who manages trait shame by "attack self." Then a very negative synergy occurs. The bully's shame is displaced onto the victim. The victim comes to represent everything the bully hates in himself (because this kind of bullying is usually boy on boy, I will use masculine pronouns) and absorbs so much shame that his thinking becomes jumbled. He starts to believe that he is "damaged goods." Life becomes insufferable, and suicide may seem like an attractive option.

WHAT MAKES A BULLY?

The Swedish psychologist Dan Olweus, long associated with the University of Bergen in Norway, is considered the foremost authority on bullying. In 1970 he conducted the first large-scale scientific study of the subject. In 1983, when three adolescent boys in Northern Norway committed suicide in response to bullying, Olweus was recruited to create an intervention to stop bullying. The Olweus Bullying Prevention Program has subsequently been used throughout Norway with some success (30 to 70 percent)[4] Its results have been less impressive in the United States, Germany, and Belgium (5 to 30 percent),[5] possibly because of cultural differences. Despite this, his research regarding bullies remains the gold standard.

Olweus sees bullying as a "component of a more generally antisocial and rule-breaking ('conduct-disordered') behavior pattern."[6] Aggressive behavior is a stabile trait, meaning that an aggressive child usually grows up to be an aggressive adult.[7] Bullies have an increased risk of alcoholism and criminality later in life. A Finnish study, "From a Boy to a Man," followed 2,540 boys from the age of eight for a decade. Boys identified as bullies in middle school often exhibited antisocial personality disorder (criminal behavior), substance abuse, and problems of anxiety and depression as young adults.[8] Olweus, following 87 boys from age 12 to age 24, found that over half of those who were bullies in grades 6 through 9 had at least one criminal conviction by the age of 24, and over a third had three or more convictions (this compared to a criminal conviction rate among non-bullies of about 1 out of 10).

While those who were bullied as children can often escape their tormentors as adults, they cannot escape themselves. They are likely to suffer from depression and low self-esteem. While girls are bullied less frequently than boys, their outcomes are worse. A Finnish study found them more likely to have had at least one psychiatric hospitalization and been prescribed antipsychotic, antidepressant, and antianxiety drugs as adults.[9]

Olweus has identified five risk factors that predispose a child to becoming a bully:[10]

1. Parents did not bond with the child when he or she was an infant.
2. Parents failed to inhibit the child's aggression.
3. Parents model aggression and physical violence as their primary problem-solving strategies (Olweus calls it "power-assertive child-rearing methods").
4. The child has an inborn penchant toward aggressive and impulsive behavior (Olweus calls it "an active and 'hot-headed' temperament").
5. The child is larger and stronger than other children his age.

Let's examine these risk factors more closely.

Lack of a Parental Bond

Olweus refers to parental bonding as the "basic emotional attitude of the primary caretaker" to the infant. He goes on to say that this kind of parent–child relationship is "characterized by lack of warmth and involvement."[11] John Bowlby, who wrote copiously about this subject, calls it "insecure attachment."[12] In prefeminist writings, the caregiver is always assumed to be the mother, but in the current culture we believe it can as easily be the father, grandparent, nanny, or adoptive parent.[13] In chapter 1 we talked about the human longing to be part of a group. The parent–child "dyad" (a group of two) is everyone's first experience of a group. Most children first show awareness of this around six months of age[14] when the architecture of the brain has reached a certain level of complexity, about the same time that infants become toddlers. Before that age, children seem equally happy with any caretaker who comforts or amuses them. After that, they want and need their mothers and become anxious around strangers. The importance of the mother–child dyad may seem obvious to us but was more or less ignored by the scientific community prior to the twentieth century. It only became a worthy object of investigation because of society's changing attitude toward children after World War I[15] and public concern over the many children orphaned and displaced by that terrible conflict.

Orphaned infants who had been hospitalized during the war lost weight on diets that should have helped them grow, grew quiet and sad despite their clean and organized surroundings, and had a shockingly high mortality rate (as high as 75 percent for two-year-olds in a report from 1915).[16] Such children also showed language deficits and lower IQs than their nonhospitalized peers. The condition was referred to as "hospitalism" and, later, "failure to thrive." The cause was thought to be malnutrition or infection of some kind. Efforts were made to further isolate babies to prevent the spread of infection, but that only made them more listless. In 1931 Harry Bakwin, a doctor in charge of the pediatric unit at Bellevue Hospital in New York City and a professor at New York University Medical School, reasoned that these infants were responding to a lack of human contact. He took down signs that had been placed around the ward emphasizing antisepsis ("Wash your hands twice before entering this ward") and replaced them with signs encouraging cuddling and cooing ("Do not enter this nursery without picking up a baby").

The problems of maternal deprivation were not only physiological. Psychological damage was also evident, not just in the form of depression,[17] which was often obvious, but more subtly in a lack of empathy. An early example of this was noted in a scientific paper by David Levy published in 1937.[18] Levy, a prominent New York psychoanalyst and one of the leaders of the child guidance movement, described an eight-year-old girl who had been adopted after years of being shuttled between foster homes who showed antisocial traits such as lying, manipulation, and superficial emotionality. He speculated as to whether there might be a "deficiency disease of the emotional life, comparable to a deficiency of vital nutritional elements within the developing organism."[19] Many child welfare workers reported that they were familiar with this kind of behavior in children separated from their mothers at an early age or shuttled between foster homes.

Meanwhile in England, John Bowlby, a perceptive and gifted psychiatrist, graduate of the Tavistock Psychoanalytic Institute, and director of the London Child Guidance Clinic, had noticed commonalities in 44 children who had been referred to his agency for thievery. In his own words:

> in several cases sympathetic discussions with the mothers of the children revealed that their apparent love for their child was only one aspect of their feelings about him. Often an intense, though perhaps unadmitted, dislike and rejection of him also came to light. Furthermore very careful enquiries showed a remarkable proportion of children who, for one reason or another, had not lived securely in one home all their lives but had spent long periods away from home.[20]

Every new mother wants to be part of the group that might be called Good Mothers. The first rule for membership is that the Good Mother loves her child so much that she would give up her life for him or her. Some of these mothers did not feel that way about their children, although they hid the truth beneath a layer of socially acceptable patter. In other cases, chaotic family lives and frequent relocations had interfered with the creation of a stabile caregiver bond.

Other caregivers may substitute for mothers, an issue that is becoming more pertinent as our culture comes to accept the idea that a same-sex couple can successfully raise a family. Neither a blood relationship nor a particular gender is necessary. For centuries the children of the British upper class have been raised by devoted nannies. In situations where parents are preoccupied with other concerns, grandparents and aunts and uncles are often successful substitutes. Extended families, a rarity in this country, offer a variety of individuals who are willing to form a strong attachment with an infant.

Shortly after the publication of my previous book on school shooters, I received an email from a young man (we will call him Carter). I include the letter verbatim because the process of his writing it was as important as its content.

> Dear Dr. Fast,
>
> [Your book][21] dredged up an old memory, one whose details I could stand to be free of. I must apologize, but I need to tell someone this, and you may be in a position to appreciate my story. If not, I am sorry for wasting your time, and I wish you the best of luck with your book.
>
> I almost disemboweled Matt P. in seventh grade, and I've spent years regretting it.
>
> For the first few years, I regretted being unable to carry out the act; later I was upset that I was willing to do such a thing. My motivations switched one hundred eighty degrees, but the guilt was constant.
>
> Matt P. was a year older than I was, bigger, and less bookish. I wasn't particularly sociable or charismatic in middle school, and was physically dominated by those further along in puberty, like Matt. I suppose this is the wont of every teenager in my position, but I was frightened and furious. I had fully expected that the adults, who I had imagined up until that time controlled the universe, would have in their foresight forbidden such actions, but they had failed . . . and I got beat up. Every time I was bounced off the lockers or shoved to the ground or called a faggot, I kept thinking that it was an unsympathetic Fate, in the person of Matt P., challenging me to do something about the apparent insouciance of the universe.

"I'm going to kick your ass, and what are you going to do about it?" he asked.

So, after getting socked in the gut one time too many after gym class, I went home, and by accident, I found the knife. When my dad left, he hadn't taken all of his tools. Under his workbench, I found a Buck Special with a drop point and a nine-inch blade, sharp as the day it was bought, lying dusty and forgotten in its sheath next to the spackle and the block planes.

I cannot explain how comforting it was to pull the knife from its sheath, and to feel the cool mass of it in my hand, and to hear the soft ringing of the blade when I brushed my thumb-tip against it. I knew then that I found my answer for Matt.

Nobody noticed that I had taken the knife. I put it in my gym bag, next to my socks and my cup, and I immediately felt better. I kept it there for a few weeks. I knew, I just knew, that I'd get assaulted again, and I just had to have the bag next to me, and be curled up on the ground at the feet of my attacker, where I could draw the knife forth.

I thought about a stab to the heart second. I first thought of the throat, which I immediately deprecated—Matt was taller than I was, and I hadn't the length of arm. I had little arm of any sort. We had learned that the heart was behind a heavy curtain of ribs, and inside a tough pericardial sac—our Life Science teacher, an ex-nurse, taught us about how tough the chest cavity was for surgeons with skill and the right tools to get through. Let alone amateurs acting under duress with hunting knives.

No, it'd have to be the gut.

My plan was to let him hit me. I'd curl up around my gym bag, with my right hand slid inside, gripping the knife. Knowing Matt, a helpless victim in a fetal position would be an invitation to lean over and deliver a wedgie or a just a thin filament of spit down the back of the neck, or perhaps just a whispered invidious remark about one's parentage. Then, I would pull the knife, brace the heel of my left hand against the pommel, and, rolling back onto my heels and standing up, I'd drive the point of the knife into his stomach, right below the xiphoid process. The trick then would be to keep the blade angled down, and let him stand up to complete the evisceration. He'd be surprised, and then he'd die, painfully.

My thoughts past this point weren't terribly clear. Matt P. would be dead, and I wouldn't have to worry about him anymore. I had very little concern for the future, which was for me at least a foreshortened and not terribly interesting place. I had the present to worry about.

I was never able to do it. Mostly, the opportunity was never right. My plan was predicated on a particular choreography of bully and bully-ee that never came out quite right. At first, I was waiting for the perfect place and time . . . and then, there was the dinner.

My school had a Grandparent's Dinner every year. Students were expected to bring their grandparents or great-aunts or uncles in for a rubber chicken dinner and a speech from the Principle. There was an exhibit of athletic trophies and academic awards and student artwork. Everybody left with a better feeling of community and some indigestion. My grandparents would not have missed Grandparent's Dinner for the world, and so I went to sign up. The reservation sheet was tacked to the Principle's door, and Matt P.'s name was on it.

Up until that point, I really didn't consider Matt to be human. He was just the entity who made my life miserable Monday through Friday, eight to two-fifteen. The notion of him having grandparents was an epiphany, pregnant with implications, like NASA finding an empty Fresca can on Mars. Were I to kill, or seriously injure Matt, some old Italian nana I'd never met would likely be very upset. Unlike her grandson, I didn't wish her any harm at all.

To say nothing of the reaction from my own grandparents . . .

Then, as now, the thought of sorrowful old people upsets me terribly. I realized with growing frustration that I could endure more bullying than I could the thought of weeping old ladies. The knife stayed in the bottom of my locker until the last day of school, when I brought it home in a shoebox underneath a stack of old quizzes.

I'd like to say that Matt P. had a similar revelation, and he made up with me and everyone else he had kicked the shit out of. To the best of my knowledge, he didn't. The funny thing was, even as I got beat up, I'd think about why I could never make Matt regret what he was doing; and I'd start to laugh. Sometimes that made him hit me harder, but eventually he started to think me laughing was funny too. I learned, quite by accident, that comedy could keep the bullies off me, and that worked until I was big enough to take care of myself.

I could never hurt him, but at the same time, I could never stop hating him. I'm a coward for never going through with it, and I'm a lunatic for how intent I was on killing him for so long. I know I chose right, but I can see how tremendously appealing the wrong choice is.

As for the mechanism—eh. My dad kept his guns locked up. I'd have used 'em in a heartbeat, but I didn't want to drag my parents into it, and I figured the gun would've drawn more attention than the knife. Besides, guns were a little too impersonal. I wanted to be able to see him die, and for him to know that it was me that killed him. Had I two dozen bullies to make an end of, expediency would've pushed me towards firearms.

This would have been a ceremony indeed; for whatever psychological or societal reasons I came close to killing for (and others DID kill for), these will always be feasts for Baal; if this kind of action is so horrible, why was his cult once so popular?

Thank you Doctor, for listening to me.

The letter itself is an example of positively managing shame by processing, or confessing. Carter wrote about "an old memory, one whose details I could stand to be free of" and how he "needed to tell someone this." Even now, years after the event, he still needed to talk about it, to *manage* it. Because I seemed knowledgeable, sympathetic, and nonjudgmental regarding people with violent impulses, Carter decided to confide in me. According to his letter, he was small and a late bloomer, and was repeatedly bullied by Matt, who was "bigger and less bookish." This is an example of the unequal power differential that is always present in bullying. For Carter, his father's knife promised a way of managing the shame through "attack other." Carter seems to have strongly bonded with his grandparents, and the fact that Matt had grandparents too humanized him. One could speculate that if Carter had grown up with no adult bond, Matt might have remained less than human, and a target for Carter's father's knife. Carter also learned that shame can be managed through humor.

A few questions occurred to me while reading this, and I wrote back asking him about resilience factors, such as friendships and memberships in groups. This was his response:

> I didn't have that many friends growing up. Most of the time, the problem is me. I didn't like social occasions from an early age, and to this day I have a problem with people. I can deal with one or two other persons in a room with me at an informal gathering, but any more than that, and I start to get nervous. Classrooms are a little easier (only a little), but parties are torture. Given the choice, I'd rather go someplace quiet and read a book. I hate doing that though, I don't want people to think I'm rude or haughty. So I smile, and endure. So I made few friends—what ones I had I was (and am) very attached to.

I also asked Carter about his connection with his parents. Carter replied that his home life had been chaotic. His parents did not earn enough money to support a family and were often in conflict. During the first eight years of Carter's life, they moved three times. He rarely saw his father, who worked double shifts through the night, or his mother, who worked part-time and had gone back to college.

> Very often, they would be tired, and frustrated and angry. My sister and I were hit when necessary, but sometimes Mom or Dad would fly off the handle and start throwing things, or slamming doors or Mom would be crying and Dad would peel out of the driveway, and come home very late at night. There would be much weeping and shouting, especially as I got older. I was never certain

what mood either of my parents was going to be in when I got home from school. Depression? Hair-trigger rage? Something like ordinary moods?

Carter and his younger sister often stayed with their maternal or paternal grandparents, who were loving and attentive. Another source of resilience for him was a golden retriever he got when he was eight.

> For the next sixteen years, he [the golden retriever] was the most even-tempered and reliable member of my family, even though he couldn't speak English and had trouble answering the phone. He was often the only one my sister and I could go to when we were upset, and while he couldn't give advice, he was a good listener.
>
> Years later, reflecting on my mother's depression throughout my childhood and adolescence, and my father's long absence, someone remarked that, effectively, I had been raised by the dog.
>
> I still prefer golden retrievers to people, most of the time.

So while his parental bond may have been fragile, his attachment to his grandparents was robust, and he could use it as a basis for understanding the sentience and humanity of another human being. Once he had experienced this revelation, he could transfer his empathic feelings to others.

The dependability of the caregiver bond also shapes our response to *temporary* loss of the caregiver, a common event in everyone's life. Consider a toddler who has formed a successful bond with his father. He approaches his father with the expectation of a piggyback ride around the backyard. The father, who is engrossed by a phone call about the bake sale he is organizing for daycare, gently pushes him aside.

Depending on his temperament, he may cry and scream as though his heart is broken. Rejection seems tragic and permanent for a little guy with a foggy sense of past and future. When his father gets off the phone, he comforts him and takes him for a piggyback ride around the yard. Soon the child is giggling, and the temporary rejection is forgotten. The child has learned that people are reliable, that a few moments of being ignored may not be a sign of permanent abandonment, that hugging and comforting by a close companion can ease the pain. The next time, separation will be easier for him. A year from now he will be able to think to himself, *Well, Daddy is busy right now but he will play with me later,* with only a hint of sadness and no shame at all. He knows, after a number of repetitions, that his membership in the dyad of Me and My Dad is secure.

Now imagine a different kind of caregiver, a woman who, for whatever reasons, numbs herself to her shame with some kind of addiction. Her toddler may never learn how to properly manage the discomfort of temporary separation because the addiction has made her unreliable. Her judgment may be impaired, her memory subject to lapses, her perception of reality altered. She says, *I'll be with you in a minute,* but often the minutes stretch into hours, and sometimes she remains emotionally or physically unavailable for days. Other people, *alleged* providers of childcare, come and go but do not stay long enough to create a real caregiver bond. To complicate matters, this mother's feelings toward her toddler may be ambivalent or resentful. Children may be viewed as nothing more than an impediment to her getting high.

All children realize that they should be loved by their caregivers. Toddlers blame the absence of this love on themselves and attribute it to a personal deficit: *I am not loved because something is wrong with me.* As a result, toddlers may find it difficult to believe that any person would love someone as damaged as they are. This kind of shame is not easily managed. It may endure for a lifetime, shaping one's personality in myriad ways that spoil the quality of life. Such people may consider themselves unworthy of a good job, a loving spouse, or other satisfactions. Their anger toward the hand they have been dealt may be turned against themselves in the form of anorexia, cutting, and suicide attempts. If the anger is turned outward, they may be unable to accept responsibility for their own failures and shortcomings. They may come to resent those who might have aided and befriended them. In the worst cases, their thoughts may become confused, they may harm others for reasons that temporarily seem logical with no sense of the consequences, as was very nearly the case with Carter.

Which of these scenarios becomes the reality depends on the balance of risk factors and resilience factors. Having an extended family is often a resilience factor because many adults are available for the child to attach to, if the parents are in crisis of some kind. Special talent in the arts or sports is also a resilience factor because they increase a child's sense of self-worth. Being born into a middle-class or wealthy family is a resilience factor because parents have more resources when a crisis arises. When Donald Trump was expelled from high school, for example, his parents had the resources to send him to a military academy where experienced teachers "straightened him out."[22] Unfortunately, resilience factors do not balance out risk factors in a tidy or calculable way. There are no algorithms to predict who will become a delinquent and who an asset to society. James Garbarino, an authority on violence and children, reminds us that "Rarely, if ever, does one single risk factor tell the whole story or determine a person's future. Rather, it is the buildup of negative influences and experiences that accounts for differences in how youth turn out."[23] He likens dealing with risk factors to juggling balls. One can manage two easily, or three with a little practice, but add a fourth and keeping the balls in the air becomes a challenge. The more risk factors, the greater the likelihood of dropping the ball.

Parents' Failure to Inhibit Child's Aggression

Little children naturally express themselves physically, and sometimes violently, because their responses are unfiltered, quick, and thoughtless. Because they the patience, self-moderation, impulse control, and verbal skills required to identify and articulate what they are experiencing, they act out. They perform a mime show choreographed by anger or frustration. When a parent tells a child to "Use your words," rather than to strike out, he or she is acknowledging that talk is a safer, more socially acceptable and precise means of communicating feelings—including negative, frightening feelings like shame and anger—and one that, when it becomes habit, will help the child attain a better life. Children who have learned to identify their own feelings and have the self-control to step back and formulate their thoughts—and the vocabulary to express them—are less likely to engage in a violent act than children who do not have these resources.

If the parent tolerates a child's acts of aggression, or encourages them, the aggression is likely to increase.[24] Some children are harder to rein in because of developmental delays, autism, impulsivity, or attention deficit disorder. Again, wealthy parents have the advantage in obtaining specialized help. Some children may consider parental tolerance of their aggression as an expression of indifference, a lack of love and caring, or even rejection. Children who feel unloved are willing to go anywhere for a sense of family. They may obtain this in school, if they are appealing to teachers and have a hunger to learn, or they might find it in a neighborhood street gang, often a stepping stone to a criminal career.

Parents Model Aggression and Physical Violence

Some parents model aggression and physical violence as their primary problem-solving strategy ("power-assertive child-rearing methods" in Olweus's words). Such parents are often raised "by the stick" themselves. The way our parents disciplined us is imprinted in our own child minds as the "right way," and it is often difficult, despite our best intentions, to avoid falling under their spell when we ourselves become parents. The distinguished criminologist Cathy Widom has demonstrated convincingly that violent parents do, more often than not, rear violent children,[25] but how much of that is genetic, or related to parenting style, remains unclear.

A parent who responds violently to provocations is modeling a style of problem-solving based on superior size and strength and the power to intimidate. Violent behavior comes with a beguiling reward—an intoxicating sense of power—but one gained at a high price. The writings of extremely violent people continually describe the self-respect they attain through their misbehavior.[26] An act of violence makes the offender feel that he is acting in a decisive way, that he or she has taken control of the situation through his or her own strength, directly, immediately, and incontestably. Shame is replaced by a feeling of grandiosity. A second, neurological process occurs at the same time. The body is pumped up with adrenalin and neurotransmitters are released,[27] creating a highly pleasurable sensation that indiscriminately obliterates bad feelings in the same way as alcohol or drugs. On Nathanson's compass of shame, it combines two poles, avoidance and attack other. Caregivers who violently enforce their dictums are attempting to manage their own shame at the expense of their family. They reinforce a cycle of violence *and* a cycle of shame.

Child Has an Inborn Penchant Toward Aggressive and Impulsive Behavior

Some children are born more aggressive or headstrong than others. Whether children are ever born without any capacity for empathy and what we call conscience remains to be seen. At certain times in history, psychologists have espoused a "bed seed" theory of antisocial behavior. There seems to be a pendulum in thinking about this subject that swings back and forth between the decades. In 1954, when the pendulum was in full swing toward nature (as opposed to nurture), William March wrote a best-selling novel called *The Bad Seed*[28] about a little girl, the product of an affluent home and loving parents, who murders a playmate out of spite. People found the idea creepy enough to propel it to best-sellerdom. It became a hit Broadway show and a popular movie.

Authorities on antisocial behavior, including Hervey Cleckly, who wrote the classic treatise on the subject,[29] and Robert Hare,[30] who created the "psychopath checklist," agree that both biological and environmental factors contribute to the making of the psychopath or sociopath (a term used informally to identify a milder level of the problem).

The best evidence for this comes from an area of research called "twin studies." In a twin study, researchers locate pairs of identical and non-identical twins who were separated at birth and adopted by different families. The quality in question—in this case psychopathic—is measured for each of the twins, often by a questionnaire, and the results are compared. If the scores are more equal between identical twins than fraternal twins, that suggests that the problem is genetic, since identical twins share all their DNA while fraternal twins share only half. If their scores vary randomly, it suggests that the effect may be due to the environment. Twin studies of psychopathic behavior suggest that psychopathy is biological and environmental, nature and half nurture.[31] However, we do not know what genes, or combinations of genes (alleles), are responsible and precisely how they affect behavior to bring about these conditions.

The idea that children are born with a criminal inclination is offensive to some who choose to believe, based on experience or ideology, that all children are born good or are blank slates upon which any future can be writ. Some years ago I gave a lecture at New York City's Administration for Children's Services, the organization that provides services to children of families who have been reported for violent or neglectful treatment of their children. I spoke to a group of 20 women employees who had dedicated their lives to working with children who had been taken from their homes because of conditions dreadful beyond what most of us can imagine. I asked them how many believed that some children were born bad. Not one raised her hand.

When Olweus writes of this factor, he emphasizes that the "temperament of the child . . . is *in part* inherited . . . The effect of this factor *is less powerful than those of the [previously] mentioned conditions*" (my italics). I believe he makes this point because he does not want to give the impression that any child, regardless of the temperament with which he or she is born, lacks the potential to be a worthy and productive adult.

Size and Strength of the Child

The fifth factor concerns the size and strength of the child. A male bully is usually physically stronger and larger than others his age. That is usually the source of his authority.

Angus Watson, a British journalist who writes on a variety of subjects, described his own experience as a school bully when he was nine. While he appeared as a good citizen to his teachers and older students, he was feared by his classmates—and rightly so. He was bigger and stronger than others in his class and, by his own admission, nastier.

> I discovered that one way of amusing my friends was to taunt other children. I became a ringleader and people began to look up to me, which suited me just fine.
>
> I became an expert at giving boys dead arms, dead legs and knuckle dusters (a stiff rap to the skull with the central knuckle). I could hit an earlobe from five yards with a high-velocity elastic band, push a boy over in the mud and mock him for any physical defect. Several boys would look up nervously when I came into a teacher-free room.
>
> [I]t's possible I helped make life a misery for several other children. Weaker boys were just accessories to my fun. My cronies and I didn't think of ourselves as unpleasant thugs but as heroes: as far as we could see, we were the winners and weaker people were there for our amusement, to add glory to our adventures. What to an observer may have seemed horrific was, for us, innocent fun. It didn't seem we were doing anything wrong; it was just how things worked. I was a bigger boy fulfilling his role in child culture. Violence was currency passed from strong to weak.[32]

After describing a particularly nasty and theatrical act of cruelty committed by a fellow bully, Watson escalated his aggression.

> Bullying took on a crueller and more imaginative twist. Breaking expensive Caran d'Ache pencils while their owners watched, teasing them about their mothers' hairstyles, throwing sticks dipped in sheep-poo at them, and so on. Pretty horrible stuff, and certainly nothing to remember with pride. So why did I do it? . . .
>
> [I]t was part of my childhood culture. My big brother whacked me with happy regularity, as did all my dormitory captains at boarding school. One particular prefect would make us drink water until we were sick. Another made my friend cut me with an army tin opener.
>
> My friends and I used to stab each other, and ourselves, with compasses for amusement. We used to spray deodorant from very close on to our skin, making it blister. I still have scars from that. Pain was all around. Bullying, I suppose, was a way of passing this on to the weaker boys.[33]

Watson had been shamed by a variety of older children, and this was his opportunity to manage the emotion by inflicting it on other, smaller children and also on his friends and himself. Using one shame management strategy (attack other) does not stop a bully from occasionally using another (attack self).

By his own account, the event that cured Watson of his bullying involved the discovery of girls.

> Then, in the summer holidays when I was 12, I hung out with a group of girls for the first time, in the seaside village where we used to go on holiday . . . For their amusement, I roughed up a couple of younger boys down on the seafront. The girls pointed out what an idiot I was and said they didn't want to be friends with someone who behaved like this . . . Whether it was a sudden revelation, growing older or, more likely, an increasing desire to impress girls, everything became clear.
>
> [T]he long-term taunting and physical bullying stopped, and I encouraged my friends not to bully, too. I suddenly saw how awful I looked.[34]

Watson wanted to join a group of higher status, Boys Who Socialize With Girls, but was rejected because of his bullying behavior. He changed his behavior in response to "reintegrative shaming"[35]—the shame that brings one back into a group. He was not simply pretending to change: the shaming brought about a change of consciousness, an awakening of empathy.

WHAT MAKES A VICTIM?

Children, when asked why some students are bullied, replied that it was because they were *different*; they were obese, red-headed, spoke with a funny accent, or wore thick glasses.[36] Many adults were of the same belief. In fact, "difference" has little to do with it. Children become bullying victims because they are smaller and weaker than other children their age.[37] They give off subtle signals that they will internalize shame rather than fight back. They may cower or tear up easily. They might be considered, in a logical corollary of Bowlby's theory of bonding, as "overattached" to their mothers ("Momma's boy" was a bully's taunt in the old days).

Bullying requires a confrontation between weak and strong, a "power differential." It may be easier to understand the importance of the power differential by imagining a bullying incident *without* it. If the power differential does not exist—if the bully chooses a target who is his equal in size and strength and who externalizes shame—the victim will fight back. This is no longer bullying; it is a duel. It is a fight entered upon by both parties over an insult or some other question of honor in order to determine status. Who is the better fighter, the stronger, the cleverer, the quicker? Perhaps there is even a choice of weapons to maintain the fairness of the fight. Fists, knives, or guns? It is something entirely different from a bullying incident. (Note: this is not an endorsement of dueling, a practice outlawed nearly everywhere in the modern world. Restorative practices provide better ways of repairing honor and do not involve injury or death.)

Olweus divides victims into two categories: the "submissive" and the "provocative."[38] The submissive victim appears to be cautious, sensitive, quiet, and insecure, with little sense of his own value. The submissive victim internalizes his or her shame, transforming it into negative self-talk and masochistic behavior. A younger boy will cry; an older boy will hide. He will make excuses to stay home, avoid the school bus, or skip classes where he knows the bully is waiting.[39] The second kind of victim is provocative, both anxious and aggressive. This child may disrupt the class by attention-seeking behaviors, talking too much, laughing inappropriately, or fidgeting in a way that distracts nearly everyone. Often the provocative victim has problems with concentration, hyperactivity, or a narcissistic need to be the center of attention.

DIRECT BULLYING AND RELATIONAL BULLYING

As boys are associated with direct bullying, girls are associated with relational bullying, the spreading of rumors designed to humiliate the victim and socially isolate her. This difference in bullying styles corresponds with the broad stereotypes of male and female social behavior, but of course men engage in relational bullying too, and women occasionally become involved in fistfights.

All online bullying, or cyberbullying, is relational bullying. Cyberbullying has even greater potential for harm than real-world bullying because the perpetrator can remain anonymous and the size and composition of the audience remains unknown. Who is reading this Facebook page filled with disparaging remarks about me? My parents? My teachers? Everyone in the world?

The audience can be vast if some detail of the event makes it "go viral." If one with whom you are not intimate sees you with your clothes off, it is embarrassing enough. If 1,000 people, or a 100,000 people witness it, it becomes literally mortifying. In 2010 a 12-year-old Canadian named Amanda Todd, during a video chat with a stranger, exposed her breasts in response to his polite and flattering encouragement. Over the next two years he stalked her relentlessly, anonymously posting his video of her revealing her breasts on her Facebook page. Classmates began calling her "porn star." Eventually she changed schools. Somehow the stalker learned of her move and, maintaining his anonymity, cultivated online friends at her new school. He again posted the video, creating another wave of humiliation among her peers. On October 14, 2012, no longer able to bare the shame, Amanda took her own life.[40] The stalker was eventually identified as a 35-year-old Dutch man named Aydin Coban, a technologically sophisticated cyber-criminal who was also wanted in the United Kingdom and the United States for similar crimes involving enticing minors to commit immoral acts.[41]

MEGAN TAYLOR MEIER

Suicide is the third leading cause of death among teenagers, and studies have estimated that half of these suicides occur in response to bullying. I end this chapter with the tragic case of Megan Meier, who took her own life in 2006. Like Amanda Todd, her suicide was provoked by an adult who engaged her in cyberbullying.

Megan Meier and her family lived in Dardenne Park, a bedroom community of St. Louis. Waterford Crossing was a new development of clapboard and stone colonials with broad green lawns, and the inference of rising social status was reflected in the name of the street where Megan lived: Waterford Crystal Drive. She had recently turned 13 and began having mood swings. They occurred suddenly, with little provocation. One expects a certain amount of drama from a girl who has just entered her teens, but these were of a different magnitude. In an interview, her mother said that Megan had always been unhappy about her weight, even in kindergarten. In elementary school she began to feud with some of her classmates, and, by third grade, the hostilities had reached the point where she confessed to her mother that she wanted to kill herself. Olweus might have described her as a provocative victim. A psychiatrist diagnosed her as having attention deficit hyperactive disorder (ADHD), prescribed an antidepressant, a mood stabilizer, and medication for an attention deficit disorder.

Those of us who have had no direct experience with ADHD may have difficulty understanding the extent of its ill effects on a child's social life. As described by Dara R. Blachman and Stephen P. Hinshaw:

> Children with ADHD have been repeatedly found to experience extremely
> high rates of peer rejection . . . even those children with ADHD who are not

aggressive tend to be rejected because of their overzealous and insensitive behaviors ... Children with ADHD often serve as "negative social catalysts," fueling conflictual social interactions among their peers.[42]

Blachman and Hinshaw studied the socialization of girls in a summer camp, two-thirds of whom had been diagnosed with ADHD, and found that the girls with ADHD had made fewer friendships than the undiagnosed girls and were more likely to have *no friends at all*. Among the ADHD girls who had made friends, the relationships had more *sturm und drang* than the normal girls, "particularly with respect to increased levels of negative features such as conflict and relational aggression."[43]

In 2004, when Megan was in sixth grade, her mother, Tina, who was a realtor, sold a house four doors down to Lori and Curt Drew, who had a daughter Megan's age. The girls developed a close, on-again/off-again relationship in which Megan seemed to have the upper hand. They had a pattern: inseparable for two or three days and then Megan needed time to herself. Her friend would sometimes feel rejected and her parents "ticked off" at the way their daughter was being treated.

The Drews were considered one of the less popular families in the neighborhood. "They seem to have been regarded as local inconveniences, their offenses good-humoredly endured but regularly remarked upon, like those of a barking dog."[44] Their daughter was prim and obedient while Megan had a "wilder, more domineering personality."[45] She loved going fishing with her dad, watching horror movies, and playing with her chihuahua, Barry. She had a vivid imagination and a reputation for fearlessness, on one occasion picking up a frog and waving it in the face of a squeamish boy. She also had a dutiful, empathic side to her personality and sympathy for the underdog; for years, she had helped a blind student at her school find his next class when the bell rang.

While sixth grade "wasn't horrible,"[46] in her mother's words, seventh grade posed challenges. By that time she had lost 20 pounds and was not unattractive. Some pictures from that period show her wearing volumes of eye shadow and lip gloss, sucking in her cheeks to look like a fashion model, and practicing expressions of the sort we see in lipstick adds. While this kind of play is typical for a child her age, who is grappling with becoming an adult woman and meeting our cultural definitions of beauty, her focus on her weight and her poor self-image raised the stakes. "Megan was trying desperately to fit in,"[47] her mother told an interviewer, months after her daughter's death, but her classmates were reluctant to accept her, and her desperation to belong may have aggravated the situation.

Curious about romance and looking for a place to practice chatting with boys in vitro, Megan and the Drews' daughter, during one of their on-again periods, secretly set up a MySpace page. They created an avatar with a false name and borrowed an image they found on the Internet of an attractive teenage girl. Both mothers learned of the experiment independently and forbade their daughters to continue but never spoke of it to each other. They were not close friends.

Megan's seventh-grade experiences were sufficiently troubling that her parents transferred her to a nearby Catholic school. Immaculate Conception had smaller classes, mandatory uniforms, and assigned seats at lunch to keep cliques in check. The initial results were encouraging. Megan seemed to be making friends and was paying less attention to her hair and makeup. But the clique-ish behavior, forbidden in the classroom, had migrated onto the Internet. Megan began pestering her parents for a MySpace account so she could chat with friends outside of school. Tina was reluctant to agree after the fiasco of the previous year. Furthermore, the rules of MySpace prohibited anyone under 14 from having an account. Megan was still 13. After much campaigning and negotiating, Tina agreed with these caveats:[48]

1. Your dad and I are the only ones who know the password.
2. It has to be set to "private."
3. We have to approve the content.
4. We have to be in the room at all times when you're on MySpace.

Megan's MySpace page went online on September 13, 2006. Megan's online self strove to be urban and sophisticated. She gave her home as "getto st. louis, MISSOURI, United States," and laced her bio with words like "hip-hop" and "bling." In less than a week Megan received a friend request from 16-year-old Josh (because her MySpace page was set to private, only people granted "friend" status could chat with her and leave messages). Unbeknownst to her, Josh, his physical description (blue eyes, brown wavy hair, six foot three), and his Dickensian childhood (dad abandoned family, mom struggled to feed three little boys) were the creation of Lori Drew, or, according to another account, of Lori's daughter and Ashley Grills, an 18-year-old who worked for the direct mail company the Drews ran out of their home. Josh was tailored to appeal to Megan's boy tastes and her sympathy for the underdog. He lived 10 minutes away, in O'Fallon, near enough to be boyfriend material, but was homeschooled (to explain why none of her friends from O'Fallon knew of him) and had no phone.

When she was not at school, Megan was at the computer chatting with her new friend, who did not care about her weight and thought she was really pretty. This went on for a month. According to her father, "She was the happiest she had ever been in her life."[49] She was looking forward to having her braces removed on the 15th of October and to her birthday party on the following day.

Word spread among the Drew's daughter's friends about the game being played with Megan's life. On October 15 another girl was given the password to Josh's account and invited to take a turn at impersonating him. She typed in a message from Josh: he had heard that Megan was mean to her friends. Megan, devastated, typed back in a frenzy. *How did he know? Where had he gotten this information? Who was this person anyway and what the hell did she say?*

After school the following day—the day of her birthday—Megan rushed home and logged onto her MySpace account. Her father had worked the early shift and was upstairs napping, and Tina, although aware that Megan was distressed about something, had to get her younger daughter to the orthodontist. After all, *sturm und drang* were not uncommon elements of Megan's life. There was no reason to suspend scheduled activities. Tina ordered Megan off the Internet and left the house. When she checked in with Megan from the orthodontist's office, Megan admitted that she was still on the Internet. Friends were mocking her. Tina called back 20 minutes later and Megan was sobbing. "Mom, I can't even begin to explain."

Had she learned that Josh was a vicious hoax?

When Tina got back at 5:00, she found Megan sitting at the computer, typing desperately in a kind of emotional meltdown. Members of the chat group were lobbing insults at her, calling her a slut, and, even worse, fat.

When Tina gently criticized her daughter for engaging in what might have seemed a ridiculous fight about her weight, Megan fired back: "You're supposed to be my mom. You're supposed to be on my side!"[50] And ran up to her room.

About 20 minutes later Tina reported having an awful feeling. She ran upstairs and found that Megan had hanged herself by a belt in her closet.

Megan was rushed to the hospital by ambulance, but efforts to resuscitate her were to no avail. Josh's online identity vanished overnight, and the conversations that went on that afternoon could not be retrieved. Megan's father, preoccupied with saving his daughter's life, only had time to glance at the last line of text, yet he recalled it vividly. "Everybody in O'Fallon knows how you are,"[51] a Josh impersonator had written. "You are a bad person and everybody hates you. Have a shitty rest of your life. The world would be a better place without you."

A month passed before the Meiers learned from the mother of one of the other girls who had been involved in the hoax that Josh was the creation of females in the Drew household. When Steve Pokin, the journalist who first reported the story, was preparing his column for the St. Charles County *Suburban Journal*, he asked Lori Drew why she had created the website. Megan had called her daughter a "lesbian," she replied, and this provided a way for her to monitor whatever else Megan might have to say about her.

The news coverage brought a tidal wave of scorn. The Drews were harassed, threatened, and ostracized. Attempts to prosecute Lori Drew for causing events that led to the suicide of Megan Meier were unsuccessful. Jack Banas, the prosecuting attorney for St. Charles County, said that "[Lori Drew] made a huge, fatal mistake by trusting these kids. But there are undisputed facts and disputed facts, and even if you believe all of them, they still don't give you a criminal pattern in the state of Missouri."[52] The case made wide ripples. The Drews stopped publishing their newsletter. Their daughter disappeared—transferred to another school, everyone assumed. Her whereabouts were kept secret out of fear for her life. The Meiers got divorced and Tina Meiers created a nonprofit organization, the Megan Meier Foundation, to fight bullying and cyberbullying. A number of counties in Missouri and throughout the country passed legislation against harassment using computers or cellphones.

I think it is not too great a leap to assume that Tina Meiers, in her attempt to sell Lori Drew a house, implied that its purchase would bring membership in an Upscale Community. When Lori Drew discovered that she and her husband were not embraced by the community but barely tolerated, she felt deceived. Worse yet, even Tina's daughter rejected Lori's daughter. She had called her a lesbian. The creation of Josh was an "attack other" strategy, shame displaced, an attempt to mislead Megan as Lori and her daughter had been misled by Megan's mother. It may have seemed like an innocent enough prank, but they had failed to consider how fragile Megan's self-concept was, how dramatic her shifts of mood, and how impulsive her behavior.

NOTES

1. Centers for Disease Control, "Youth Risk Surveillance Survey—United States, 2013," *Morbidity and Mortality Weekly Report*, Surveillance Summaries 63, no. 4 (June 13, 2014).
2. Ibid.

3. *"Bad Teacher* Cast Discusses Bad Nicknames," Young Hollywood, 2011, http://www.younghollywood.com/videos/yhstudio/june/bad-teacher-cast-discusses-bad-nicknames.html.

4. Luke A. Egan and Natasha Todorov, "Forgiveness as a Coping Strategy to Allow School Students to Deal with the Effects of Being Bullied: Theoretical and Empirical Discussion," *Journal of Social and Clinical Psychology* 28, no. 2 (2009): 198–222.

5. Ibid.

6. Dan Olweus, *Bullying at School* (Oxford: Blackwell, 1993), 35.

7. L. Rowell Huesmann et al., "Stability of Aggression over Time and Generations," *Developmental Psychology* 20, no. 6 (November 1984): 1120–1134.

8. Andre Sourander et al., "What Is the Early Adulthood Outcome of Boys Who Bully or Are Bullied in Childhood? The Finnish 'From a Boy to a Man' Study," *Pediatrics* 120, no. 2 (2007): 397–404.

9. A. Sourander et al.,"Childhood Bullying Behavior and Later Psychiatric Hospital and Psychopharmacologic Treatment: Findings from the Finnish 1981 Birth Cohort Study," *Archives of General Psychiatry* 66, no. 9 (September 1, 2009): 1005–1012.

10. Olweus, *Bullying at School*.

11. Ibid., 39.

12. John Bowlby, *Attachment: Vol. 1, Attachment & Loss*, 2nd ed. (New York: Basic Books, 1983).

13. Dan Olweus, "Bully/Victim Problems in School: Facts and Intervention," *European Journal of Psychology of Education* 12, no. 4 (1997): 501.

14. I. Bretherton and K. A. Munholland, "Internal Working Models in Attachment Relationships: A Construct Revisited," in *Handbook of Attachment: Theory, Research, and Clinical Applications*, ed. Jude Cassidy and Phillip R. Shaver (New York: Guilford Press, 1999).

15. The change was also associated with movements to end child labor and provide universal education. Activists such as Lewis Wicks Hines and Edgar Gardner Murphy played critical roles.

16. Robert Karen, *Becoming Attached: First Relationships and How They Shape Our Capacity to Love* (New York: Oxford University Press, 1998), 19.

17. Bowlby called this "anaclitic depression."

18. David Levy, "Primary Affect Hunger," *The American Journal of Psychiatry* 94 (1937): 643–652.

19. Karen, *Becoming Attached*, 17.

20. John Bowlby, "Forty-Four Juvenile Thieves: Their Characters and Home-Life," *International Journal of Psycho-Analysis* 25 (1944): 19.

21. Jonathan Fast, *Ceremonial Violence: A Psychological Explanation of School Shootings* (New York: The Overlook Press, 2008).

22. "Donald Trump Biography: Reality Television Star," Biography.com, 2015, http://www.biography.com/people/donald-trump-9511238#synopsis.

23. James Garbarino, *Lost Boys; Why Our Sons Turn Violent and How We Can Save Them* (New York: The Free Press, 1999), 10.

24. Olweus, "Bully/Victim Problems in School"; Olweus, *Bullying at School*.

25. C. S. Widom, "Does Violence Beget Violence? A Critical Examination of the Literature," *Psychological Bulletin* 106, no. 1 (1989): 3, and "The Cycle of Violence," *Science* 244, no. 4901 (1989): 160–166.

26. Gilligan, *Violence*; for many examples of deriving self-respect through violence, see Lonnie H. Athens, *The Creation of Dangerous Violent Criminals* (Urbana: University of Illinois Press, 1989).

27. Serotonin (5-HT), norepinephrine, and dopamine.

28. William March, *The Bad Seed*, reissue ed. (New York: Harper Perennial, 1954).

29. Hervey M. Cleckley, *The Mask of Sanity: An Attempt to Clarify Some Issues About the So-Called Psychopathic Personality* (Augusta, GA: E. S. Cleckley, 1988).

30. Robert D. Hare, *Without Conscience: The Disturbing World of the Psychopaths Among Us*, 1st ed. (New York: Guilford Press, 1999).

31. Jeanette Taylor et al., "Genetic and Environmental Influences on Psychopathy Trait Dimensions in a Community Sample of Male Twins," *Journal of Abnormal Child Psychology* 31, no. 6 (2003): 663; Soo Hyun Rhee and Irwin D. Waldman, "Genetic and Environmental Influences on Antisocial Behavior: A Meta-Analysis of Twin and Adoption Studies.," *Psychological Bulletin* 128, no. 3 (May 2002): 490–529.

32. Angus Watson, "Experience: I Was a Bully," *The Guardian*, March 19, 2010, http://www.guardian.co.uk/lifeandstyle/2010/mar/20/i-was-a-bully.

33. Angus Watson, "Why I Used to Be a Bully," *The Telegraph*, June 7, 2004, http://www.telegraph.co.uk/education/educationnews/3340735/Why-I-used-to-be-a-bully.html.

34. Watson, "Experience."

35. John Braithwaite, *Crime, Shame and Reintegration* (Cambridge, UK: Cambridge University Press, 1989).

36. Olweus, *Bullying at School*.

37. Ibid.

38. Ibid.

39. Ibid.

40. Gillian Shaw, "Amanda Todd's Mother Speaks Out About Daughter's Suicide," *Vancouver Sun*, October 14, 2012.

41. Kelly Sinoski, "Extraditing Dutch Man for Amanda Todd Case Could Take Years: Expert," *The Vancouver Sun*, April 19, 2014.

42. Dara R. Blachman and Stephen P. Hinshaw, "Patterns of Friendship Among Girls with and Without Attention-Deficit/hyperactivity Disorder," *Journal of Abnormal Child Psychology* 30, no. 6 (2002): 625.

43. Ibid., 636.

44. Lauren Collins, "Friend Game," *The New Yorker*, January 21, 2008, 36, http://www.newyorker.com/reporting/2008/01/21/080121fa_fact_collins.

45. Ibid.

46. Ibid.

47. Ibid.

48. Ibid.

49. Steve Pokin, "'My Space' Hoax Ends with Suicide of Dardenne Prairie Teen," *St. Charles County Suburban Journal*, November 11, 2007, http://www.stl-today.com/suburban-journals/stcharles/news/stevepokin/my-space-hoax-ends-with-suicide-of-dardenne-prairie-teen/article_0304c09a-ab32-5931-9bb3-210a5d5dbd58.html.

50. Ibid.

51. Ibid.

52. Collins, "Friend Game," 41.

CHAPTER 3

The Bullying of Lesbian, Gay, Bisexual, and Transgender Teens

PART 1: IT'S NOT EASY BEING GREEN

On September 13, 2011, a headline appeared in *The New York Times:* "Eight Suicides in Two Years at Anoka-Hennepin School District." Officials of the district denied that their educational policies had played any part in the suicides. True, the suicides had begun soon after the board had promoted a policy that prohibited any discussion of gender orientation in the classroom, but how could that single provision have led to eight suicides in two years? Only two of the students were gay, they insisted.

Parents, teachers, and friends of the deceased disagreed. They claimed that at least four of the students had been gay, and others had been tormented by school bullies because their behavior seemed "gender inappropriate." The bullying had been frequent, violent, and humiliating, involving urinating on the victims, stabbing them with pencils, punching them, kicking them, and shoving them into walls and lockers. The bullied children were the target of gender slurs and predictions that they would burn in hell forever for their behavior.[1] When they complained to school administrators, they were told to "lay low," to "ignore" the harassment, or, in one case, to "try to stay out of people's way."[2] On many occasions they were assured that the problem would be taken care of. And eventually it was, but the path was longer and more circuitous than anyone could have imagined.

A closer examination of these tragic deaths can help us understand important aspects of scapegoating, suicide clusters, the complexity of gender identity, and how "attack other" behavior can become "attack self." Most important, it can lead to a way of discouraging gay teens from committing suicide. Research studies have shown that lesbian, gay, bisexual, and transgender (LGBT) teens attempt suicide four times more frequently than their heterosexual classmates.[3] Why is this the case? How can we stop these tragic deaths or at the very least improve their odds of survival?

The bullying of minorities, be it because of race, gender, or religion, differs somewhat from the bullying described by Olweus in the previous chapter. Olweus writes about children for whom bullying is a trait, an integral part of their personality, and victims whose tendency to absorb shame, to "attack self," makes them likely candidates for persecution. The bullying of minorities is in some ways a different matter. When a section of society agrees to recognize a minority group as the cause of their particular social woes, bullying of that group becomes *sociosyntonic*. By this I mean that their persecution becomes acceptable within the culture of that subgroup. It becomes an option for anyone in need of processing shame through the "attack other" mode, and it is particularly appealing to those who belong to a low-status group. If the culture's hatred toward the scapegoated group is sufficient, maiming or killing may be tolerated, punished mildly, or even approved of.

Examples are common enough. Blacks were disdained by white Southerners who blamed abolition for the loss of their gracious antebellum lifestyle. For many decades in the South, a white man could kill a black man with few repercussions. In Italy and France, crimes of passion—men killing their wives after finding them involved in infidelities—were punished by mild prison sentences.[4] Murdering one's wife, while not a virtuous act, represented a kind of honorable response to being cuckolded. During World War II, the Nazi Party attempted to eradicate Jews, homosexuals, gypsies, and other minorities whom they blamed for diluting the purity of the Germanic race, causing their ignominious defeat in World War I and the humiliating terms of the Treaty of Versailles.[5]

Homosexuals have been scapegoated by some cultures throughout history and remain so despite dramatic social changes in recent years, such as the right to serve as an openly gay man or woman in the military and the legalization of gay marriage. The word "homophobia" entered the English language in 1920, but it originally referred to a fear of men and the male sex as experienced by women. Its modern usage, "fear or hatred of homosexuals and homosexuality,"[6] first appeared on Halloween of 1969 in an article in *Time* magazine, four months after gay men had fought off the police at New York's Stonewall Inn, a watershed in the battle for gay rights.

Homophobia has been seen as helping the male heterosexual culture meet a variety of psychological needs, such as the affirmation of masculinity. The degree to which our culture values raw masculinity is apparent in its worship of the solitary cowboy (the Marlboro Man), the "self-made man" (Sam Walton, who founded Walmart), the philanderer (President Clinton), the fearless NASCAR driver, and the football player who crushes his opponent. For some heterosexual men, any shred of sexual desire they may feel for another man sends them into a panic. They are the insiders, but might they really be the outsiders? The presence of gays may make straight men feel the way women do around aggressive men: a sense of being prey. It knocks them off the top of the food chain. The invalidation of homosexuals as reliable workers, often transmitted through cubicles by "harmless joking," serves to reduce competition for jobs. Myths that they are child molesters[7] or sex maniacs, or have a full-time agenda of converting straight men into homosexuals, make them threatening in social situations and the workplace. This kind of behavior is particularly apparent during tough economic times.

Another need, both individual and institutional, involves reproduction and immortality. Members of a faith community are often encouraged to have large families so the religion will flourish and continue across the generations.[8] In the same way, heterosexual parents often see their biological children as providers of a sort of immortality. Although adoption and childbearing are becoming more common in the gay and lesbian community, the concept of homosexuality often evokes fear of the extinction of the family or faith community.

"Internalized homophobia" is a term that has been applied to homosexuals who have absorbed the antigay attitudes of their communities. This is sometimes available for public view in the realm of politics, where duplicitous behavior is encouraged by the need to please many constituents of differing ideologies. Mark Foley, a Republican congressman from Florida from 1994 to 2006, represented a conservative district and often aligned himself with antigay legislation, such as voting for the Defense of Marriage Act in 1996. Reports of inappropriate instant messages to a male page resulted in the public admission of his homosexuality.[9] Larry Craig, a senator from Idaho known for his campaign against gay rights, resigned in 2008 after soliciting sex from a plainclothes police officer in a public restroom.[10] David Dreier, another Republican congressman from California who held office for more than 20 years and who voted in favor of Defense of Marriage Act, against the inclusion of homosexuals as a protected class in hate crimes, against the Mathew Shepard Act, and against the military's Don't Ask, Don't Tell was eventually outed by the gay media.[11] Ed Schrock, a Republican senator from Virginia, also opposed much gay rights legislation, and chose not to run for a third term after he was accused of having sought sex with gay men through a phone service.[12] In a research study, 121 New York City teenagers stated their belief in a number of false gay stereotypes: that gay men were effeminate and gay women masculine, that gay men disliked gay women and vice-versa, and that homosexuals were innately unhappy,[13] even though they themselves were gay and did not correspond to these stereotypes. The point is, people can and do compartmentalize their lives, embracing cultural misbeliefs that they know in their own hearts are false.

A cornerstone of Freud's psychoanalytic theory was the Oedipus complex, a term he first used in the *Interpretation of Dreams*[14] in 1899 and revisited in *Three Essays on the Theory of Sexuality*.[15] In Sophocles' ancient tragedy, from which the idea is drawn, Oedipus unwittingly kills his father and later marries his mother, Jocasta, the dowager queen. Freud believed that boys between the ages of three and five experienced their fathers as their rivals and their mothers as the object of their love (the opposite, the Electra complex, applied to girls of the same age). The successful resolution of the Oedipal complex, the transference of love from the mother to a woman of the same age outside the family, led to "healthy" or normal adult sexuality, which Freud believed to be exclusively heterosexual. If the Oedipus complex was not properly resolved—if the boy became overly attached to his mother and remained so—the result would be overidentification. He would become womanly and seek male love objects. Freud referred to homosexuality as "inversion," a term borrowed from the nineteenth-century German sexologist von Krafft-Ebing.[16] The use of the word "inversion" is itself a form of heterosexualism, with its implication that homosexuality is an upside-down way of doing things.

While several types of psychotherapy were popular in postwar America, psychoanalysis dominated the field. When the American Psychiatric Association published its first catalogue of psychiatric disorders in 1952,[17] psychoanalytic thinking informed most of the diagnoses. Homosexuality was listed under the subtitle "Sexual Deviation" and began a list that concluded with "pedophilia, fetishism and sexual sadism (including rape, sexual assault, mutilation)."[18]

One of the remarkable books of postwar America, *Sexual Behavior in the Human Male*,[19] was written by Alfred Kinsey, a professor of biology at Indiana University, who had no stake in promoting psychoanalysis. Kinsey and his crew of researchers conducted lengthy interviews with 17,000 men about their sexual behavior. Based on his findings, Kinsey suggested that gender orientation might be best understood as a gradient spread across a scale of seven degrees, where zero represented those who were entirely heterosexual and six those who were entirely homosexual. Those at three, in the middle of the scale, were equally attracted to members of both sexes. He concluded from interviews and other research that homosexuality was common and natural in man and beast. He estimated that about 10 percent of the population was gay, a figure widely disputed. These findings were considered remarkable at a time when the majority of gay men and women were closeted and represented a paradigm shift in the way we thought about love and sex.

Some practitioners of the period discounted his research. Irving Bieber, an influential New York psychoanalyst, wrote a book in 1962 about homosexuality based on his dialogues with patients and consultations with colleagues. Bieber described homosexuality as a psychiatric problem whose etiology consisted of overbearing mothers and timid fathers. (It did not occur to him that sons of other gender predilections might find their mothers overbearing or their fathers timid, or that gay men might seek psychotherapy for problems unrelated to gender orientation.) In 1963 Bieber was interviewed by *The New York Times* for an article, the title of which reflected the opinion of the *Times* and the times: "Growth of Overt Homosexuality in City Provokes Wide Concern."[20] Beiber expressed disapproval of homosexuals' organized attempts to present themselves as "just another minority, since their minority status is based on illness rather than racial or religious factors."[21] Charles W. Socarides, another well-known New York psychoanalyst of the era whose homophobia overshadowed his common sense, was reported to be worried about homosexuals seeking public acceptance. "The homosexual is ill and anything that tends to hide that fact reduces his chances of seeking and obtaining treatment. If they were to achieve social acceptance it would increase this difficulty."[22]

Many factors had combined to make gay men convenient punching bags for the determinedly heterosexual culture of the 1950s. Their socially assigned role as depraved outcasts, combined with the paranoia of Cold War Communism and the antics of Senator Joe McCarthy, drove the US State Department to recognize them as a risk to national security. Because they led secret lives and engaged in forbidden behaviors, they might easily be convinced to leak valuable state secrets or undermine the operations of the government. Employees of federal, state, and local governments suspected of being homosexuals were dismissed from their jobs.[23] The FBI kept lists of known homosexuals, and the US Post Office tracked homosexually oriented mailings. Politically motivated police raids on gay bars became commonplace around the United States and Canada. Laws were passed prohibiting cross-dressing.[24]

Activist groups such as the Mattachine Society, formed in 1950 in Los Angeles by labor organizer Henry Hay Jr., and the Daughters of Bilitis, formed in San Francisco in 1955 by Del Martin and Phyllis Lyon (1955), were among the first attempts to give social and political power to homosexual men and women (although Martin and Lyon insisted that at the beginning they were simply interested in finding a place to dance together where they would not be gawked at).[25] The public dialogue around civil rights for African Americans and the passage of the Civil Rights Act in 1964 contributed momentum to the idea of social inclusion for all. Change was in the air.

Throughout history, oppressed and voiceless groups have rioted when their social situation became intolerable.[26] Rioting (attack self/attack others) is a common form of shame management when the shame is intense, it is shared by a number of people, and no more prosocial or peaceful method of managing it exists. Like other shame management strategies, rioters are usually unaware of their motivations beyond a general sense of rage and frustration. Because the shame is hidden, the self-destruction of their own neighborhood and injuring of members of their own community often appears to outsiders as nonsensical and counterproductive. But riots draw attention to social problems. They create milestones for a movement and a common history that empowers and unites.

Because of laws against cross-dressing, the presence of a transgendered individual at a bar was sufficient to have the establishment shut down. As a result, the transgendered community in San Francisco's Tenderloin district, unwelcome at gay meeting places, would congregate at Gene Compton's Cafeteria at 101 Taylor Street, which was open 24 hours a day. (Closed in 1972, a wall plaque marks its former location.) On a warm night in August of 1966, some of the customers became raucous and the management called the police. When the police attempted to arrest one of the patrons, dishes and furniture flew, and the huge plate-glass window in front of the cafeteria became one of the victims. The next night the diner refused service to anyone who entered cross-dressed. Fighting spread onto the street. A newsstand was burned down, and the plate-glass window, replaced hours earlier, was broken again. The third night a massive demonstration was staged against Compton's new policy of refusing service to the transgender community. The riot led eventually to the establishment of a National Transsexual Counseling Unit, the first peer-run support and advocacy unit of its kind.

During the summer of 1969 the police staged frequent raids on the Stonewall Inn in New York's Greenwich Village with the pretense of determining if liquor was being served (it was a private club and had no liquor license). During the early hours of the morning of June 28, the patrons decided that enough was enough and fought back. The riot overflowed into Sheridan Square, a predominantly gay neighborhood at the time, and the crowd swelled to almost 400 according to *The New York Times*. "The young men threw bricks, bottles, garbage, pennies and a parking meter at the policemen."[27] Minor celebrities became involved, elevating the status of the event. Dave von Ronk, a well-known folk singer who lived on the square, was accused of having thrown a "heavy object"[28] at a patrolman. That night Stonewall, like the Compton Cafeteria riots, gave birth to a cohesive community of New York's gays and lesbians that transcended race, class, and age.

JAIMIE NABOZNY

Human rights campaigns often turn up individuals who find themselves forced into the part of David in response to some entrenched bureaucratic Goliath. Like it or not, they are destined to change history.

Jamie Nabozny was born in 1975 and grew up in Ashland, Wisconsin, a *rust belt* community at the northern end of the state, where winters are long and cruel and the winds across Lake Superior chill the soul. The economy, prosperous during the era of Smoke Stack America, had grown reliant on tourism. In elementary school, Jamie was a good student and "enjoyed a positive educational experience."[29] Around 1988, when he entered middle school (seventh and eighth grade), he fully realized what he had long suspected, that he was gay, and he decided to make no secret of it. There is nothing extraordinary about realizing one's gender orientation at this age. Research shows that most gay teens achieve clarity about their sexual orientation around age 14,[30] when the hormones kick in. What was unusual was his decision to reveal it. More than a few of his classmates began addressing him as "faggot." They struck him and spat on him. One boy in particular, Roy Grande, a bully whose shame management style would, in later years, lead to multiple felony convictions, made Jamie's life miserable. When Jamie told his guidance counselor, Ms. Peterson, that he was openly gay and being harassed for it, she ordered the bullying to stop and placed the worst offenders on detention. After a brief hiatus the harassment resumed. By then Ms. Peterson had been replaced by Mr. Nowakoski, who arranged a meeting with Mary Podlesny, the principal. According to Jamie, "In the very beginning the principal said things to me like, 'I'll take care of it,' 'I'll deal with it' and nothing changed, the harassment continued."

When school resumed after winter break, the bullying was worse. Jamie was seated in science class beside Roy Grande and his friend Jason Welty. When the teacher left the room, Roy and Jason began groping Jamie. They pushed him to the floor and pretended to rape him, tearing his shirt in the process. Twenty students looked on, many of them laughing.[31] Afterwards, Jamie ran to the principal's office. She responded that "boys will be boys"; if he was going to be "so openly gay" he should expect this kind of behavior from his fellow students. Jamie fled from the school. No action was taken against Roy and Jason but Jamie was forced to speak to a counselor because he had left school without permission.

In eighth grade, shortly after the school year began, several boys attacked Jamie and his brother in the men's room, knocking the books out his hands and hitting him. Jaime's parents demanded a meeting with the principal. The bullies were confronted but denied that the incident had occurred. No action was taken against them, and Jamie was forced to return to his regular school schedule. It was, in Jamie's words, "a green light" for bullying. The harassment worsened, and Jamie and his parents became frequent visitors to Mary Podlesny's office. Each time she promised the situation would improve, but nothing changed. By the end of the school year the attorney for the school district suggested that Jamie take time off from school. He stayed home for a week and a half. When he returned, the harassment became unbearable. For what may have seemed like the hundredth time, Jamie appealed to the principal for help, "and she just looked at me and shook her head and said, 'Jaime, if you don't have an appointment than I don't have anything to say to you.' I left school, and went home and I attempted to kill myself."

When his mother discovered that Jamie had taken a handful of pills, she rushed him to the hospital. His stomach was pumped, and he spent some days in the psychiatric unit as was customary at the time.[32] He finished eighth grade in a Catholic school, where his classmates and teachers left him in peace. Unfortunately, the school went no further than eighth grade.

Because Jamie's parents could not afford to send him to a private high school, he had no alternative but to enter ninth grade at Ashland High School. His parents assured him that things would be different, that it would be a fresh start, but Roy Grande and his friends were enrolled there. Around the third week of school, a boy named Stephen Huntley, a friend of Roy Grande's, approached Jamie in the boys' room, struck him in the back of the knees so he fell into the urinal, and urinated on him. The principal's secretary sent Jaimie home to change clothes. The principal's solution was to isolate Jaimie from the bullies by putting him in classes that met in other parts of the building. Huntley went unpunished.

In Jaimie's opinion, the new schedule did not offer sufficient protection. He improved his chances of surviving high school by arriving early and hiding in the library, then rushing from one class to the next with his head down, minimizing his time in the hallway. A teacher who was particularly sympathetic to Jamie's plight arranged for him to have lunch in her classroom during a period when it was empty.[33]

Despite all this, the bullying continued. He felt

> numb between my ninth grade year and the last incident that happened to me, because I really didn't show my emotions at school. I'll tell you I showed them at home, I would go home and lock myself in my room and cry, and my parents were at the end of their ropes, trying to figure out what to do and trying to help me.[34]

Living in a constant state of fear, Jamie became depressed, exhibited symptoms of posttraumatic stress disorder, and developed learning problems. Arriving in his special education class, he found to his dismay that Stephen Huntley and Roy Grande had preceded him. After a second suicide attempt and another stay in the psychiatric unit, Jaimie and a friend hitchhiked to Minneapolis, the only place he knew for certain that gay people existed.

> [I] figured I would be safe there. I got down there and quickly realized that there's not a lot that I could do when you're seventeen to survive on the streets, or at least not things that I was willing to do and so I called home and told my parents, "You know how bad it is for me at school, just let me live here [in Minneapolis] and go back to school and be safe.

Jamie's parents convinced him to return home by promising that he would not have to go back to Ashland High School. The Department of Social Services disagreed, and its word was law until he was 18.

In tenth grade his parents moved farther from school and he had to take the school bus. The other students on the bus called him "fag" and "queer" and pelted him with whatever objects were on hand—nuts and bolts on one occasion. He began walking to school despite the distance.

One morning, arriving early to hide in the library, he found the doors locked. He sat down cross-legged in the hallway, praying that his presence would remain unnoticed. Minutes later a group of eight boys led by

Stephen Huntley approached him. Stephen kicked Jamie in the stomach repeatedly to the amusement of his friends. Then he said that if Jamie ever told anybody about this, he would kill him. Jamie reported the incident to Ms. Hanson, who referred him to the school's police liaison, Dan Crawford. Crawford convinced him not to press charges and referred him to Assistant Principal Blauert. Blauert was unable or unwilling to suppress his own laughter at this turn of events. He told Jamie that he "deserved such treatment because he was gay."[35]

Later that week the beating took its toll, and Jamie collapsed. He spent five days in the hospital.

> I had to have emergency abdominal surgery for internal bruising and bleeding. My spleen had ruptured and I had a tear in my stomach. And I knew I wasn't ever going to be safe at school and I knew I had to leave Ashland.

In yet another meeting with school administrators, Jamie and his parents were told that the administration was "unwilling to help him and that he should seek educational opportunities elsewhere."[36]

He ran away to Minneapolis a second time. He called his mother and told her that if she wanted to stay in touch with him, she had to let him stay there. Otherwise she would not hear from him again until he was 18, the age of emancipation in Wisconsin. His mother agreed. It was, she said, the most difficult decision she ever made. As it turned out, simply being in Minneapolis was no cure. He visited a community health center where he was diagnosed with posttraumatic stress disorder and depression. He received therapy and, perhaps more important, a referral to a crime victims' advocate.

> I ended up going to what was, at the time, the Gay and Lesbian Community Action Council, and I ended up meeting with their Crime Victims Advocate who happened to be a lawyer and she told me that what happened to me was wrong and it was illegal and I needed to sue my school. And I went home and I called my parents and I told them about this crazy lesbian lawyer at the Community Action Council, and her crazy ideas about suing the school.
>
> And my mom was silent for a second and I could tell she had tears in her eyes, and she said, "Jaime, you need to do this, too many kids are suffering out there. And you have the ability to stand up and fight back." And she said, "Somebody needs to say this is wrong."
>
> And so I went back to the crazy lesbian lawyer and I said, all right, I'll do it.

On February 6, 1995, the Naboznys hired a local lawyer and sued Mary Podlesny, the middle school principal; William Davis, the high school principal; Thomas Blauert, the high school assistant principal; and the Ashland School District for violating Jamie's Fourteenth Amendment rights. Adopted after the Civil War, the amendment addresses citizenship rights and equal protection. Although it was initially drafted to protect the freed slaves, it became the foundation of other important decisions such as *Roe v. Wade* and *Bush v. Gore*.

The school administrators asked the court for a summary judgment: Was there any basis for having a trial, or was the charge without merit? Having considered the complaint, the judge ruled against Jamie. His attorney had failed to produce evidence that he was discriminated against based on his gender. (The judge sidestepped the issue of whether he deserved equal protection based on his sexual orientation.) He further ruled that Jamie's lawyer failed to produce evidence to establish that the school administrators had done anything to create or increase the risk of Jamie being harmed by other students. Also, it did not really matter since in the judge's opinion the bullies were not state actors (meaning that they were not acting on the part of the state of Wisconsin) and were therefore not subject to regulation under the Bill of Rights. The judge also granted qualified immunity to all of the defendants against all of Jamie's claims.

The case was brought to the court of appeals by Lambda Legal, a non-profit legal organization dedicated to gaining "full recognition of the civil rights of lesbians, gay men, bisexuals, transgender people."[37] The decision was overturned, and a jury trial began.

The case, the first of its kind, was reported in newspapers and on television and began to draw national attention. David E. Springer, a partner at Skadden, Arps, Slate, Meagher & Flom, an international law firm with a feared litigation department, offered his services pro bono.

> And not only did he [the Skadden & Arps attorney] take my case, but he came out as a gay, HIV positive man to his entire firm. And he said this is the case that he wanted to be remembered for, not all of the other cases that he had done.[38]

One of the highlights of the trial was when Mary Podlesny took the witness stand and claimed under oath that she could not remember ever meeting with Jamie or his parents. Another involved Roy Grande. Because he was currently serving a prison sentence on an unrelated charge, he appeared in court in his prison oranges. He admitted to, and apologized for each and every incident of harassment to which he had subjected Jamie.[39] In November of 1996 the "small town jury"[40] found the school administrators liable for failing to stop antigay violence against Jamie

Nabozny. While the jury was out determining the damages, defendants offered a settlement of $900,000, and Jamie's lawyers accepted. Jamie was more than satisfied:

> I think it was the best possible outcome for the case . . . school administrators now have a personal responsibility to protect students from harassment and if they do not they can be individually sued, much like a doctor for malpractice. I've always said I don't care why people do the right thing; they just need to do the right thing. And if it means they're afraid of losing their house or their life savings, then hey, they'll protect kids and that's what needs to happen.[41]

Lambda Legal agreed:

> This historic victory was the first legal challenge to antigay violence in public schools. The 1996 precedent on appeal, followed by the million-dollar verdict and settlement, electrified the nation's education community and led to an explosion in legal advocacy for LGBTQ youth.[42]

Jamie Nabozny's experiences in middle school and high school may seem uniquely cruel and nightmarish, but they were typical of the gamut through which many gay and lesbian teens had to pass back then and perhaps not so much worse than what LGBT teens encounter today in parts of the United States.

While many Americans considered *Nabozny v. Podlesny* an important victory in the age-old battle for "liberty and justice for all," others felt that any validation of LGBT life undermined the stability of the traditional American family.

Barb Anderson was one such person.

NO HOMO PROMO

In 1994 in Minnesota's 11th school district, the Anoka-Hennepin District, Barb Anderson, a former district teacher and a researcher for the conservative Minnesota Family Council, was outraged to learn that homosexuality was being taught as "normal" in her nephew's health class. She believed that if homosexuality was discussed with a boy, he would want to try it, adopt it as his sexual orientation, and in all likelihood contract AIDS. She and four other like-minded parents, learning that the district's sex education curriculum was due for re-evaluation, volunteered to serve on the review committee. Seven months later they drafted a report that concluded, "The majority of parents do not wish to have there [sic] children taught that the gay lifestyle is a normal acceptable alternative."[43] Every school was to review its curriculums and educational materials, identifying and disposing of any content related to LGBT individuals and behavior, regardless of how its exclusion would affect students' education in that area of study. All LGBT services such as hotlines and counseling centers were to be removed from health resource lists.[44]

On their recommendation, the report was adopted as district-wide policy: homosexuality must "not be taught/addressed as a normal, valid lifestyle." The policy seems to have been passed sub rosa. The local newspapers carried no mention of it. It was not announced to parents, nor included in the district's policy handbooks. There appears to be no administrative document describing it. Principals were told about it and then instructed to explain it to their teachers.[45]

A number of gay rights initiatives and counterinitiatives were on the table at this time. President Clinton had passed Department of Defense Directive 1304.26[46] "Don't Ask, Don't Tell," which prohibited discrimination against homosexual or bisexual service members so long as they remained "closeted." (Prior to this even closeted homosexuals soldiers who revealed their sexual orientation were considered deviates and security risks and were, at various times in American history, hospitalized, court-martialed, incarcerated, or dishonorably discharged.) The AIDS epidemic of the 1980s had brought questions of inheritance and death benefits among gays and lesbians to the forefront of the public discourse. The liberal media was supporting a gay marriage intiative while conservative politicians on the House Judiciary Committee introduced a Defense of Marriage Act, which defined marriage as "a legal union between one man and one woman"[47]

In March of 1997, five months after *Nabozny v. Podlesny*, the Office for Civil Rights of the Department of Education, published a special "Sexual Harassment Guidance" addendum to Title IX of the Education Amendments of 1972 (perhaps at least partially in response to the Nabozny lawsuit). It restates explicitly the message of the 1972 amendment: sexual harassment is forbidden in schools that receive Federal funding, regardless of the gender or the gender orientation of the bully or the victim, and it gives plenty of examples. To better understand the purpose of such "special guidances," think of a mother with a home full of rowdy middle-school boys. She makes a rule—*no more basketball in the living room*—but after a few weeks of good behavior, the boys are back playing basketball in the living room. A lamp is broken, a precious vase cracked. The mom calls a meeting, has all the boys sit down, makes sure eye contact is established, and repeats the message in a more emphatic manner. *No. More. Basketball. In. The living room. Who doesn't understand what I just said?*

HATE CRIMES

The year after the issuance of the "Sexual Harassment Guidance," Mathew Shepard, a 21-year-old political science student at the University of Wyoming in Laramie, was beaten, tortured, and murdered by two men he met in a bar one night. In June of the same year, James Byrd Jr., a 49-year-old black man living in Jasper, Texas, was tortured and murdered by three white men who had offered him a ride in their truck. While neither incident involved the institutional bullying of homosexuals in the public schools systems, they both served as object lessons in how higher status minorities (white men in low-paying, dead-end, manual-labor jobs) could treat lower status minorities (gays, blacks) as less than human. Both crimes generated a flurry of books, plays, documentary films, and television reports that forced law-makers and their constituents to explore their own consciences about what sort of behavior could be tolerated in postmillennial America.

The United States had passed a Federal Hate Crimes law in 1969.[48] Because it was intended to add teeth to the Civil Rights Act of 1964, it focused on school integration and voting rights, specifying crimes motivated by race, color, religion, or national origin (but not gender orientation). Furthermore, the law was activated only when the victim was engaged in a federally protected act such as voting or attending school. The attempt to pass another law broadening its scope to include acts of violence toward gays and lesbians (and transgendered people in its later versions), regardless of where they take place, was first presented during the 107th Congress (2001) by Representative John Conyers, Jr., an African American Democrat from Detroit, who had served nearly a half-century in Congress. It was supported by 210 groups, including the AFL-CIO, the American Medical Association, the American Psychological Association, and the NAACP, but it also had its detractors. James Dobson, founder of Focus on the Family, told his radio listeners that the bill's real purpose was to "muzzle people of faith who dare to express their moral and biblical concerns about homosexuality."[49] John Boehner, Republican of Ohio and House minority leader at the time, said that the bill made no sense. "We're going to put into place a Federal law that says that not only will we punish you for the crime that you actually commit, the physical crime that you commit, but we're also going to charge you with a crime if we think that you were thinking bad things about this person before you committed the crime."[50] Michelle Bachmann, Representative from Minnesota's Sixth Congressional District (which overlapped with Minnesota's 11th School District)[51] said, "I feel that this hate crime legislation could be considered the very definition of tyranny in that it gives government literally the key to deciding what the thoughts of Americans should be."[52]

John Conyers, undeterred, sponsored the bill in every Congress over the next eight years, and in every Congress it was killed, sometimes in the House, sometimes in the Senate. Finally in the 111th Congress, hanging onto the red, white, and blue coattails of the National Defense Authorization Act, it made its way through the House and Senate and was signed into law by President Barack Obama on October 28, 2009.

Alex Merritt and Ben Franklyn

In Minnesota's 11th district, a student named Alex Merritt was being harassed by his social studies teacher, Diane Cleveland, whom he saw before lunch; and by Walter Filson, whose class in law enforcement he took after lunch. They bullied him in tandem, riffing on what they perceived as his homosexuality or bisexuality although Alex was neither.[53] During lunch Cleveland would sit with Filson, recapping the witticisms she had made to Alex; then he would pick up on her bullying themes in his after-lunch class. For example, when Alex told Cleveland that he wanted to do a report on Ben Franklin, she responded, "Why? Do you have a thing for older men?" After lunch, Filson referred to Alex as "Mr. Ben Franklin" and repeated the taunt about Alex's attraction to older men.[54] The two teachers modeling this kind of behavior sent a message to students throughout the school: that Alex was available as a punching bag for those who needed to manage their own shame through "attack other" mode. "I got death threats from random kids, saying things like 'Shut up, you queer;' and, 'I'm going to kill you, you queer,' "[55] Merrick told a journalist for a local paper.

Despite his reluctance, Alex eventually told his mother about it and in May of 2008 she filed a complaint with the Minnesota Department of Civil Rights. The school board settled for $25,000. Alex, who had transferred to a high school in another district 25 miles away (he graduated in the spring of 2009) said that the money couldn't "fix a broken heart or bring back all my friends."[56] The school board gave Cleveland a slap on the wrist and apparently ignored Filson's bad behavior altogether.

In the wake of this humiliating and costly experience, and perhaps also in consideration of the recently enacted Mathew Shepard law, the school board decided to review its Sex Education Curriculum Policy, which had remained unexamined for the prior 14 years. A revised version of the Sexual Orientation Curriculum Policy, document 604.11, was cautiously drafted by the district's legal department, committed to paper, and released throughout the school system and to the public. It is reprinted here in its entirety.

604.11

SEXUAL ORIENTATION CURRICULUM POLICY

It is the primary mission of the Anoka-Hennepin School District to effectively educate each of our students for success. District policies shall comply with state and federal law as well as reflect community standards. As set forth in the Equal Education Opportunity Policy, it is the School District's policy to provide equal educational opportunity and to prohibit harassment of all students. The Board is committed to providing a safe and respectful learning environment and to provide an education that respects the beliefs of all students and families.

The School District employs a diverse and talented staff committed to serving students and families from diverse backgrounds.

The School District acknowledges that one aspect of that diversity regards sexual orientation. Teaching about sexual orientation is not a part of the District adopted curriculum; rather, such matters are best addressed within individual family homes, churches, or community organizations. Anoka-Hennepin staff, in the course of their professional duties, shall remain neutral on matters regarding sexual orientation including but not limited to student led discussions. If and when staff address sexual orientation, it is important that staff do so in a respectful manner that is age-appropriate, factual, and pertinent to the relevant curriculum. Staff are encouraged to take into consideration individual student needs and refer students to the appropriate social worker or licensed school counselor.

Anoka-Hennepin District No. 11
Coon Rapids, MN 55433
Adopted February 9, 2009

At first glance, it may have appeared to parents as no more than another ripple in the river of memos about school lunches, snow days, and home and away games; it might have seemed to be a brief, reasonable, and respectful document. At second reading, they might have paused over the sentence "the Anoka-Hennepin staff, in the course of their professional duties, shall remain neutral on matters regarding sexual orientation" and wondered what it means to remain *neutral*. Does it mean to say, "I don't care if you're straight or gay, I will treat you with the same respect as I would treat anyone else?" Or does it mean that when an openly gay teen is being humiliated or physically abused in the classroom, a teacher will refrain from defending him for fear of appearing less "neutral"? History shows that when an authority, be it an individual or a nation, remains neutral in the face of aggression, it is taken as covert approval of the aggression and encourages further abuse. To do nothing in the face of cruelty is to enter a tacit agreement with the abusers.

Teachers were confused by the "neutrality" document and expressed fear of losing their jobs during a very bad economy. The district responded with a PowerPoint that illustrated in concrete terms how to remain neutral while helping a gay student who was being bullied. If a teacher heard a gay slur, one slide explained, he or she should say, "That language is unacceptable in this school." If further enforcement was required, he or she might continue, "In this school we are required to welcome all people and to make them feel safe." Notice the inclusion of the word "required," as though managing a classroom was no more following a list of orders. Teachers were reminded never to show "personal support" for gay students in the classroom.[57] It is questionable whether any learning institution can function in a democratic society if teachers are required to submerge their own beliefs in the process of educating children, particularly when these beliefs involve civil rights.

On October 16, after eight months of this "neutrality," Thomas John Hayes, or T. J. as he was known to his friends, committed suicide. He was 16, a student at Blaine High School (one of the five high schools in the Anoka-Hennepin School District). He was not, as far as people knew, gay. A month later Samantha Johnson, 13, an eighth grader at Fred Moore Middle School, who had been trying unsuccessfully to start a Gay-Straight Alliance, committed suicide. Eleven days later another Blaine High School student, Aaron Jurek, 15, committed suicide. After Christmas vacation, Nick Lockwood, 18, an Andover High School senior, followed in their footsteps. On May 4, July Marie Barrick, 15, a Champlain Park High School student, took her own life, and two months later, Justin Aaberg, a student at Anoka High School, followed their lead. Next was Cole Wilson, an Anoka High School senior, two months later. The suicide of Jordan Yenor, 14, on May 14, 2011, a student at Northdale Middle School, made a total of eight suicides in just under two years. One student compared the experience to living in a horror movie.[58] Another student recalled, "People were dying one after another. Every time you said goodbye to a friend, you felt like, *Is this the last time I'm going to see you?*"[59]

For every child who took his or her own life, an unknown number of District 11 students contemplated the act. During the period in question, some 700 students from the district visited mental health counselors, an exceptionally high number. The counselors reported an "explosion" of suicidal ideation and dangerous behaviors, including students cutting themselves with knives and razor blades and asphyxiating themselves while playing what they called the "choking game."[60] Incidents of cutting increased from about one a week to several a day, according to one middle school teacher.[61] Some children were hospitalized because they were assessed by professional clinicians as posing a danger to themselves.

Eleven months passed before anyone publically suggested a connection between the Neutrality Policy and the suicides. During a school board meeting on August 23, 2010, Justin Aaberg's mother approached the microphone, her eyes filled with tears. She placed a picture of a handsome 15-year-old with cornsilk hair and blue eyes on the desk before her, explaining that this was her son, that he had been openly gay, and that he had hanged himself six weeks ago. It was only after his death that she learned of the district's sexual orientation policy, which she believed left gay students feeling isolated and doubting their self-worth. She also shared what she had heard from teachers about their confusion regarding the use of the word "neutrality" and how it compromised their ability to defend bullied students.[62] She demanded the policy be revoked. "What about my parental rights to have my gay son go to school and learn without being bullied?"[63] Aaberg asked, openly weeping now, while the board stared back, expressionless.

"Just so you know," the board chair responded, "there are two distinct policies. One's a curriculum policy; the other's a bullying policy." In other words, although both policies addressed sexual orientation, neither one was technically a sexual orientation policy. This important distinction may have been pointed out to him by the school board's attorneys, since institutions that received Federal monies were forbidden to have special policies regarding the treatment of minorities. He went on to say that no student in the district could be harassed for any reason, and teachers were expected to take immediate disciplinary action if they witnessed a bullying incident.

On another occasion, Brett Johnson, the district communications director, told a television news reporter that the school board was not ignoring the problem. They had hired "two certified mental health counselors" to travel between the schools and provide support (the Anoka-Hennepin School District has more than 39,000 students). "While the recent suicides are troubling," he went on, "District 11 officials say the number of deaths are not out of line with what other school districts are experiencing."[64] This simply was not true.

Superintendent Carlson took it upon himself to personally investigate the suicides. Could one person with an important full-time job and no background or training in mental health care accurately assess what was possibly one of the worst adolescent suicide clusters in recent years? Usually such tasks are left to the Centers for Disease Control and involve a team of experienced researchers, who may spend months in the field. Carlson, undaunted, conducted "a series of conversations among district officials, as well as with parents who knew the [deceased] students."[65] Shortly thereafter he communicated his findings in a 74-second telephone voicemail message relayed robotically to every household in the district with a school-aged child.

> Based on all of the information we've been able to gather, none of the suicides were connected to incidents of bullying or harassment . . . The continuation of inaccurate information is not helpful. Once again we have no evidence that bullying played a part in any of our students deaths . . . In a few incidents people told the school board and district leaders that employees stood by while students were bullied. These statements are also not true. We have no evidence of that occurring."[66]

This kind of message, which denies that persecution exists, contributes to what has been called an "invalidating environment"[67] and constitutes a powerful form of shaming. Jefferson Fietek told me that prior to Carlson's telephone message, he would receive one or two text messages a month from gay students who needed his support. After the message, the rate rose to eight or ten a day. When he began to receive text messages from students in crisis while being interviewed by CNN, the interviewer demanded to know if the interruptions had been prearranged.

They had not.

The local evangelical community supported Carlson's "findings." In a blog entree titled "Gay Activists Manipulate Suicide Tragedy for Ideological Purposes," Tom W. Prichard, the president of the Minnesota Family Council, wrote that the suicide of Justin Aaberg was not the result of bullying but rather of sadness over his "male lover having an affair." Prichard based this assessment on information gleaned from parents of students in the district (but not Justin's parents, classmates, or teachers). He said that God had created us "male and female with sexual expression designed for a lifelong union between a man and a woman" and that "fighting against this reality is the reason alternative forms of sexual expression . . . will put people at greater risk [of suicide]."[68]

Barb Anderson, interviewed on a radio program called *Americans for Truth About Homosexuality*, attributed the District 11 suicide cluster to the presence of LGBT support services and advocacy groups and their attempts to make gay children feel legitimized. She admitted that bullying of gay students existed in the schools but added that they had no one but themselves to blame for being open about their gender orientation. "These kids are locked into a lifestyle with their choices limited," she told Peter LeBarbara, a former director of the Minnesota Family Council, who hosted the show, "and many times this can be disastrous to them as they get into the behavior which leads to disease and death."[69]

The battle over maintaining the dignity, respect, and safety of homosexuals in Minnesota's District 11 did not go on in a vacuum. Similar skirmishes were taking place in well-to-do suburbs in Helena, Montana; Alameda, California; and Oak Park, Chicago.[70] Gay students were undergoing the same repertory of insults: being urinated on, stabbed with pencils, shoved into lockers, and hospitalized with broken ribs. While liberal parents were suing school boards to put a stop to such behavior, other parent groups were upping the ante, campaigning to remove books such as *And Tango Makes Three* from school libraries for fear that exposure to the true-life tale of two male zoo penguins raising a baby penguin would normalize homosexuality and "turn" straight first graders gay.[71]

While the District 11 suicide cluster was defined by place—a Minnesota county—it overlapped with another series of adolescent suicides, this one highly publicized. Although it spread across the country, it occurred during the last three weeks of September 2010, so it might have been considered a cluster in terms of time. On the ninth of the month, Billy Lucas, a 15-year-old openly gay boy from Greensberg High School in Indiana, hanged himself after years of being tormented about his sexuality.[72] On the nineteenth, Seth Walsh, a 13-year-old boy in Tehachapi, California, committed suicide after a "relentless barrage of taunting, bullying and other abuse at the hands of his peers."[73] On the twenty-second, Tyler Clementi, a new freshman at Rutgers University in New Jersey and a fine violinist, jumped from the George Washington Bridge after learning that his roommate had secretly broadcast his tryst with another man on the Internet. The following day Asher Brown, an eighth grader in Harris, Texas, who had been bullied throughout middle school, shot himself in the head. Earlier that day he had been knocked down two flights of stairs for the amusement of his tormentors. On the twenty-ninth, Raymond Chase, a 19-year-old gay African American and sophomore at Johnson & Wales College in Rhode Island, took his own life after being rejected as a lover by a heterosexual male friend.

The Department of Education's Office of Civil Rights issued another "guidance letter" on the subject of bullying to all the schools and higher learning institutions in the United States that were receiving Federal funds. The letter was not specifically about gender bullying. The subject did not appear until page 7, sandwiched between sexual harassment and disability harassment. It described a typical case of bullying of a gay high school student. Because the student self-identified as gay and the harassment was homophobic, the school in the example did not believe that the aggressive acts were covered by Title IX. Title IX makes sexual harassment illegal but seems ambiguous (to some) about the bullying of LGBT students. Eleven states that wanted to be clear about where they stood in relation to this issue had passed their own anti-LGBT bullying legislation. Some schools believe that the law applies only to boys harassing girls and, on rare occasion, the opposite. The "guidance" clears up any possible misconceptions.

> Title IX prohibits harassment of both male and female students regardless of the sex of the harasser—*i.e.*, even if the harasser and target are members of the same sex. It also prohibits gender-based harassment, which may include acts of verbal, nonverbal, or physical aggression, intimidation, or hostility based on sex or sex-stereotyping.[74]

The letter goes on to state that the school has an obligation not simply to end the harassment and punish the bullies but also to "eliminate the hostile environment."[75]

In October President Obama recorded a video supporting gay teens for a website called "It Gets Better." The site was created by Dan Savage, an openly gay journalist, and his partner, Terry Miller, shortly after the suicides of Justin Aaberg and Billy Lucas. It encouraged the well-known and little-known, the gay and the straight, to upload videos expressing the idea that gay life gets better after one reaches the age of majority and can behave, dress, and think as he or she likes without the fear of being beaten or shamed. Savage and Miller were brutally bullied when they were young but had reached a point in their lives where they managed their shame and anger through social action, by writing and lecturing on the subject of gay rights, rather than turning those emotions against themselves.

THE BALLAD OF DEZ AND SARAH

At the end of January, two young women, seniors at Champlin Park High School (another of the five high schools in the Anoka-Hennepin district) felt the sting of discrimination and responded with social action rather than self-harm. They challenged the system in a peaceful yet powerful manner, with a strong sense of conviction in their cause. Their actions had far-reaching effects.

During the darkest days of winter, when the heart longs for the sound of a robin or the sight of a crocus poking through the snow, Champlin Park High School students buoy their spirits with a week of activities called Snow Days. Traditionally, the week begins with the Pep Fest and the coronation of a popular senior class boy and girl as the school's king and queen. Those who have been chosen as members of the Royal Court walk in twos across the field house, to the stage where the thrones await. The coronation is followed by a formal prom. Desiree Shelton, or "Dez" as she was known to her friends, and Sarah Lindstrom were among those elected to the Royal Court. They were "out" lesbians and engaged in a romantic relationship with one another. They had campaigned together for election to the Royal Court, seeing this as an opportunity to make "a political and public statement about gender roles and the visibility of LGBT students and couples at CPHS."[76] Lindstrom later told an interviewer that, while she had heard about the suicides, she had not known any of the students personally and was unaware that any were LGBT related.[77] While this may seem strange, the suicides were dispersed among five large high schools and one middle school and mostly involved students with whom seniors rarely deign to socialize: freshman.

The coronation traditionally began with the 12 members of the Royal Court processing through a decorated arch erected for the occasion at the far end of the field house and then forming boy and girl couples according to their own preference (or the decision of an administrator if they had no preference). As they walked the length of the field house, the announcer introduced each couple over the PA system and shared some interesting facts about them. Finally, they took their place on stage, and stood by during the coronation of the king and queen.

Being openly gay and in a relationship, Shelton and Lindstrom decided to process as a couple. Two boys volunteered to process together to "maintain the couple format." Six days before the ceremony, the young women were approached by a teacher who told them that the plan was not acceptable. They would meet with the principal on the following day to discuss the matter.

They immediately sought out Mathew Mattson, the assistant principal who was in charge of the Snow Days activities. He told them that the administration had discussed the matter and agreed that "it is tradition for only a boy and a girl to process in together."[78] They feared it would make the two boys who had agreed to walk together "uncomfortable" and that the sight of two women walking together would make some of the students "uncomfortable."

Shelton and Lindhurst brought a number of sympathetic and supportive teachers with them to the meeting with Principal Michael George the next day. He repeated his concerns, adding that the final decision would not be made until he consulted with Dennis Carlson, the district superintendent. A follow-up meeting was scheduled for January 27, a Thursday. The Royal Court was to be held on the following Monday.

On Thursday the young women were told that the procession would be cancelled and the event would begin with everyone seated on stage. This new arrangement, the principal believed, "would make everyone comfortable."[79] Mattson said that even if the young men believed they were comfortable marching in a pair, they might not be "three months from now when a picture of them processing together surfaces and rumors get started that they are gay . . . they might then get bullied, commit suicide, and their parents would blame the school district."[80] They also discussed the possibility of canceling the event altogether. Principal George added that at a school board meeting earlier that week parents had "praised them for keeping gays out of the schools and were otherwise hostile toward gays and lesbians."[81] This made them worry about "student safety"[82] if the young women walked in the procession together.

On Thursday afternoon, Ms. Shelton told her mother that the school would not permit her to march alongside Ms. Lindstrom.

"That's bullshit," her mother replied. "You need to go get them."[83]

That evening they contacted the National Center for Lesbian Rights and the Southern Poverty Law Center for advice. The former organization, founded in 1977, tackled a broad range of gender orientation and expression issues through education, litigation, and advocacy; the latter, the prowling pit bull of civil rights advocacy, was the very same agency that had sunk its teeth into the leg of the Ku Klux Klan in the 1980s and shook it until all that remained was a pile of old bedsheets.

The two civil rights organizations arranged for the young women to meet with an attorney from Faegre and Benson, a 100-year-old Minneapolis law firm. After hearing their stories, the attorneys spent the night drafting a letter to the school district and preparing legal papers in case the need for an emergency injunction arose.

Superintendent Carlson received the letter Friday morning. His treatment of Shelton and Lindstrom, it stated, violated the young women's First and Fourteenth Amendment rights and if the school did not rescind these discriminatory actions by noon on Friday, a temporary restraining order would be filed. The letter insisted that the "District [must] make clear to Principal George and to all District staff that it is *unlawful and a violation of the First Amendment for schools to censor student expression of their sexual orientation, gender identity, or support for lesbian, gay, bisexual and transgender (LGBT) rights*" (my italics).[84]

A mediation session with all parties was immediately planned for Saturday with the hope of avoiding the Monday court date. The young women and their attorneys met with district leaders and US District Court Judge Susan Richards Nelson in her Minneapolis chambers. In one hour the young women had won their dispute. They would process together, holding hands, the length of the field house.[85] And their friend Chelsea, who was also gay, could walk with her girlfriend; and any member of the Royal Court could march with anyone they liked, be it boyfriend, girlfriend, best friend, or great grandmother, were she still alive and ambulatory. Carlson also agreed to include Gay-Straight Alliance clubs and other student groups in future planning of events to make sure that *all* groups were included and no one was left out. Then Carlson and George took the young women out to lunch. During the meal Carlson reminisced about a couple he knew who had ostracized their lesbian daughter. He had been "horrified."[86]

On Monday evening, Shelton and Desiree, holding hands, dressed in tuxedos and pink ties with matching yellow roses in their lapels and no little trepidation, set foot on the red carpet that traversed the field house. To their relief, they were met with wild applause and cheers. They seemed to have the support of the entire school. Dozens stood. Cellphones flashed, recording the moment for posterity. "It felt amazing!" Shelton said later, although she admitted that she was too nervous to register exactly what was going on.[87]

Had Carlson been converted? Had he gone to bed that night imagining that he would change the world when he woke? That he would meet with Barb Anderson, and other members of the Parent Action League carrying the flag of gender equality and bring them around with a stirring speech about the constitution? Or did he imagine that he had dodged a bullet? That all this fuss would go away and they could return to business as usual, balancing the concerns of certain outspoken homophobic board members with the needs of the students, as he had once characterized his own administrative style?

In fact, District 11 would never return to business as usual.

On April 25, the district received a memorandum from the Department of Justice and the Office of Civil Rights informing them that they were now the subject of an investigation in response to a complaint of harassment and discrimination on the basis of gender orientation and nonconformity to gender stereotypes.[88] A month later, Carlson received a letter from the Southern Poverty Law Center and the National Center for Lesbian Rights informing them that they had been retained by a group of students who had been harassed because of their sexual orientation or gender presentation. The Southern Poverty Law Center investigation suggested that the district had taken only a few superficial steps to addressing the problem and remained a "hostile and alienating environment" for LGBT students. By failing to respond in a meaningful way, it was violating the law and the constitutional rights of the clients they were representing. The letter went on to invite the school board to meet with the attorneys to explore a settlement in order to avoid litigation. Otherwise,

> Without prompt and meaningful action to remedy the current hostile environment and to compensate our clients for the harm caused by the District, we intend to file a federal lawsuit seeking full redress as well as injunctive relief going forward.[89]

Carlson fired off a press release, cannily suggesting that since the plaintiffs were recommending training in gay and lesbian issues, rather than pursuing a lawsuit they should donate resources for training. As for the Sexual Orientation Curriculum Policy, Carlson believed it encouraged

> discussion of sexual orientation in a respectful manner . . . The policy is appropriate for the community . . . The district's Sexual Orientation Curriculum Policy is constitutional. The Supreme Court has recognized that public school officials have a valid interest in taking neutral positions on matters of public controversy.

Regarding the students named in the lawsuit as bullying victims, Carlson explained that an outside law firm retained to investigate the cases had found that "the district's response was prompt, reasonable and appropriate. Staff investigated and gave appropriate consequences, *including suspension* [my italics]. Due to data privacy laws, victims and their families are not always made aware of the discipline given to offenders."[90] In other words, the bullies had been punished but the victims and their parents had not heard about it because of the district's respect for their privacy.

The claim of suspension is worth closer examination. One of the plaintiffs, referred to as D.M. in the lawsuit, was African American, the adopted child of a same-sex couple. Because his parents were gay, *and* he was small for his age, *and* he participated in gymnastics, a "girl's sport," he was subjected to the repertoire of homophobic gestures and speech previously described. The bullying began in fifth grade and escalated year by year. His fathers, Michael McGee and Jason Backes, made every effort to convince the school to protect him and train his classmates in civil behavior. They received the usual District 11 responses: that the situation would be investigated, that teachers and staff would look into it.

By seventh grade D.M.'s grades began to slip—prior to this he had been an honor roll student—and he had told his fathers that he did not want to return to Jackson Middle School. No intervention had been overlooked in the fathers' efforts to correct the situation. They had recorded every incident, notifying the school, meeting with everyone from the classroom teacher to Superintendent Carlson. In nearly every case they were given the usual assurances followed by the usual inaction. They had watched their son's sense of self-worth deteriorate before their very eyes and were unable to stop it.

In the beginning of eighth grade, as the aggression continued to escalate, a classmate called D.M. a "nigger." D.M. told his parents, who told his school counselor. The offending student was immediately suspended (the suspension referred to by Carlson). It was necessary to suspend the student because district policy stated that acts of racial harassment would be punished by suspension. After that, the bullying continued, but the bully in question confined himself to gay slurs.[91]

The day after Carlson's press release, lawyers from the Southern Poverty Law Center, the National Center for Lesbian Rights, and Faegre & Benson, LLP, filed their lawsuit. It named as defendants, the Anoka-Hennepin School District, the school board, Superintendent Carlson, the principal of Anoka High School, the interim principal of Anoka Middle School for the Arts, and the principal of Jackson Middle School. The aim of litigation was not so much to award damages or to extract a confession of guilt but rather to change the offending system. A month into the trial, the judge asked the US Office of Civil Rights to join the discussion so that its complaint might also be resolved.[92]

The Parent Action League struck back, commandeering a school board meeting in January. They trash-talked Dan Savage; warned of the risk of AIDS, which they continually referred to as GRIDS (gay-related immunity deficiency, a name proposed in 1982 before the true nature of AIDS was understood); misquoted biblical verses; promoted conversion therapy; misinterpreted a Supreme Court Case (*Meyer v. Nebraska*, a case about teaching German during World War I) as a decision supporting the Neutrality Policy; and made continued references to a covert gay agenda that was forcing good Christians "into the closet." They demanded that conversion therapy be listed in school resources and that the school create a new division in support services for "students of faith, moral conviction, ex-homosexuals and ex-transgenders."[93] Confrontations such as this continued throughout the summer and fall and into the winter months.

In February an agreement was struck to replace the Sexual Orientation Curriculum Policy with a Respectful Learning Environment Policy. In March a consent decree was announced. It required that the district retain a consultant who was an expert on sex-based harassment to review the current bullying policies and procedures and develop a new and comprehensive plan to replace it, a plan that addressed gay bullying in the middle schools and high schools. The district was also to hire a Title IX coordinator, to insure that the new policies and procedures were compliant, and an expert consultant in mental health to help students who were victims of harassment. Student and faculty handbooks were to be rewritten so they included resources and procedures for LGBT students. The district was to implement an electronic system for keeping detailed records of every incident of harassment that took place and improve its system for responding. It also included an elaborate system of monitoring, evaluating, and, if necessary, reorganizing the antibullying infrastructure should it prove less than effective.

The estimated cost of the implementation was $500,000.[94] The six plaintiffs were to receive $270,000 to divide among them.[95]

NOTES

1. Southern Poverty Law Center, *Jane Doe et al v. Anoka-Hennepin* (Complaint), 13–39 (US District Court, Court of Minnesota, 2011).
2. Ibid., 4.
3. P. Gibson, "Gay Male and Lesbian Youth Suicide," in *Alcohol, Drug Abuse, and Mental Health Administration. Report of the Secretary's Task Force on Youth*

Suicide: Vol. 3, *Prevention and Interventions in Youth Suicide* (Washington, DC: US Department of Health & Human Services, Public Health Service, Alcohol, Drug Abuse, and Mental Health Administration, 1989).

4. This practice ended in both countries in the early 1970s.

5. Thomas J. Scheff, *Emotions, the Social Bond, and Human Reality: Part/Whole Analysis* (Cambridge, UK: Cambridge University Press, 1997); James Gilligan, *Violence: Our Deadly Epidemic and Its Causes* (New York: Putnam, 1996).

6. C. T. Onions, ed., *The Oxford Dictionary of English Etymology* (Oxford: Oxford University Press, 1966).

7. Cleta L. Dempsey, "Health and Social Issues of Gay, Lesbian, and Bisexual Adolescents," *Families in Society* 75, no. 3 (1994): 160–167.

8. Gregory M. Herek, *Hate Crimes: Confronting Violence Against Lesbians and Gay Men* (Thousand Oaks, CA: SAGE, 1992).

9. Charles Babington and Jonathan Weisman, "Rep. Foley Quits in Page Scandal," *The Washington Post*, September 30, 2006, http://www.washingtonpost.com/wp-dyn/content/article/2006/09/29/AR2006092901574.html.

10. "Senator, Arrested at Airport, Pleads Guilty," *The New York Times*, August 28, 2007, http://www.nytimes.com/2007/08/28/washington/28craig.html.

11. John Byrne, "Anti-Gay Congressman David Dreier, Said to Be Gay, 'Lived with Male Chief of Staff,'" *The Raw Story*, n.d., http://www.rawstory.com.

12. William Falk, "That Wasn't the Week That Was," *The New York Times*, September 5, 2004, http://www.nytimes.com/2004/09/05/opinion/05falk.html.

13. Paul A. Paroski, "Health Care Delivery and the Concerns of Gay and Lesbian Adolescents," *Journal of Adolescent Health Care* 8, no. 2 (March 1987): 188–192, doi:10.1016/0197-0070(87)90263-4.

14. Sigmund Freud, "The Interpretation of Dreams," *Psychology Today*, 1899.

15. Sigmund Freud, *Three Essays on the Theory of Sexuality*, trans. James Strachey (Mansfield Centre, CT: Martino Publishing, 2011).

16. Richard von Kraft-Ebbing, *Psychopathia Sexualis*, trans. Victor Robinson (Rochester, NY: Pioneer Publications, 1953).

17. American Psychiatric Association, *Diagnostic and Statistical Manual of Mental Disorders*, 1st ed. (Washington, DC: American Psychiatric Association, 1952).

18. Ibid., 39.

19. Alfred C. Kinsey, *Sexual Behavior in the Human Male*, 1st ed. (Bloomington: Indiana University Press, 1948).

20. Robert C. Doty, "Growth of Overt Homosexuality in City Provokes Wide Concern," *The New York Times*, December 17, 1963.

21. Ibid.

22. Ibid.

23. Barry D. Adam, *The Rise of a Gay and Lesbian Movement*, Social Movements Past and Present (Boston: Twayne, 1987).

24. Ibid.

25. Kay Tobin and Randy Wicker, *The Gay Crusaders* (New York: Arno Press, 1975).

26. H. Edward Ransford, "Isolation, Powerlessness, and Violence: A Study of Attitudes and Participation in the Watts Riot," *American Journal of Sociology* 73, no. 5 (March 1, 1968): 581–591.

27. "4 Policemen Hurt in 'Village' Raid; Melee Near Sheridan Square Follows Action at Bar," *The New York Times*, June 29, 1969, http://query.nytimes.com/mem/archive/pdf?res=F20714FA3D5D1A7B93CBAB178DD85F4D8685F9.

28. Ibid.

29. *Nabozny v. Podlesny*, Lambda Legal, accessed December 6, 2013, http://www.lambdalegal.org.

30. Anthony R. D'Augelli et al., "Predicting the Suicide Attempts of Lesbian, Gay, and Bisexual Youth," *Suicide and Life-Threatening Behavior* 35, no. 6 (2005): 646–660.

31. *Nabozny v. Podlesny*.

32. Bill Brummel and Geoffrey Sharp, *Bullied: The Jamie Nabozny Story*, 2010, http://vimeo.com/30915646.

33. Ibid.

34. "Jamie Nabozny," Speak Truth to Power, April 5, 2011, http://blogs.nysut.org/sttp/defenders/jamie-nabozny/.

35. *Nabozny v. Podlesny*.

36. Ibid.

37. "About Us," Lambda Legal, accessed January 3, 2014, http://www.lambdalegal.org/about-us

38. "Jamie Nabozny."

39. Brummel and Sharp, *Bullied*.

40. *Nabozny v. Podlesny*.

41. "Jamie Nabozny."

42. *Nabozny v. Podlesny*.

43. Sabrina Erdely, "One Town's War on Gay Teens," *Rolling Stone* 2, no. 2 (2012), http://www.rollingstone.com/politics/news/one-towns-war-on-gay-teens-20120202.

44. Southern Poverty Law Center, *Jane Doe et al.*

45. Erdely, "One Town's War."

46. This was necessitated by US Federal Law Pub. L. 103-160 (10 U.S.C. § 654).

47. House Comm. the Judiciary on. Defense of Marriage Act. 28 USC 115 Sec 1738 C, 1996.

48. 18 U.S.C. §245 (b)(2)

49. David Stout, "House Votes to Expand Hate-Crime Protection," *The New York Times*, May 4, 2007, http://www.nytimes.com/2007/05/04/washington/04hate.html.

50. Ibid.

51. Ken Avidor, Karl D Bremer, and Eva Young, *The Madness of Michele Bachmann* (Hoboken, NJ: Wiley, 2012). PAL's membership list is kept secret.

52. "Right-Wing Hysterical Over Hate Crimes Bill", US House, C-Span, 2009, http://www.youtube.com/watch?v=7jgYFIG7BRg&feature=youtube_gdata_player.

53. Emily Johns, "In Gay Slur Settlement, All Are Paying a Price," *Star Tribune/St. Paul*, August 13, 2009, local ed., http://www.startribune.com/local/stpaul/53189752.html.

54. Ibid.

55. Ibid.

56. Ibid.

57. Erdely, "One Town's War."

58. Ibid.

59. Ibid.

60. The choking game (it goes by different names in different parts of the country) refers to any one of several techniques to produce euphoria, or a change in consciousness through temporary strangulation. This differs from auto-erotic asphyxiation. The 2006 Youth Risk Behavior Study in Ohio found that 19 percent of 17- and 18-year-olds had tried it.

61. Jefferson Fietek as quoted in Rachel Janik, "From 'No Homo Promo' to 'Model for the Nation,'" Medill Equal Media Project, October 2, 2012.

62. Ibid.

63. Erdely, "One Town's War."

64. Steve Ericson, "District 11 Deals With Another Student Suicide," CTN News, Channel 15, May 20, 2011, http://www.ctnstudios.com/index.php?option=com_content&view=article&id=553:district-11-deals-with-another-student-suicide&Itemid=100.

65. "Anoka-Hennepin Disputes Bullying-Suicide Connection," MPR News, December 7, 2010), http://www.mprnews.org/story/2010/12/17/anoka-hennepin-bullying-suicides.

66. Ibid.

67. Marsha Linehan, *Cognitive-Behavioral Treatment of Borderline Personality Disorder* (New York: Guilford Press, 1993).

68. Tom Prichard, "Gay Activists Manipulate Suicide Tragedy for Ideological Purposes," Minnesota Family Council, September 28, 2010, http://mnfamily-council.blogspot.com/2010/09/gay-activists-manipulate-suicide.html.

69. "AFTAH Interview with Barb Anderson—Discusses Radical Sex Ed and School Promotion of Homosexuality," Americans for Truth About Homosexuality, November 27, 2010, http://americansfortruth.com/2010/12/01/112710-aftah-interview-with-barb-anderson/.

70. Erik Eckholm, "In Efforts to End Bullying, Some See Agenda," *The New York Times*, November 6, 2010, http://www.nytimes.com/2010/11/07/us/07bully.html.

71. Ibid.

72. Jesse McKinley, "Suicides Put Light on Pressures of Gay Teenagers," *The New York Times*, October 3, 2010, http://www.nytimes.com/2010/10/04/us/04suicide.html.

73. Ibid.

74. Russlynn Ali, "Dear Colleague Letter," Office of the Assistant Secretary for Civil Rights, US Department of Education, October 26, 2010, 8, http://www2.ed.gov/about/offices/list/ocr/letters/colleague-201010.html.

75. According to Section 504 and Title II.

76. *Desiree Shelton & Sarah Lindstrom v. Anoka-Hennepin School District, Champlain Park High School et al.* (n.d.), 29.

77. Bambi Weavil, "Rare Interview with Sarah Lindstrom: 'We Gave Them Confidence to Come out & Be Themselves,'" *Out Impact*, February 17, 2011.

78. *Desiree Shelton & Sarah Lindstrom v. Anoka-Hennepin*, para. 33.

79. Ibid., para. 36.

80. Ibid., para. 37.

81. Ibid., para. 38.

82. Ibid.

83. Beth Hawkins, "Bullying Gay and Lesbian Kids: How a School District Became a Suicide Contagion Area," *Minnesota Post*, December 7, 2011, http://www.minnpost.com/politics-policy/2011/12/bullying-gay-and-lesbian-kids-how-school-district-became-suicide-contagion-a.

84. Samuel Wolfe, Shannon Minter, and Michael A. Ponto, "Letter from Southern Poverty Law Center Regarding Injunction on Behalf of Desiree Shelton and Sarah Lindstrom," January 28, 2011.

85. Hawkins, "Bullying Gay and Lesbian Kids."

86. Ibid.
87. Chris Williams, "Sarah Lindstrom and Desiree Shelton, Lesbian Couple, Cheered By School After Winning Rights," *Huffington Post*, January 31, 2011, http://www.huffingtonpost.com/2011/02/01/sarah-lindstrom-desiree-shelton-lesbian-students_n_817057.html.
88. Paul H. Cady, "Memorandum Re: Department of Justice Investigation of Complaint," US Department of Justice, Office of Civil Rights, April 25, 2011, http://i2.cdn.turner.com/cnn/2011/images/07/18/doj.investigation.pdf.
89. Samuel Wolfe and Shannon Minter, "Proposed Meeting to Resolve Claims," May 24, 2011, http://www.splcenter.org/sites/default/files/downloads/case/Anoka-Hennepin-Letter.pdf.
90. Mary Olson and Brett Johnson, "Support, Not Litigation, Is the Best Path to Aiding GLBT Students in Anoka-Hennepin," press release, Educational Service Center, July 20, 2011, http://i.cdn.turner.com/cnn/2011/images/07/20/a.h.response.splc.nclr.pdf.
91. Southern Poverty Law Center, *Jane Doe et al.*
92. "Civil Rights Division Educational Opportunities Case Summaries," US Department of Justice, accessed March 25, 2014, http://www.justice.gov/crt/about/edu/documents/casesummary.php.
93. Andy Birkey, "Conservative Christian Parents Fight for Right to Discriminate against LGBT Students at Anoka Hennepin," *Twin Cities Daily Planet*, January 13, 2012, http://www.tcdailyplanet.net/news/2012/01/13/conservative-christian-parents-fight-right-discriminate-against-lgbt-students-anoka-.
94. *Jane Doe et al & U.S. v Anoka-Hennepin* Consent Decree (USDistrict Court for the District of Minnesota, 2012).
95. Ibid.

CHAPTER 4

The Bullying of Lesbian, Gay, Bisexual, and Transgender Teens

PART II: WAS IT A CLUSTER AND WHAT WAS ITS CAUSE?

When the media learned of the extent of the Anoka-Hennepin suicide cluster, its etiology became a subject of fierce debate. People were of two opinions.

Progressives took it for granted that the Sexual Orientation Curriculum Policy encouraged the bullying of gay children, which led to some taking their own life. The overlap of Anoka-Hennepin School District with the congressional district of Michelle Bachmann, a conservative congresswoman contemplating a run for the presidency and a friend of the Parents Action League and the Minnesota Family Council, seemed incontrovertible evidence that she was not suited for the White House. Thus the Anoka Hennepin suicide cluster became a political football.

Conservatives argued that there was no "cluster"; gay students, they insisted, were being encouraged by liberals to pursue a gay lifestyle as though it were a form of "normal behavior" and the depressing effects of that "choice" was what drove them to suicide. In an email to Rolling Stone, the Parent Action League appealed to common sense.

> How could not discussing homosexuality in the public-school classrooms cause a teen to take his or her own life . . . ? Because homosexual activists have hijacked and exploited teen suicides for their moral and political utility, much of society seems not to be looking closely and openly at all the possible causes of the tragedies.[1]

Superintendent of Schools Dennis Carlson agreed but took a different tack. In an editorial on Minnesota Public Radio, he denied the usefulness of simple fixes.

> Will a change in policy end bullying or harassment? Will it decrease student depression? Will it prevent students from self-destructive behavior or from committing suicide?
>
> If it were that simple, we would make a policy change instantly. Unfortunately, there are no easy answers or quick fixes because human behavior, especially that of adolescents going through tremendous physical and emotional change, is complex, and it is complicated by the stresses many families in our communities are now feeling.[2]

WHAT IS A SUICIDE CLUSTER?

The Centers for Disease Control have defined a suicide cluster as "a group of suicides or suicide attempts, or both, that occur closer together in time and space than would normally be expected in any given community."[3] "Community" can refer to groups defined not only by time or place but also by ideology, some shared experience, or occupation. For example, the US military, during the first four months of 2013, lost 161 soldiers to suicide, one every 18 hours, surpassing the number of troops ever killed in combat.[4] This constitutes a suicide cluster, even though the troops were scattered around the world.

Suicide clusters defined by a time or place are easily verified because cities, counties, states, and the Federal government all keep statistics of deaths and their causes for public health purposes. Likewise, a surge in suicides in the military is easy to spot because the military keeps track of fatalities at its bases, and not simply those incurred in battle. A larger problem of identification is posed by suicides that occur in many locations and appear to be based on some shared experience.

An example of this is "Gloomy Sunday" (*Szomorú Vasárnap*) a popular Hungarian song of 1933, which became associated with a number of suicides in its native land.

> Sunday is gloomy, my hours are slumberless
> Dearest, the shadows I live with are numberless
> Little white flowers will never awaken you
> Not where the black coach of sorrow has taken you
> Angels have no thoughts of ever returning you

Wouldn't they be angry if I thought of joining you?
Gloomy Sunday[5]

In 1936, while investigating the suicide of a shoemaker named Joseph Keller, Budapest police discovered a suicide note quoting lyrics from "Gloomy Sunday." Further investigation identified 18 more suicides inspired by the song; two had been committed after its victims had heard it played (with exquisite melancholy, one assumes) by a gypsy band.[6] By March the song had been translated into English and recorded by Billy Holiday, among others. An article in *The New York Times* dated April 5, 1936, relates the story of 13-year-old Floyd Hamilton Jr., "whose body was found hanging in the living room of his home yesterday . . . the boy had in his pocket the words of 'Gloomy Sunday,' a song which was blamed for many suicides in Hungary."[7] A *Times* article from the following month tells of Phillip Tangier Smith Cooke, a student at Hobart College. While classmates were dancing at the senior ball, Cooke shot and killed himself with a rifle in the bedroom of his frat house. Testimony at the inquest "indicated a connection with the song, 'Gloomy Sunday,' recently held responsible for many suicides in Hungary."[8] Whether the song brought about the melancholy that might lead to suicide, triggered suicide in a person who had already planned to commit the act, or so aptly described the melancholy that one boy wanted to keep it as a "suicide note" to explain his emotions to others is impossible to determine. An unnamed authority estimated that 200 suicides worldwide had been caused by the melancholy melody.[9]

Suicide clusters have attracted interest throughout history. Accounts are found in the Bible and in Greek and Roman history. In his *Lives*[10] (ca. 400 BC), Plutarch recounts the story of the Maidens of Miletus (Μίλητος), an ancient Greek city near what is today Balat, Turkey.

A certain dreadful and monstrous distemper did seize the Milesian maids, arising from some hidden cause . . . for all on a sudden an earnest longing for death, with furious attempts to hang themselves, did attack them and many did privily accomplish it. The arguments and tears of parents and the persuasions of friends availed nothing, but they circumvented their keepers in all their contrivances and industry to prevent them, still murdering themselves. And the calamity seemed to be an extraordinary divine stroke and beyond human help, until by the counsel of a wise man a decree of the senate was passed, enacting that those maids who hanged themselves should be carried naked through the market place. The passage of this law not only inhibited but quashed their desire of slaying themselves. Note what a great argument of good nature and virtue this fear of disgrace is; for they who had no dread upon them of the most terrible things in the world, death and pain, could not abide the imagination of dishonor and exposure to shame even after death.[11]

James Frazer, in *The Golden Bough*,[12] a classic work of religious scholarship, argues that temple prostitution was ubiquitous throughout the Near East (although in recent years some biblical scholars have taken issue with this), and virgins were often engaged in sexual rituals that took the form of fertility rites or divine marriages. It seems likely that the maidens of Miletus were involved in similar kinds of rituals, rituals that had once been tolerable but now, due to some change in implementation, had become unbearably shameful. Assuming the rituals involved divine marriage, here is a possible scenario: For centuries at this temple, intercourse with the gods had been play-acted, but then a priest decided to replace the act with real intercourse, perhaps to woo a wealthy supporter, who in turn for his donation was allowed to play the part of the god during the ritual. The maiden who was next in line decided she would rather die than engage in this degradation of her faith and avoided the shame of the new arrangement by hanging herself. The other Maidens, considering this a pretty good solution to an intolerable state of affairs, followed her example. The solution suggested by the "wise man" in Plutarch's narrative was effective because the tableau of having their naked corpses carried through the marketplace seemed even more shameful then whatever sort of acts, sexual or otherwise, they were being forced to engage in.

ANTISUICIDE CLUSTERS

Dave Phillips, then a young sociologist at the State University of New York at Stony Brook and intrigued by the reports of an increase in suicides following the death of Marilyn Monroe in 1962, wondered whether suicide clusters regularly followed a highly publicized suicide.[13] He found that the research literature was equivocal. Durkheim,[14] whose thinking dominated the field of suicidology for many years, argued that it might occur occasionally among those who were close to the victim, but they were likely to have committed suicide in any case. Phillips found "the dearth of studies linking suicide and suggestion ... somewhat puzzling, in view of the general importance ascribed to contagion and suggestion in other areas of sociology."[15]

In an attempt to better understand the phenomena, Phillips reviewed the suicides reported on the front page of the five US newspapers with the largest circulation during the period of 1946 to 1967. Because the number of monthly suicides varied according to the time of year, he calculated the average number for each month. If his hypothesis was correct, suicides following a "celebrity" suicide would exceed the average. He found that this was indeed the case and concluded that the rise in suicides was the result of "suggestion." Suicide was being offered (and accepted) as a suggestion for solving a problem.

> A person who finds no meaning in life may kill himself; but, on the other hand, he may join a religious or political movement that provides him with meaning. An intensely lonely person may "choose" suicide as a solution to his loneliness or he may instead join a movement like the Samaritans that provides him with companionship. Alcoholics may kill themselves or join Alcoholics Anonymous; terminal cancer patients may commit suicide or join faith-healing cults.[16]

This is a cognitive explanation in that it involves mobilizing ego strengths; the rational actor thinks out the course of his or her life. I suggest, as I have throughout this book, that people make important life choices based on their emotional needs and their desire to remain in relationship to an individual, group, or community.

We might better understand this by imagining some close-knit group that has been meeting for years, a book group or a poker game. One member who has been having a rocky time of it suddenly bursts into tears, throws down his cards or her knitting, and runs out the door. The rest of the group gets up and runs after him or her. We do not just abandon someone we have come to love, even if it is someone we have worshipped from afar, such as Marilyn Monroe. We might also assume, as Phillips suggests, that they were people with little else to live for and perhaps serious problems they wished to escape. Some who adored Marilyn Monroe may have committed suicide to be with her; others may have done so simply to avoid abandoning her. They wanted to rescue her from isolation, even in death. I offer a scrap of evidence to support this alternative view.

While suicides increased by 200 in the month following Monroe's suicide, other front-page suicides (20 percent of the 34 cases Phillips examined) were followed by a *decline* in the number of suicides. Apparently there are suicide clusters and *antisuicide* clusters. Phillips ignores the latter, but it seems to me that any event that reduces the number of suicides warrants a close investigation. In August of 1948 the suicide rate decreased by 100 after the suicide of Henry Brooks, a financier. In April of 1951, the suicide rate decreased by 96 following the suicide of John C. Lang, a police witness. In the most extreme example, in April of 1957, the suicide rate decreased by 138 following the suicide of E. Herbert Norman, the Canadian ambassador to Egypt. A closer look at these three suicides is certainly worth our time.

HUNTED AS SLAYER, BROOKS ENDS LIFE[17]
1948, August 28
New York Times, p. 1.

The hunt for Henry M. Brooks, once a wealthy stock promoter, for the slaying of Joseph R. Watkins, a pressing creditor and business associate, ended yesterday in the Albion Hotel at Asbury Park, N.J. He was found there with a bullet through his right temple. "Death by suicide," the county medical examiner said . . .

WITNESS ENDS LIFE BY SHOT[18]
1951 April 20
New York Times, p. 1

P.B.A. Treasurer Dies in Bronx Park—Testified at Jury Inquiry Into Funds—Investigation Barely Under Way

Patrolman John C. Lang, 47 years old, treasurer of the Patrolmen's Benevolent Association, left his six-room apartment in the Bronx at noon yesterday, walked over to a quiet spot in Bronx Park and killed himself with a bullet through the temple from his own service revolver . . . He had testified for forty-five minutes on Monday before a New York County grand jury investigating the affairs of the association, principal line organization in the Police Department, had spent hours "downtown, waiting to be recalled on Tuesday and finally was sent off with word that he would be summoned back later . . .

Canadian Envoy Ends Life;
Named in U.S. Red Inquiry;
E. Herbert Norman Jumps From Building in Cairo
—Case Angers Ottawa[19]
By OSGOOD CARUTHERS
Special to *The New York Times*.
April 05, 1957, Page 1

CAIRO, April 4—E. Herbert Norman, Canadian Ambassador to Egypt, killed himself today by plunging from the roof of a nine-story building. He had been suffering from strain of overwork and extreme depression over the revival of charges by a United States Senate subcommittee that he had been a Communist.

In these cases people contemplating suicide deferred or abandoned the idea because they did not want to be associated with suicides of a lower status group: murderers, cops on the take, or Communist spies. Recall that in the 1950s Communists were possibly the most shamed group in the country, reviled and persecuted by Senator Joseph M. McCarthy and the House on Un-American Activities Committee. Returning to our imagined book group and poker game, there may be members who, when they become upset and run out the door, elicit a sigh of relief from those who remain behind. *Thank goodness we're rid of that lowlife!*

DID THE SUICIDE OF THE ANOKA HENNEPIN SCHOOL DISTRICT REALLY CONSTITUTE A CLUSTER?

So the question is: Were the nine Anoka-Hennepin School District suicides that occurred in 2010 and 2011 significantly more than the average number of teen suicides for that time and place?

What is the *average* number of suicides? What constitutes *a lot* of suicides? What constitutes a few? Is Minnesota a state where an unusually large number of people commit suicide every year? Or did something occur during the years 2010 and 2011 that prompted this particular group of teens to take their own lives?

The average suicide rate for the planet Earth is 11.4 per 100,000 (Guyana has the highest rate, at 70.8 per 100,000, and Kuwait the lowest rate, at 1 per 100,000).[20] According to recent census data, the population of the United States is almost 309 million,[21] and the suicide rate has risen over the past decade from 10.5 to 12 per 100,000.[22]

The Western states (Texas, New Mexico, Oklahoma, etc.) have the highest suicide rate (13.6); the Southern states (Mississippi, Louisiana, Georgia, etc.) the second highest (12.6); the Midwestern states (Minnesota, Ohio, Wisconsin, etc.), the third highest (12.0); and the Northeastern states (Maine, Vermont, New Hampshire, etc.) the lowest (9.3).

Like many statistics, these inform and mislead. Men, women, and adolescents all commit suicide in different numbers for different reasons, and averaging them together conceals important distinctions. Adult women attempt suicide most often—three times as often as adult men—but usually do so by overdosing on pills, an act that can be undone if discovered in time. Men, preferring firearms, attempt less often but succeed about four times as often as women.[23]

In May of 2013, a *New York Times* article, looking back on the decade of 2000 to 2009, the period for which the Centers for Disease Control and

Prevention have the most comprehensive data, announced that suicide rates had risen "sharply"[24] in the United States among men in their 50s (baby boomers). While the national average suicide rate had increased by less than 3 per 100,000, the rate for male baby boomers had increased by nearly 50 percent[25] (from 20 to 30 incidents per 100,000). Baby boomers, the *Times'* reporter suggested, were responding to "years of economic worries . . . Historically [male] suicide rates rise during times of financial stress and economic setbacks."[26] Nearly 1,000 comments followed the Internet posting of the article, many describing loved ones who had lost their jobs during the Great Recession of 2008. One woman wrote of her brother:

> After four years of no job offers, unemployment running out, having no health insurance . . . his dignity was shot. He had lost hope of ever working again. . . . I would give anything and everything to have him back.[27]

Were we to graph the Dow Jones average and the suicide rate of American male adults from 1900 to the present, the two lines would mirror each other, with suicides increasing during recessions and decreasing during times of affluence. Men's sense of worth derives from their ability to work and support a family. To lose that role is to experience shame of the deepest sort.

Adolescents commit suicide for a different reason. Eric Erikson, in his classic study of human development *Childhood and Society*,[28] identifies the central task of adolescence as separating from one's parents and creating the foundations of an adult identity. (One authority[29] has suggested that the central developmental task of a gay child is to reject the degrading myths about homosexuality in order to affirm his or her emerging sexuality.)

What is the foundation of an adult identity? At the very least it is finding some passion that can lead to a vocation; forming an intimate bond with another person that may become a model for marriage later on; discovering a morality that dictates a right and wrong way to behave; and adopting a spiritual belief regarding the reason we have been put on Earth, why we live, and what becomes of us when we die. It is no coincidence that high school society is a cartoonish analog of the adult world, a sandbox where children can play at being scholars, techies, criminals, musicians, or actors; where they can practice falling in love and breaking up; where they can worship their athletes and disdain their slackers.

Suicide rates for teenagers are very low compared to those of older men and women. Most adolescents sense that their time of life is, despite the occasional periods of horrifying humiliation, a vital period of learning and becoming, shaped by a glimmer of what pleasures and frustrations adulthood may hold.

In 2006, teens between the ages of 15 and 19 had a national average suicide rate of a little more than 7 per 100,000.[30] In Minnesota, the rate was 9.2 per 100,000.[31], [32] Incidentally, the percentage of students who had *thought* about killing themselves (had suicidal ideation) had been in steady decline for the decade prior to the suicide cluster.[33] The Anoka-Hennepin School District, with 39,000 students (it is the largest school district in Minnesota), might anticipate that during a two-year period seven teenagers would commit suicide (3.6 a year). The number that actually occurred during the first year of the alledged suicide cluster, the period beginning on October 16, 2009, with the suicide of T. J. Hayes and ending on October 3, 2010, with the suicide of Cole Wilson, was seven.

This was twice the number expected and all within a radius of 20 miles. (While the Anoka-Hennepin School District is the largest in in the state, the five high schools and the middle school where the suicides took place are clustered around the intersection of Andover, Anoka, Blaine, and Champlin Park.)

WAS THE CLUSTER CAUSED BY THE SEX EDUCATION CURRICULUM POLICY?

Correlation occurs when two events happen at the same time. This is obviously very different from saying that the one event caused the other yet even seasoned researchers frequently make this mistake.

In order to demonstrate causation, we should be able to show that the change was not caused by some event extraneous to the events we are investigating. Furthermore, the cause must precede the effect. Finally, we should be able to explain the mechanism of the causation without resorting to improbable explanations (e.g., etheric theories, extraterrestrial intervention, or witchcraft).

By comparing adolescent suicide rates throughout Minnesota with those of the Anoka-Hennepin School District, we can dismiss the influence of extraneous events[34] such as a celebrity suicide of the type studied by Dave Phillips[35] or a lethal media product such as Gloomy Sunday. No "external" events occurred during the time in question that caused a suicide increase across other similar communities. The average statewide suicide rate for Minnesota from October 2009 to October of 2010 continued a trend of small yearly increases, led by a more substantial increase among men aged 55 to 59, as previously mentioned (the baby boomers). If an extraneous event did occur influencing adolescents toward suicide, it would have also affected neighboring school districts, but since neighboring districts did not report a rise in suicides (or any suicides at all to my knowledge), we can assume that this was not the case.

Did the cause precede the effect? Was the Neutrality Policy put into effect prior to the occurrence of the cluster?

The Neutrality Policy was dated February 2009, four months before summer vacation. School started up again in September, and the first suicide occurred in October of that year. The cause preceded the effect but not by too much, which seems logical. The timing seems reasonable, allowing for a few months of the snowballing of homophobic aggression and the school staff figuring out how to respond to the demand for "neutrality."

Further evidence for causation might be established if the suicides stopped when the policy was repealed. The last reported Anoka-Hennepin School District suicide, that of Jordan Yenor, occurred on May 14, 2011, 10 days before the letter from the Southern Poverty Law Center arrived on Superintendent Carlson's desk demanding "prompt and meaningful action to remedy the current hostile environment and to compensate our clients for the harm caused by the District" and threatening to file a Federal lawsuit seeking "full redress" and "injunctive relief."[36]

In February the Sexual Orientation Curriculum Policy was repealed, and the following month the court handed down its consent decree. There have been no adolescent suicides in Anoka-Hennepin School District since then. While I still cannot conclusively prove that one caused the other, the evidence is compelling.

One more factor should be considered here, an economic cataclysm that struck Anoka County during the time in question, one that was likely to have create a suicidal climate for Baby Boomers: a record number of mortgage foreclosures. *Big mortgages.* During the years preceding and following the suicide cluster, Anoka County (most of the Anoka-Hennepin School District lies within Anoka County) had the highest and fastest-growing rate of foreclosures of any Twin Cities' suburb. In 2006 there had been 849 foreclosures; in 2007, 1,848; and by 2008, 2,343.[37] In the 12-month period between July 31, 2008, and July 31, 2009, foreclosures rose to around 10,154,[38] the highest rate ever for Minnesota, while home values dropped precipitously. The suicide cluster began three months later.

Jan Buckman, who ran the foreclosure prevention hotline, excitedly told a local paper, "It's explosive, unbelievable, like a train wreck with people who have over-extended themselves crashing against changing interest rates . . . this is very, very real and it's getting worse." More recently, the county's 20-bed homeless shelter had to accommodate 80, and that did not include "suburbanites who preferred sleeping at rest stops, couch-hopping or spending the night freezing in cars."[39]

"To be homeless in the suburbs is the end of the line," the director of the Anoka County homeless shelter noted. "It's a different culture here. The homeless in the suburbs don't scream, panhandle or knock down doors. They hide." In a recent homeless census conducted during the darkest days of winter (January 25), investigators counted 1,463 homeless individuals. The number of homeless teens (150) was up 40 percent from the previous year. Fifteen homeless people were sleeping outside in 12-degree weather and another 25 were found sleeping in their cars. Twelve families were living in unheated sheds or fishing houses.[40]

It is likely that parents of students, teachers and administrators, their family members, or their close friends were among the 10,000 Anokans who lost their homes to foreclosure during the year prior to the suicide cluster and had to rent more modest domiciles, move in with relatives, or couch-surf until they could get back on their feet. It was an epidemic of shame, the kind that cries out for a scapegoat. It is possible that "attack other" adults created a climate that bristled with homophobic aggression. The humiliations endured by lesbian, gay, bisexual, and transgender (LGBT) students, itemized in the complaint of the Southern Poverty Law Center, includes incidents of such cavalier cruelty that, were it not a legal document, it would strain belief.

A REASONABLE EXPLANATION OF *HOW* A CAUSED B

Finally, we need to establish some kind of reasonable explanation for how the Neutrality Policy could have doubled the suicide rate for Anoka Hennepin teens. Because we are viewing this incident through the lens of shame theory, we consider suicide as an extreme example of "attack self," and we look for a variety of shame-instilling circumstances, rather than any single monolithic cause. We also examine why the shame could not be managed in less lethal and tragic ways. We begin with an examination of group membership.

For gay teens, the most important group memberships are family, friends, school community, and perhaps church, depending on the role religion plays in the family. Gay teens anticipate that their membership in these groups will be jeopardized or terminated by the public revelation of their homosexuality. They will experience a precipitous drop in status and find themselves members of a group with a powerful tradition of being reviled by the dominant culture. Let us not forget that many adults do not like teenagers very much to begin with.[41] Teens seem to be having more fun than we are but doing less (or no) work. We support them, but they do not obey us. Occasionally they wreck the car or cause other damage, and we get the bill. Sometimes they get arrested and we have to bail them out.

In one well-conducted study, 95 percent of gay adolescents listed isolation as the primary problem in their lives.[42] They felt "separated" and "emotionally isolated" from peers because of their sexual orientation. The same study[43] identified family difficulties as the second most common problem. Those who do not come out to their families worry about being discovered. One young lady said of this experience,

> I always had to watch myself. I always had to make sure that I was not acting too butch, or dressing too much like a dyke. I always felt like I was trying to be someone who I wasn't, always trying to fit in where I knew I didn't fit. I really felt all alone, I thought I was the only person in the world who felt this way.[44]

Those who do come out are often estranged or disowned. Even the most liberal, adoring, flexible, and forgiving parents may tell their child that this is only a phase that they may outgrow. While such comments seem "neutral" enough, they betray the parents' discomfort with homosexuality and emphasize the heteronormative nature of society.[45]

Around 50 percent of gay adolescents have experienced physical violence at the hands of family members.[46] Conflicts are more common between a homosexual son and other male family members. In one account, two brothers altruistically administered frequent beatings to their gay brother to "toughen him up" so that he could deal with schoolyard bullies.[47] A father may have such shame regarding homosexuality that the sight of a formerly beloved son holding hands with another boy is unbearable. Thus the membership in the family becomes less secure. The third most frequently identified problem is the violence experienced at the hands of peers. Forty percent of LGBT students reported being victimized by their peers. Thus it is not only family membership that is jeopardized but also friendships and membership in the school community.

For some children, the loss of a church community may be as shameful as the loss of family and school. Consider the little girl who, reaching puberty, discovers that despite all efforts to honor religious beliefs and obey her parents—to be, in other words, the best child she can possibly be—she finds herself having romantic daydreams about a member of the same sex. If the gay child belongs to an Orthodox or Evangelical faith with homophobic policies and has fully embraced the ideology of her faith, that teen will come to believe that she is loathsome. If an Evangelical Christian, she will burn in hell for eternity. If an Orthodox Jew, she will be an abomination in the eyes of God. How terrible! Will these children be willing to forfeit the faith in which they were raised in order to maintain a positive sense of identity? Or will they choose to live out their lives pretending to be who they are not?

There is one more group from which gays are banished that should be mentioned here, and that is the group within which other groups exist—the group of all groups—the "dominant culture." The assumptive superiority of the dominant culture, if it is to remain dominant, is constantly reinforced by a subtle, persistent, and often unconscious shaming. The educator Derald Wing Sue has referred to the manifestation of these shamings as acts of "microaggression."[48] These include actions and expressions that reinforce patriarchy, heterosexism, and whiteness. Microaggression can be interpersonal or institutional, the former consisting of subtle comments and actions that enforce the user's status and diminish that of the victim. Most of us are trained in delivering interpersonal microaggressions from an early age by our parents, unconsciously, out of their love for us and their fear that in our naiveté we will lose whatever social status they have struggled to make available to us. Like the relentless buzz of the traffic on the nearby interstate, we become numb to microaggressions until they are pointed out to us. Even then, some of us are likely to argue that to pay such careful attention to our speech—to parse every word, as it may seem—will only make the minorities in question feel more victimized or mire everyone's communications in the minutia of political correctness. Such arguments hark back to the 1950s, when racist, sexist, and homophobic jokes were defended as being "just fun." In fact, the pleasure of such jokes lay in the comfort achieved by buttressing up the raconteur's status by diminishing the status of the group being ridiculed.

Some of the most harmful microaggressions are nonverbal and occur at the institutional level in the form of racial profiling; discriminatory hiring and promotional practices; segregation of private schools, clubs, and churches; and "educational curricula that marginalize or ignore the history of minorities."[49] Institutional bias is often written into an institution's standard operating procedures. While such rules appear to apply equally to all, they often provide an advantage to members of the dominant culture.

While one or two microaggressions might seem trivial, a barrage of them on a day-to-day basis can beat a person down. The accumulation of these slights has been referred to as "minority stress"[50] and "death by a thousand cuts." They negatively impact self-image, as well as physical and psychological health.

Thus it seems that shame theory provides a reasonable explanation for how the school board policy occurring against a background of financial crises and the possibility of homelessness, could have caused a suicide cluster of gay students, students who empathized with gay students, and even students who bullied gay students. While this is still not definitive and incontrovertible evidence that A caused B, it reinforces our case.

POSITIVE WAYS TO MANAGE LGBT SHAME

African American youth, a minority group that parallels or surpasses LGBT youth as a target of senseless discrimination, have African American parents who can teach them how to survive and even thrive in the world of whiteness (e.g. "If you want to succeed you've got to work twice as hard as the white man"). They can name great black actors, writers, and activists; celebrate their history (albeit for only one month a year); and trace their ancestry back to Africa, the cradle of the human race. But who is there to teach the gay adolescent about survival in the world of heterosexism? Not parents or siblings or uncles or aunts, except on rare occasion.

Homosexual shame, like all shame, is best managed by conversation with an empathic and non-judgemental listener. If a listener can be found who has suffered shaming in a similar context, yet achieved satisfaction or even happiness in life, all the better. If Dan Savage's "It Gets Better" videos comfort gay teens and prevent suicides, they do so because they are versions (albeit one-sided) of these kinds of conversations. Telephone help lines and walk-in support services with well-trained counselors and therapists are often life-savers. Gay-Straight Alliances and other clubs that provide a safe container for self-disclosure are among the best ways for a school to facilitate this. (Some of the high schools in the Anoka Hennepin School District had Gay-Straight Alliances, but the clubs were not permitted in the middle schools.)[51] If access to all such resources is forbidden, as was the case in the Anoka-Hennepin School District, then the shame remains unmanaged and easily turns to violence against the self.

Openly gay teachers may make themselves available for conversation and informal counseling. While their existence is not advertised, it becomes known to gay students and shared among them because it is a lifeline. Coleen Cashen, a school psychologist at Northdale Middle School, and

Jefferson Fietek, chair of the theater department at Anoka Middle School for the Arts, are two openly gay employees of the district who, prior to the passage of the Neutrality Policy, provided counseling and emotional support to middle-school gay students. Following the passage of the Neutrality Policy, Cashen was told by other teachers, "You have to be careful, it's really not safe for you to come out," and said that she was afraid to display a picture of her family on her desk.[52]

One day after passage of the Neutrality Policy, Fietek noticed his students tittering as they passed around a community newspaper that had just outed him. Even though he was open about his sexual identity, when one of the students interrupted the class to ask if he was gay, he became terrified that his answer might violate the Neutrality Policy and jeopardize his job in the school system.[53] These fears were not without basis, particularly during the Great Recession of 2007–2008. Following his courageous public criticism of the Neutrality Policy on CNN and other media outlets, his theater budget had been slashed and his computer confiscated. He had suffered other career setbacks that had the odor of retribution.

NEUROLOGICAL VULNERABILITY

Before ending this chapter, it should be mentioned that recent developments in neuroscience support the existence of a neurological component to suicide clustering. During puberty the brain experiences a rapid rise in dopaminergic activity, meaning simply that more dopamine is produced. Dopamine is a neurotransmitter that appears to be associated with goal-oriented and reward-seeking behavior. The prefrontal cortex, the front part of the brain that makes a person behave reasonably, lags behind the rest of the brain in development. This makes middle adolescence, from 14 to 17, a period of risky behavior because "sensation seeking is high and self-regulation is still immature . . . many risk-behaviors follow this pattern, including unprotected sex, criminal behavior, attempted suicide, and reckless driving."[54] The developing brain of the adolescent may also make teens unusually vulnerable to peer pressure. Although the mechanisms of this are not yet clearly understood,[55] the behavior is known to all mothers and is reflected in the statement, *If all your friends jumped off the Brooklyn Bridge, would you do it too?* The question is rhetorical, but if an answer was required it would be, *Maybe.* Adolescents are the age group most likely to follow their friends to the grave when their lives become unmanageable.

NOTES

1. Parent Action League, "Email to Rolling Stone: Discussion of Homosexuality Leading to Suicide," Quoted by Erdeley, 2012.
2. Dennis Carlson, "Anoka-Hennepin Policy Aims to Respect All Families and Students," MPR News, June 8, 2011, http://www.mprnews.org/story/2011/06/08/carlson.
3. Patrick W. O'Carroll, James A. Mercy, and John A. Steward, *CDC Recommendations for a Community Plan for the Prevention and Containment of Suicide Clusters* (Atlanta: Centers for Disease Control, Center for Environmental Health and Injury Control, Division of Injury Epidemiology and Control, 1988), https://www.ncjrs.gov/App/abstractdb/AbstractDBDetails.aspx?id=122038.
4. Bill Briggs, "One Every 18 Hours: Military Suicide Rate Still High Despite Hard Fight to Stem Deaths," NBC News, May 23, 2013, http://usnews.nbcnews.com/_news/2013/05/23/18447439-one-every-18-hours-military-suicide-rate-still-high-despite-hard-fight-to-stem-deaths.
5. "Billie Holiday: Gloomy Sunday Lyrics," Lyricsfreak.com, accessed September 17, 2008, http://www.lyricsfreak.com/b/billie+holiday/gloomy+sunday_20017999.html.
6. Loren Coleman, *Suicide Clusters* (Boston: Faber & Faber, 1987).
7. "Boy Suicide Had Death Song," *The New York Times*, April 6, 1936.
8. "Senior Ends Life as Class Dances," *The New York Times*, May 23, 1936.
9. Coleman, *Suicide Clusters*.
10. Plutarch and William Watson Goodwin, *Plutarch's Lives* (Boston: Little, Brown, 1874).
11. Ibid., 354.
12. Sir James George Frazer, *The Golden Bough: A Study of Magic and Religion* (New Delhi: Cosmo Publications, 2005).
13. David P. Phillips, "The Influence of Suggestion on Suicide: Substantive and Theoretical Implications of the Werther Effect," *American Sociological Review* 39 (1974): 340–354.
14. Emil Durkheim, *Suicide: A Study in Sociology* (London: Routledge, 1897).
15. Phillips, "The Influence of Suggestion," 341.
16. Durkheim, *Suicide*, 351.
17. "Hunted as Slayer, Brooks Ends Life," *The New York Times*, August 28, 1948, sec. A.
18. "Police Witness Ends Life by Shot; P.B.A. Treasurer Dies in Bronx Park—Testified at Jury Inquiry into Funds," *The New York Times*, April 20, 1951, sec. A.
19. Osgood Caruthers, "Canadian Envoy Ends Life; Named in U.S. Red Inquiry; E. Herbert Norman Jumps From Building in Cairo—Case Angers Ottawa," *The New York Times*, April 5, 1957, sec. A.
20. World Health Organization, *Preventing Suicide, a Global Imperative* (Geneva: World Health Organization, 2014).
21. US Census Bureau, "USA Quick Facts from the US Census Bureau," *State & County Quick Facts*, 2014, http://quickfacts.census.gov/qfd/states/00000.html.
22. Rates are assumed to represent the annual number of suicides per 100,000, as is the custom in epidemiology.
23. Centers for Disease Control and Prevention, "Trends in Suicide Rates Among Persons Ages 10 and Older, by Sex, United States, 1991–2009," accessed

April 8, 2014, http://www.cdc.gov/violenceprevention/suicide/statistics/trends01.html.

24. Tara Parker-Pope, "Suicide Rate Rises Sharply in U.S.," *The New York Times*, May 2, 2013, http://www.nytimes.com/2013/05/03/health/suicide-rate- rises-sharply-in-us.html.

25. Ibid.

26. Ibid.

27. Ibid.

28. Eric H. Erikson, *Childhood and Society* (New York: W.W. Norton, 1950).

29. Erik F. Strommen, "Family Member Reactions to the Disclosure of Homosexuality," *Journal of Homosexuality* 18, no. 1–2 (1989): 37–58.

30. American Association of Suicidology, "Youth Suicide Fact Sheet," 2006, http://www.suicidology.org.

31. Minnesota Department of Health, "Injury and Violence Prevention Home/Leading Causes of Death," n.d., http://www.health.state.mn.us/injury/.

32. The national figure is from the American Association of Suicidology, for 2006; the Minnesota figure is from the Minnesota Department of Health 10-year average for 2000–2009; therefore this particular comparison should be considered a little fuzzy.

33. Minnesota Department of Health, "Adolescent Health: A View from the Minnesota Student Survey," presented at the MDH Maternal and Child Health Advisory Task Force, June 10, 2011.

34. This is sometimes called a "quasi-experimental design."

35. Phillips, "The Influence of Suggestion."

36. Samuel Wolfe and Shannon Minter, "Proposed Meeting to Resolve Claims," May 24, 2011, http://www.splcenter.org/sites/default/files/downloads/case/Anoka-Hennepin-Letter.pdf.

37. Paul Levy, "Anoka County Expects $2.5 Million Grant for Foreclosure Aid," *Star Tribune*, February 25, 2009, http://www.startribune.comlocal/north/40266167.html.

38. "Zillow Metrics (Counties): Homes Foreclosed (Out of 10k)—Anoka, MN," accessed June 5, 2014, http://www.quandl.com/ZILLOW/MCOUNTY_HOMESSOLDASFORECLOSURESRATIO_ALLHOMES_ANOKAMN-Zillow-Metrics-Counties-Homes- Foreclosed-Out-of- 10k-Anoka-MN.

39. Paul Levy, "Homelessness Rising Dramatically in Twin Cities Suburbs," *Star Tribune*, April 29, 2012, http://www.startribune.com/local/149442415.html.

40. Levy, "Homelessness Rising."

41. Mike A. Males, *The Scapegoat Generation: America's War on Adolescents* (Monroe, ME: Common Courage Press, 1996).

42. Emery S. Hetrick and A. Damien Martin, "Developmental Issues and Their Resolution for Gay and Lesbian Adolescents," *Journal of Homosexuality* 14, no. 1–2 (1987): 25–43.

43. Ibid.

44. Gerald P. Mallon, *We Don't Exactly Get the Welcome Wagon: The Experiences of Gay and Lesbian Adolescents in Child Welfare Systems* (New York: Columbia University Press, 1998), 119.

45. Derald Wing Sue, *Microaggressions in Everyday Life: Race, Gender, and Sexual Orientation* (Hoboken, NJ: Wiley, 2010).

46. Hetrick and Martin, "Developmental Issues."

47. Richard Isay, *Being Homosexual: Gay Men and Their Development* (New York: Vintage, 2010).

48. Sue, *Microaggressions*.

49. Ibid., 8.

50. Ilan H. Meyer, "Prejudice, Social Stress, and Mental Health in Lesbian, Gay, and Bisexual Populations: Conceptual Issues and Research Evidence," *Psychological Bulletin* 129, no. 5 (2003): 674–697.

51. Personal communication, Jefferson Fietek, November 29, 2014.

52. Rachel Janik, "From 'No Homo Promo' to 'Model for the Nation,'" Medill Equal Media Project, October 2, 2012, http://www.equalmediaproject.com/features/no-homo-promo-model-nation.

53. Sabrina Erdely, "One Town's War on Gay Teens," *Rolling Stone* 2, no. 2 (2012), http://www.rollingstone.com/politics/news/one-towns-war-on-gay-teens-20120202.

54. Laurence Steinberg, "Commentary: A Behavioral Scientist Looks at the Science of Adolescent Brain Development," *Brain and Cognition* 72, no. 1 (February 2010): 4, doi:10.1016/j.bandc.2009.11.003; Amanda E. Guyer et al., "Probing the Neural Correlates of Anticipated Peer Evaluation in Adolescence," *Child Development* 80, no. 4 (2009): 1000–1015, doi:10.1111/j.1467-8624.2009.01313.x.

55. Guyer et al., "Probing the Neural Correlates."

CHAPTER 5
The Bullying of Women by Men

The bullying of women may involve psychological, emotional, or economic torment.[1] Physical violence may range from slapping, pinching, and hair pulling to rapes and beatings that result in death. This last outcome occurs frequently enough that the World Health Organization has created a term for it: *femicide*.[2] Technically, femicide refers to any kind of killing of females, including the drowning of female babies, a practice still common in some very poor parts of the world, but most cases of femicide involve intimate partner violence. It is true that sometimes it is the women who are the bullies and the men victims, but these incidents are few and are often a response to years of torment and abuse,[3] as in the case of *The Burning Bed*,[4] described later in this chapter. Males have the edge on aggression.

DOMESTIC VIOLENCE: SHAME AND CONTROL

Gilligan, who believes all violence is motivated by shame, acknowledges that the "standard" explanation, that men become violent because they want to control their partner is true, but he feels we must delve deeper into the issue:

Why this need for control?

"I can only conclude," he writes, "that their desire for omnipotence is in direct proportion to their feeling of impotence."[5] They feel shamed by their own sense of worthlessness in the world. This may be their everyday sense of themselves, established over the years by parents or peers who bullied them, by school failure, by rejection by girl or boyfriends, or it may be that some life-altering crises such as public humiliation or long-term unemployment has pushed them beyond the tipping point. The husband is among the first fired during a cutback in staff. He displaces the shame onto his wife and then "beats it out of her." Now he becomes doubly ashamed of himself: he is unemployed *and* a wife-beater. Certain that his wife will find another partner if he allows her to dress attractively, or work as a waitress at the local diner, or attend classes at the local college, he becomes her jailer. Now he believes himself to be such a bad person that, if abandoned, *he* will never find another wife. With every act of brutality, he becomes more ashamed of the kind of husband he has become, more desperate to keep his wife, more enmeshed in this cycle of shame and violence.

While impotence or powerlessness may be a necessary precondition for domestic violence, one cause is rarely sufficient. "Shame is a necessary but not a sufficient cause of violence, just as the tubercle bacillus is necessary but not sufficient for the development of tuberculosis."[6] There are always additional risk factors. If a child grows up in a culture where women are disrespected and treated like chattel, or where violence is considered a good problem-solving strategy, or where the murder of women can be justified by holy writ, domestic violence will come more easily to him.

Speaking from my own experience, living with a member of the other sex for a long time (30 years in my case) is occasionally difficult. I have wondered if the essential incompatibility of men and women, both physical and psychological, might be a contributing factor. Men and women view the world and their place in it so differently that their actions may appear nonsensical or "crazy" to their spouses. A popular writer[7] hunting for an appropriate metaphor imagined them as visitors from different worlds, men from Mars and women from Venus. If this difference of cultures constituted a risk factor for domestic violence, then same-sex marriages might be more harmonious than heterosexual unions. Gay and lesbian marriage, rather than directing Western civilization into a modern-day Gomorrah, as some conservative elements have suggested, might become models for *all* successful unions.

While all the evidence is not yet in, this appears not to be the case. A friend of mine, a divorce lawyer dealing with the first wave of gay and lesbian divorces, says that gay couples come to him with the same issues as heterosexuals couples.[8] This is confirmed by the literature.[9] A review of 19 studies of long-term gay and lesbian relationships conducted during a 16-year period suggests that domestic violence occurs with the same frequency in couples regardless of whether they are gay, lesbian, or heterosexuals. So maybe we are not so different from each other after all.

MANAGING INTIMACY

Lansky[10] suggests that domestic violence might be considered a strategy (but not a good one) for managing intimacy. In order for two people to continue in a relationship they must often practice "complex regulatory maneuvers" in order to maintain a "stable organizational system." In other words, they must be able to moderate their intimacy, to control the emotional distance between them. To say that a marriage is mutually affirming acknowledges a healthy use of moderating intimacy on the part of both partners. To say that a marriage is stifling or enmeshed suggests the partners are too intimate and have sacrificed their personal identity for their identity as a couple. The expression "they seem to live parallel lives" suggests the opposite: that the couple has failed to establish a supportive degree of intimacy. They are living under the same roof in order to procreate, or for economic reasons, or due to some other convenience of circumstance, but they are not emotionally engaged with each other. Certain people can tolerate only a limited degree of intimacy, while others may long for more (in the world of simplistic clichés, men represent the former and women the latter). Pathological descriptions of couples such as *folie a deux*, or "sadomasochistic relationship," suggest that the process of distance regulation has become highly dysfunctional, that the couple is enmeshed in a way that will cause misery or harm.

WITCH HUNTS

In the past, most cultures considered women as chattel, the unmarried woman being the property of her father, the married woman of her husband. Because she was an owned object, he could do with her as he pleased. We find this expressed in print as early as Ephesians 5: 22–24:

> Wives, submit to your husbands as to the Lord. For the husband is the head of the wife as Christ is the head of the church, his body, of which he is the Savior. Now as the church submits to Christ, so also wives should submit to their husbands in everything.

Wives were physically punished for their "disobedience." In 1427, Bernardo of Siena, a Catholic priest, admonished his male congregants to treat their wives with at least as much mercy as they would their hens and pigs.[11] Yet surviving documents of women from medieval times suggest that at least some were treated well. Some owned property and, during peaceful times, rose to important positions in society.

In the beginning of the sixteenth century, Western society underwent a seismic shift. Prior to this time the Roman Catholic Church, known then as the Holy Roman Empire, had dominated the culture of northern Europe, but the people under its sway had become more and more dissatisfied with its abuses. The lavish displays of wealth at a time when peasants had little or nothing, the Papal taxes, the granting of "indulgences," where the rich could buy absolution for their sins and a place in heaven, and the deceitful behavior of the Pope's personal council (the *Curia*) all pointed to a faith that had grown corrupt on its own power and influence. At the same time, enormous scientific discoveries were changing people's worldview. Documents such as Vesalius's treatise on human anatomy and Copernicus's discovery that the earth rotated around the sun were promoting revolutionary ideas about human beings and their place in the universe. The invention of the printing press and the translation of many important theological and philosophical works into the vernacular were making these documents available to those untrained in Church Latin.

Martin Luther, John Calvin, and others, attempting to rectify the corruption of the church, created "protesting" or Protestant churches in parts of Germany (comprised of many small states at the time), the Baltic countries, Scandinavia, France, Switzerland, the Netherlands, and Scotland.

This led to two terrible wars: the French Wars of Religion (1562–1598), brought about by the rise of Calvinism, and the Thirty Year War (1618–1648). The results were plague, famine, and death. The casualties were estimated at 8 million, an astonishing number at a time when the entire population of Europe was around 100 million.[12]

At the same time, in the same countries, somewhere between 40,000[13] and 100,000[14] women were executed for being witches. We imagine witches as dreadful old crones in pointed hats, but those accused of witchcraft were a diverse lot, as illustrated by this roster of witch executions from the town of Würzburg in 1598.

The steward of the senate, named Gering; old Mrs. Kanzler; the tailor's fat wife; the woman cook of Mr. Mengerdorf; a stranger; a strange woman; Baunach, a senator, the fattest citizen in Würzburg; the old smith of the court; an old woman; a little girl, nine or ten years old; a younger girl, her little sister; the mother of the two little aforementioned girls; Liebler's daughter; Goebel's child, the most beautiful girl in Würzburg; a student who knew many languages; two boys from the Minster, each twelve years old; Stepper's little daughter; the woman who kept the bridge gate; an old woman; the little son of the town council bailiff; the wife of Knertz, the butcher; the infant daughter of Dr. Sculz; a blind girl; Schwarz, canon at Hach .[15]

What is one to make of this list? Some are little girls, some are old, some are fat, one is beautiful, one is strange, three or four are men. Our initial reaction might be that the Catholics were burning the Protestants in retribution, but this was not the case. Nor were Protestants burning Catholics. Records from this time show that witches were burned regardless of their faith or the faith of their families or loved ones.[16] Most of the executions took place in the countries divided by the Reformation and the fewest in the countries such as Spain and Italy that remained predominantly Catholic despite their large population.

Prior to the reformation, priests had exclusive rights to explaining and interpreting the Christian faith to the laity. They had mostly discouraged witch trials, explaining that witches did not exist and that those who believed in magic and sorcery "had been seduced by the Devil in dreams and visions into old pagan errors."[17] As a result, while people had been accused of witchcraft throughout the Middle Ages, convictions had been few and punishments for the most part lenient. But during the Reformation attitudes changed. Martin Luther encouraged a process called *sola scriptura*, "by scripture alone," which urged people to read the Bible and interpret its meaning for themselves. In order to facilitate this, he took it upon himself to translate the Bible from the ancient Greek *Septuagint* into German as it was spoken at this time. The work took him over a decade to complete and involved the help of many others. It was published using the printing press in 1534. Despite his best efforts to maintain accuracy, some meanings were altered in translation. The young British scholar, Dan Horn, describes the transformation of a particularly troublesome verse from Exodus:

> The original Hebrew manuscripts of the Old Testament work use the word "Kashaph" (כָּשַׁף) of which the precise meaning is unknown, but is usually translated as "sorcerer." This describes those who practice magic (both good and evil), and is genderless. The Greek Septuagint (completed by 132 BCE) translates this verse from the Hebrew using the Greek word "Pharmakeia," meaning "one who administers medicine or drugs." The Latin Vulgate, the standard text of the Roman Catholic Church, renders this passage as "maleficos non patieris

vivere," maleficos meaning "Evil-doers.". . . Martin Luther's translation of the passage translates the Greek "Pharmakeia" into the German "Zauberinnen," meaning "witches." Similarly the King James Version translates the passage into English as "Thou Shalt not Suffer a Witch to Live.[18],[19]

Other literary works of the period contributed to the fear of witches and the temptation of mortals. Shakespeare's Macbeth (1606) introduced the idea of witches as old crones conspiring against the established order. In John Milton's *Paradise Lost*, (1667) Satan is not merely an embodiment of evil but a character with human traits who has challenged God's authority and been cast out of heaven. His agenda is to tempt all men and women into evil acts. Protestant works, like *Paradise Lost*, tended to depict the devil and demons, as well as demonic possession, as real-world phenomena. "The powerlessness of humanity to resist the will of the devil was rhapsodized."[20] *Malleus Maleficarum*, or *The Hammer of the Witches* (1487), the work of a would-be witch prosecutor, Heinrich Kramer, who was expelled from Innsbruck by the local Catholic Bishop after trying to conduct his own trials, was conceived to convince the public of the evil that witches might do. A public unaccustomed to literary exaggeration was terrified by the accounts of succubae and demonic babies contained in its pages.

I would suggest that members of both faiths were ashamed of having brought about an age of horror, plague, poverty, famine, and endless war. Protestants were ashamed of themselves for abandoning the faith of their fathers (or grandfathers) and the Catholics, for allowing their Church to become so wormy with corruption that it could barely stand. The underlying process of shame management was primitive and brutal, of the sort that men resort to in times of the worst social chaos. The solution was to shift the shame onto the women and then obliterate it in a bonfire. Witches were neither Protestants nor Catholics but practitioners of magic, a practice loathed and despised by the Church of Rome and the Reformers. It brought the men back together.

THE RULE OF THUMB

For many hundreds of years men have evoked the "rule of thumb" to provide an historical justification for wife-beating. Legal scholars have been hard pressed to find this particular law anywhere in print. In 2001 an expert on Welsh Medieval law, Sara Elin Roberts, claimed to have traced it to an ancient Welsh document called "Laws of Women." It stated that "a man may beat a woman with a stick or rod as thick as his middle finger and as long as his forearm" but only under certain conditions: if she had insulted his beard, wished dirt on his teeth, been unfaithful to him, or given away his property.[21] He could only strike her three times on the body but not on the head. Clearly this law was so appealing to would-be wife beaters, not only in granting permission to perform an act of violence upon their spouse but also because it appeared legalistic in its moderating language, that for hundreds of year it was transmitted orally, finding its way from tiny Wales to remote corners of Britain and the New World. The term used to reference it, the "rule of thumb" was an equally ancient location describing a quick and dirty way of taking measurements by holding straight the arm and sighting along the upraised thumb.[22] I imagine the two became associated as the result of a drunken construction worker struggling to excuse an act of violence toward his wife. *But your Excellence, the stick were no thicker than me thumb! What of the 'rule of thumb?'*

Prior to the reign of King Charles the II (1660), British Common Law allowed a husband to apply "moderate correction." Such corrections specifically *excluded* beatings in favor of temporarily confining the wife to the household (like making a child sit in the corner). In fact, no British law, Common or Parliamentary, *ever* permitted wife beating *under any circumstances.*

This sentiment was carried to the New World by the Massachusetts Bay Colonists and incorporated into their Body of Liberties in 1641. "Every married woman shall be free from bodily correction or stripes by her husband, unless it be in his own defense from her assault."[23]

Although the "rule of thumb" appears in American case law, it is usually in decisions where it is rejected as an authority. In an 1868 North Carolina case, the judge stated, "It is not true that boys have a right to fight; nor is it true that a husband has a right to whip his wife. And if he had, it is not easily seen how *the thumb* is the standard of size for the instrument which he may use, as some of the old authorities have said" (*State v. Rhodes*, 1868). A second North Carolina judge agreed: "We assume that the old doctrine that a husband had the right to whip his wife, provided that he used a switch no larger than his thumb, is not the law in North Carolina." (*North Carolina Reports*, Vol. 70, Sec. 60, p. 44). (In 1982, the US Commission on Civil Rights issued a report on wife abuse, called "Under the Rule of Thumb." Old myths die hard.)

In these early nineteenth-century cases, the husband's right to a *moderated* assault on his wife was sometimes upheld. In 1824 the Mississippi Supreme Court declared that a husband should be allowed to moderately chastise his wife in order to avoid dishonoring the family (*Bradley v. State,* 1824) yet backed away from defining precisely what "moderately" meant in this context.

In another North Carolina decision involving a husband who had choked his wife, the judge declared that

> the law permits him to use towards his wife such a degree of force as necessary to control an unruly temper and make her behave herself and unless some permanent injury be inflicted, or there be an excess of violence, or such a degree of cruelty as shows that it is inflicted to gratify his own bad passions, the law will not invade the domestic forum, or go behind the curtain. It prefers to leave the parties to themselves. (*State v. Black*, 1 Winst., 266, 1864)

In both of these cases the wife seems to have risen in status from private property, such as the horse that pulls the plow, to that of the unruly child in need of discipline. A father's duties include instilling good character in his child, and that might justify, in the nineteenth century, a measured and salutary beating. But if the wife is neither property nor a child but rather an adult with Constitutional rights, it is the state's duty to protect her from harm. There is no question that Lincoln's Emancipation Proclamation, enacted in 1863, made thoughtful people—I include magistrates and judges—reconsider all types of slavery, overt and subtle, and this certainly contributed to the verdict in the landmark case[24] of *Fulgham v. the State of Alabama* decided in 1871.

Mr. Fulgham had been chastising one of his children when his wife interceded, believing his punishment excessive. "The child ran, pursued by the father, and both followed up by the wife." Mr. Fulgham turned his attention to his wife,

> striking her twice on the back with a board, and she returned the blows with a switch. The blows inflicted on the wife made no permanent impression. Both were high tempered, and were emancipated slaves, and were husband and wife.[25]

The court responded,

> The privilege, ancient though it be to beat her with a stick, to pull her hair, choke her, spit in her face or kick her about the floor, or to inflict upon her like indignities, *is not now acknowledged by our law* [my italics] . . . the wife is entitled to the same protection of the law that the husband can invoke for himself . . . All stand upon the same footing before the law as citizens of Alabama, possessing equal civil and political rights and public privileges.[26]

The first law providing a mandatory punishment for wife beating was passed in 1882 in Maryland. Offenders were offered a choice between

40 lashes at the whipping post or a year in jail. The whipping post was a broad tree or a column. The offender was stripped to the waist and told to embrace the post so he could be tied at the wrists. This left him immobilized while he was whipped the specified number of times.

The success of the Maryland law was apparent when, a few years later, a citizen of Pennsylvania drafted a similar bill and sent it to Robert Adams Jr., one of the state's senators. This version differed in two ways. First, it discarded the option of a year in prison. Deletion of the prison sentence represented a conscious decision on the part of many judges and justices who told of the countless wives who had come to them, pleading for the charges against their husbands be dropped so they and their children would not starve while the husband was serving a prison sentence.

Second, it reduced the number of lashes to 30, to be administered "within the prison inclosure [sic], and in the presence of a duly licensed physician or surgeon and of the keeper of said prison or one of his deputies, but in the presence of no other person."[27] Many prosecutors at that time agreed that the best way to punish a wife-beater was a "summary conviction before a magistrate and the whipping post within an hour,"[28] but others were more concerned about the shamefulness of a public lashing, hence the call for privacy and limiting the guest list. People were feeling that the time had come to move beyond public displays of corporal punishment.

An editorial in *The New York Times*, July 4, 1886, expressed these doubts:

> . . . would not the injured wife be even more unwilling to expose her husband and the father of her children to the disgrace of the whipping post than she is to cause his imprisonment, and would she not suffer as keenly after having caused the infliction of that punishment as she does when the imprisonment of her brutal companion has brought her to beggary?[29]

Despite its apparent wisdom, the Pennsylvania law was not passed.

CRIMES OF PASSION

Crimes of passion are killings committed in a rage immediately after the discovery of a betrayal or rejection by a partner in a romantic relationship. For example, a man returns early from a business trip and finds his wife in the arms of her lover. Depending on his temperament, he may pass instantly from the shame of his betrayal to rage. Before his better self can stop him, he strikes out with his fists or whatever weapon is at hand. Such killings are usually femicides. In a national survey of data from 2009, 93 percent of female victims (1,579 out of 1,693) were murdered by someone they knew, an acquaintance or family member. Of these, 63 percent (989 out of 1,579) were wives, common-law wives, ex-wives, or girlfriends of the offenders.[30] Only seldom were the new boyfriends the victims. In a Washington State report of 313 domestic violence fatalities that occurred between 1997 and 2004, only 19 (6 percent) of the victims were new boyfriends.[31] Since men are, more often than not, the aggressors in sexual situations, the logical assumption would be that the boyfriend is to blame for jeopardizing the marriage. Assuming the husband is a "rational actor"— that rare fellow beloved to economists and foreign policy wonks—and if someone *had to be* senselessly murdered, it should be the boyfriend. Killing the wife is an irrational act, an atavism. This lack of forethought is why it is sometimes called a "crime of passion." Because it is impulsive, it resembles a kind of temporary insanity and thus, in the eyes of many male judges and lawmakers of past centuries, warranted a light punishment, if any.

The crime of passion, or *crime passionnel* as it is known in France, is not a legal defense in the United States, although it is often used as a form of argument ("the heat of passion") to support a reduction of homicide to manslaughter, which has a lesser sentence. However, for centuries it was actual law in Catholic countries such as France and Italy. Because France remained a predominantly Catholic country prior to the Revolution, laws pertaining to marriage and family life were canonic and mostly unchanged since Medieval times. A woman had almost no rights. She was the property of her father prior to marriage and the property of her husband afterward. The court was oblivious to acts of adultery, defamation, and abuse committed by the husband, but adultery by the wife was punished by separation from the family and indefinite detainment in a convent, financed by the seizing of a portion of her estate. What remained of her wealth was divided between her children and relatives.[32]

During the French Revolution, ideas of *liberté, fraternité,* and *égalité* were in the air, and feminist groups such as the *Société fraternelle de l'un et l'autre sexe* began to publish papers demanding equal treatment for women in the eyes of the law. Between 1789 and 1792 motions were passed in the National Assembly giving women the right to civil marriage, divorce, and representation in the government.[33]

Bourgeois nineteenth-century historians praised those women who martyred themselves for family, religion, and country. Included in this category were the 16 *Carmelites Compiegne*, nuns who refused to obey orders from the Revolutionary government to suppress their monastery, and Marie Antoinette, because she remained behind in 1789 when other reactionary royalists fled France and fiercely protected her son from the rioting crowds.[34] However, women who engaged in aggressive "masculine" acts to obtain their civil rights, such as Theroigne de Mericourt, who championed women's battalions, and Olympe de Gouges, the author of the first "Declaration of the Rights of Woman" (1791), were singled out as monsters and social deviants.[35] Political cartoonists of the day depicted de Mericourt as a child-eating cannibal and mythologized de Gouges as a hysterical Fury, the founder of the apocryphal Club of Knitting Women, an idea that inspired Charles Dickens to create Madam de Farges in *A Tale of Two Cities,* who worked the names of those to be executed into the scarf she was eternally knitting. In 1905 a French psychiatrist, Alfred Guillois, wrote a scholarly paper diagnosing de Gouges, over a century after her death, as a case of *paranoia reformatoria*, relegating her political activism to the category of mental illness. (The reader is encouraged to compare this with the pseudo-scientific pathologizing of runaway slaves by Dr. Cartwright in Chapter 6.) Unlike de Gouge, de Mericourt escaped the guillotine but was considered insane and died in the hospital called *La Salpêtrière*. The period of liberalization was followed by a period of backlash, as often occurs following dramatic social change. If, in the final days, the French Revolution provided any equality of women to men, it was in the line of those awaiting the guillotine.

In August of 1800, after taking power, Napoleon decided to codify the morass of French laws, consolidating the achievements of the Revolution and creating a model to guide the rest of Europe. He chose as one of his partners in this ambitious venture the philosopher Jean Jacques Rousseau. Like Napoleon, Rousseau believed that women were inferior to men, or, at the risk of casting aspersions on this hero of Gallic culture, he cherished the source of free labor and selfless support that women provided. In his treatise on education, he wrote:

> the whole education of women ought to be relative [subsidiary] to men. To please them, to be useful to them, to make themselves loved and honored by them, to educate them when young, to care for them when grown, to counsel them, to console them, and to make life agreeable and sweet to them—these are the duties of women at all times, and what should be taught them from their infancy.[36]

It comes as no surprise then that the Code Napoleon legitimated the *crime passionnel,* a bit of Church law that preserved the family, rather than the individual, as the basic unit of society, husband at the helm. The punishment for killing a spouse might be as light as two years of custodial sentence (the equivalent of our modern-day "house arrest"). The Code Napoleon was finally revised in 1970, under pressure from an international feminist movement whose day had finally come.

The crime of passion was also a respected law in Italy. Italy's system of laws, prior to the twentieth century, was a *cioppino* of classical Roman, canonic, Germanic, and feudal law along with regional customs. When Napoleon conquered Italy in 1805, he brought the Code Napoleon with him, and it was embraced because of the two countries' common religious heritage, as well as its relative simplicity, organization, and what was then perceived as its modernity.[37] In the second half of the century, the Code, in particular the first book, which dealt with family law, marriage, and the authority of the father, was revised to reflect the more conservative views of the Italian church. It was liberalized by the jurist Sacchi in 1919, then made more conservative again during the ascendency of fascism. The famous jurist Alfredo Rocco, under the appointment of Mussolini, supervised the rewriting of legislation governing family morality and honor. "The Rocco Code," as it was called, became law in 1942, "thereafter to weigh like an albatross on the legal emancipation of women in post fascist society."[38]

Article 587 of the Rocco Code sanctioned not only crimes of passion but also "crimes of honor." While a crime of passion relieves a man of some responsibility for killing his wife because the discovery of her infidelity causes him to become irrational and violent, the crime of honor permits him to kill her in a more drawn out and premeditated manner because she has in some way dishonored her husband or brothers. In some cases, the crime of passion and the crime of honor overlap so they seem to be one and the same, as in the following quote from the Rocco Code: "Whoever causes the death of a daughter's or sister's spouse or lover at the moment in which he discovers illegitimate carnal relationship and in the state of rage determined by the offense to his or her family honor" was sentenced to three to seven years in jail; all other homicides received a minimum sentence of 21 years. The difference, however, becomes apparent when we consider child molestation. The man who seduced a minor went unpunished, providing the offender restored honor to the family of the child by marrying her or could show that she had been "corrupted" prior to the current molestation.[39] Note that the law deals only with adult men and female children. Other sorts of molestation were beyond the purview of Italian law.

Because Italy remained a Catholic country into the modern day, divorce remained illegal well into the twentieth century. In 1961 director Pietro Germi, a mainstay of Italian cinema, co-wrote and directed a film called *Divorce Italian Style* (*Divorzio all'Italiana*), about a Sicilian baron who, because he cannot get a divorce and marry his mistress, encourages his wife to have an extramarital affair. He plans to catch her having sex, kill her, serve a light sentence, and then, upon his release, marry his mistress. The film is broadly acted, with surreal fantasy sequences wherein the count imagines half a dozen horrible ways he might dispose of his wife. The enormous success of the film indicates that by the 1960s the law and the patriarchal sensibilities that it represented had begun to seem comedic or at least preposterous to many Italians. Although full legal gender equality has not yet been established in Italy, discrimination has been greatly reduced. Divorce was legalized in 1970. All references to the "cause of honor" were deleted from the Penal Code in 1981.[40]

HONOR KILLINGS

On May 30, 2014, the Associated Press reported that 25-year-old Farzana Parveen, in Lahore, Pakistan, was bludgeoned to death by her family because she had married for love against her family's wishes. Her parents accused her husband, Muhammad Iqbal, of kidnapping her, but she had gone with him willingly. Parveen and her husband had travelled to the high court of Lahore to plead their case and were waiting for the doors to open when they were set upon by her father and other family members wielding clubs and bricks. She was killed, but her husband managed to escape. The police reported that none of the killers were taken into custody except for the girl's father, who said that he did it in the name of honor. The Human Rights Commission of Pakistan claims in its 2013 report that 869 women were killed in 2013 in the name of honor.[41]

On July 18 a woman, Faddah Ahmad, a widow who was believed to have had sex outside of marriage, was brought to the municipal gardens near the football stadium in Ragga, in the north of Syria, by members of Islamic State in Iraq and Syria (ISIS), the most radical of the jihadist groups. She was buried to her shoulders, as is the practice in stoning. A truckload of stones was delivered to the gardens, but the crowd of local citizens that had gathered had no intention of participating, so the jihadists threw the stones themselves. The previous day another young woman, Shamseh Abdullah, had been stoned to death by the same group in the nearby town of Tabqa. When ISIS jihadists seize a community, they encourage a strict interpretation of Islamic law, including beheadings and the severing of hands for thieves.[42]

In the beginning of May 2014, an 18-year-old Afghani girl named Amina ran away from home to avoid marrying a man her family had chosen for her and sought refuge in a woman's shelter in the north. Counselors at the shelter negotiated with Amina's father and brother regarding the conditions of her return. Eventually her family signed an agreement that she would not be harmed and her father and brother recorded a video at the Ministry of Women's Affairs in Baghlan Province repeating their assurance of safety. Family members drove to the shelter to bring her home. According to her brother and uncle, during their drive home

"a gang of gunmen dragged her out of the vehicle and shot her to death. Everyone else was unharmed."[43] Women's activists accused Amina's family of staging her killing, and Amina became yet another victim of an "honor killing" to absolve some sort of family shame.[43]

In April 2013 a Jordanian woman in her twenties was found dead with her throat slit and multiple stab wounds to the face and chest. Her brother admitted that he had killed her "to cleanse the family honor," because she was rarely home. In the same month, police found the partially burned body of another Jordanian woman, four months pregnant, with her throat slit and her belly cut open. Murder is punished by death in Jordan, but in the case of the 15 to 20 honor killings that are reported each year, sentences may be commuted or reduced to forms of house arrest, particularly in cases where the family pleads for leniency.[44]

According to the International Honour Based Violence Resource Centre, some 5,000 honor killings occur each year internationally; 1,000 of these take place in India and another 1,000 in Pakistan. The numbers may be much higher because efforts are made to hide these crimes from authorities. Certain kinds of honor killings are legal in Afghanistan, Iran, Nigeria (in about one-third of its 36 states), Pakistan, Sudan, and the United Arab Emirates; in other predominantly Muslim countries, such as Jordan and Syria, they are illegal but the laws are only weakly or sporadically enforced. Honor killings also occur in immigrant communities in Western countries.[45]

To reiterate, crimes of honor differ from crimes of passion. Crimes of passion occur when a spouse discovers his or her partner in the arms of another, or learns of his or her infidelity, and, in a state where rage overwhelms common sense, hurts or kills one or both of the other members of the lovers' triangle. They are gender neutral (in theory at least) because any one or more of the three people involved may be male or female, although the victims are most often female. Crimes of honor involve a woman being killed, often by members of her own family, because she is perceived by them as having shamed the family. In crimes of passion, common sense is overwhelmed by the rapidity of the shame/rage cycle. In crimes of honor, the cycle unfolds more slowly. The family is aware that they are being shamed. The killing is carefully thought out and deliberate.[46]

Proper behavior of a woman is described in the Qur'an, the holy book of Islam, in the 34th verse of the fourth chapter of the Qur'an, the *Surah An-Nissa* (Chapter about Women):

> Men are in charge of women by [right of] what Allah has given one over the other and what they spend [for maintenance] from their wealth. So righteous women are devoutly obedient, guarding in [the husband's] absence what Allah would have them guard. But those [wives] from whom you fear arrogance— [first] advise them; [then if they persist], forsake them in bed; and [finally], strike them. But if they obey you [once more], seek no means against them. Indeed, Allah is ever Exalted and Grand. (translated by Abdullah Yusuf Ali)

So the Qur'an appears to advocate violence toward women but of a limited sort. However, Ibn Abbas, a companion of Muhammed, who wrote the earliest commentary on the Qur'an, explained that "strike them" refers only to a light tap. When asked about the means by which this punishment should be delivered, he advised the use of a *siwak* (toothbrush).[47] Not only was Ibn Abbas kind; he also had a sense of humor. There are sources that say that Muhammed himself never hit a woman and forbade it. Furthermore, Muhammed commented on this verse. "A light tap," he said, "that leaves no mark." The advice to stone the deceitful wife is found not in the Quran but in the Torah, in Deuteronomy. If a girl who is taken for a wife is not a virgin

> Then they shall bring out the girl to the doorway of her father's house, and the men of her city shall stone her to death because she has committed an act of folly in Israel by playing the harlot in her father's house; thus you shall purge the evil from among you.[48]

Crimes that warrant stoning are described in the Sharia (literally, "The Path to the Watering Hole"), which is like a legal code but much broader in scope: it deals with politics, economics, crime, sexual intercourse, hygiene, diet, fasting, prayer, and everyday etiquette. The Sharia is considered the infallible law of God, although like any code of behavior, the interpretation of its meaning and the rigor with which it is observed vary from person to person and from one religious community to the next. Some believe that the laws of the Sharia must be adapted to our modern world, while others try to follow it literally in its ancient form. Officially, Pakistan does not enforce Sharia law, while Saudi Arabia claims to live under pure sharia.

The six most serious offenses in the Sharia are referred to as the *Hadd*, those "considered to be against the right of God"[49] and are punished according to tradition. The first is theft, which is punished by the severing of the thief's hand; the second, illicit sexual relations, punishable by stoning or 100 lashes; the third, making unproven accusations of illicit sex (80 lashes); drinking intoxicating beverages (80 lashes); apostasy (death or banishment); and highway robbery (death). The most serious of these are *Zina*, engaging in unlawful sexual relations, infidelity, or sexual relations prior to marriage.

The Islamic Penal Code of Iran is very specific regarding the details of how stoning should be executed. Article 102 states that men shall be buried up to their waists and women above their breasts prior to the stoning. Article 104 specifies that the stones should "not be large enough to kill the person by one or two strikes; nor should they be so small that they could not be defined as stones (pebbles)."[50]

In practice, many honor killings involve the dishonoring of the family because the daughter has been married against the family's will and thereby had intercourse outside of (the arranged) marriage or has been promiscuous. Technically the crime must be witnessed by four people, and they must actually observe penetration "as the stick is inserted into the jar of kohl." In some cases if the witnesses are not present, the judge can make the decision intuitively.

In reality it does not matter whether the girl has actually had intercourse outside of marriage; what matters is the perception of the event in the community. The family unites in a truly horrifying act of shame management that involves "attack self" and "attack other" simultaneously. They kill their own daughter to redeem themselves in the eyes of God and regain their status in the community. The restoration of honor comes at a terrible price for them.

THE BURNING BED

United States courts do not recognize crimes of passion or crimes of honor, but until the mid-twentieth century crimes committed in a jealous rage were sometimes excused as "temporary insanity." The defense was first employed in 1859 by Daniel Sickles, a colorful and popular New York politician, while he was standing trial for having shot and killed his wife's lover, Philip Barton Key (son of Francis Scott Key). Sickles' defense attorney, Edwin M. Stanton, who later became secretary of war under Lincoln, told the jury that the sight of Sickles' young wife with another man drove him to madness and murder, despite his own philandering with the infamous prostitute, Fanny White, during his wife's pregnancy. Sickles walked out of court a free man.

In another well-known case a century later, the lawyer representing Francine Hughes got her acquitted with the same defense even though the murder appeared to be well-planned and lacking in spontaneous murderous rage. This case is often referred to as "The Burning Bed" and is described here in detail because, while it is in some ways typical of how domestic violence unfolds in a marriage, its shame unravels in a surprising, serpentine path, affecting many members of the community.

Mickey and Francine met at a school dance in 1963. She was 15 and he was three years older. They were both from clannish Kentucky mountain families, but Francine's mother described their family as "the worthy poor" in contrast to the "shiftless poor," an expression she might have used to describe Mickey's family. He was the third of six children, five of them boys known to the neighbors as "cocky, troublesome juveniles, quick to start fights and sass cops."[51]

Two events seem to have shaped Francine's early life. The first occurred when she was a preteen caring for her three-year-old brother, David, while their mother hung the laundry. Having heard that a clown at the gas station down the road was giving out balloons, she took her little brother by the hand, paid the clown a visit, and returned with a balloon. The rest is best told in Francine's words.

> I went back to helping mom with the laundry. I must have forgotten about David for a while. Without anyone noticing he had wandered out of the yard and down the street, trying to find the clown and get another balloon ... a girl came riding down the street on a bicycle and yelled to mom, "I think your son has got hit by a car!" ... Mom was crying so hard she probably didn't know what she was doing, but she grabbed me and shook me and she yelled, "It's your fault. You should have been watching him. I told you to watch him!"[52]

David was hospitalized for a "long time" and survived with two broken arms and an ear half torn off that had to be surgically repaired.

> He was home for weeks ... Every time I looked at him I felt a terrible guilt ... He was such a little child and so miserable with casts on both arms. I remember how bad I wanted to do things for him. I nursed him a lot.

Although we do not know the extent of his injuries, they might have altered the trajectory of his life. He never married. He spent the rest of his life living at home, being cared for by his mother.

The second event occurred when Francine was 13 and began wearing makeup and dressing in the style of teenage girls of the 1950s. After school she would visit the local drugstore, drink Coke, play the jukebox, and occasionally flirt with the boys. From her own account, her behavior was well on the side of modest and proper by standards of the day, but when her father found out, he told her that such places were for "tramps and whores" and, for the first and last time, whipped her with his belt. We can refer to these early, formative events as "distal shame."

When Francine dropped out of high school at 16 and married a sadistic womanizer, we might assume that somewhere in the back of her mind she knew that Mickey would provide her with many occasions for martyrdom (a form of "attack self") when she could atone for ruining her brother's life (by her own appraisal) and being a temptress (in her father's eyes.)

MORE ABOUT "ATTACK SELF"

I mentioned earlier that women tend to manage shame through "attack self" strategies. Most women have been encouraged by the dominant culture to make themselves submissive in order to get married, and to keep the social network intact[53] by staying married, even at the cost of their own self-esteem and physical well-being. These requirements are conducive to the "attack self" mode of shame management. We see evidence of this in a higher rate of cutting behavior (three times more frequent among women),[54] suicidal thoughts (17 percent more frequent among women),[55] and suicide attempts (29 percent more frequent among women),[56] as well as the reluctance to leave an abusive marriage regardless of the consequences. Uniting an "attack self" individual with an "attack other" individual is a dangerous proposition as we have seen.

There is no irrefutable mandate from nature for the man to be the hunter/competitor/squire and the woman the social director/housekeeper/brood mare. England, Israel, and India have had women as prime ministers. Germany and Denmark currently have women at the helm. Twenty-four of the Fortune 500 CEO positions are currently held by women.[57] By the same token, some postmillennial husbands have turned their back on the workplace and found fulfillment by staying home and raising their children. Matriarchal cultures have existed for centuries among the Mosuo people in Szechuan, China; the Paisa in Columbia; and among certain communities in India, notably in the states of Megahalaya and Kerala; and they are at least as successful as comparable patriarchal cultures and sometimes less violent. Utopian matriarchies have been described in essays and speculative fiction of feminist authors, both male and female.

In the 1870s, Lewis Henry Morgan, one of the pioneers of anthropology, wrote that gender equality in government, society, rights and privileges, and education "foreshadow the next higher plane of society. . . "[58] to which mankind was evolving. "It will be a revival," he wrote, "in a higher form, of the liberty, equality and fraternity of the ancient gentes." Elizabeth Cadis Stanton, an early feminist, took this to mean that matriarchies like the Amazons of Greek mythology had existed prior to the patriarchies of Judeo-Christian culture. "The period of woman's supremacy lasted through many centuries," she told the National Council of Women in 1891.[59] By the first decade of the twentieth century, a number of poems and novels had been published imagining Amazonian types of societies, sometimes with women who boasted superhuman powers and beauty, and the ability to reproduce asexually and conceive when they chose[60] (contraception was illegal at the time).[61] During World War II, women held jobs in factories and shipyards, filling places vacated by men who had been sent overseas. Rosie the Riveter presented a positive image of a woman who was strong and capable. Her hair was held back in a polka-dot headscarf and the sleeves of her blue overalls were rolled up to reveal the bicep of her right arm. But after the war, men returned home from the horror of killing and the women who welcomed them wanted to create the most secure, comforting environment they could. That peaceful scene did not include a battle for women's rights. Rosie the Riveter abandoned her blue overalls and polka-dot scarf for a dress and an apron and was often depicted in print advertisements cooking or serving a family.

It was during the tail end of this postwar gender conservative era that Mickey and Francine wed and moved in with Mickey's mother. Occasionally Mickey found work but more often he was unemployed and drinking. Francine got a job as a waitress at a diner, but Mickey interfered by insisting that she keep a list of all the people she served. The mere fact of her being out of the house was threatening to him.

They soon fell into a pattern that was to repeat with little variation for the next 14 years. He would find her wearing what he considered provocative clothes, or flirting with another man, or engaged in another harmless activity that jeopardized his "ownership" of her, and he would destroy some object that symbolized or facilitated her independence. In the beginning he tore off her clothes because he found them too revealing and ripped them to shreds. Later on, when she returned to school, he tore up her books and threatened to take a sledge hammer to her car. This was how he "beat" the shame out of their marriage. Once he felt shame-relieved, he would apologize and do everything he could to restore the "love" between them. This was a way of regulating intimacy, but not, as I have said, a good one.[62]

They had three children and moved about, living in cheap apartments and in a trailer. Occasionally he would find a job, work for a few weeks, then quit or be fired. Caring for the children kept Francine occupied. Somehow Mickey remained well nourished, with money for cigarettes and a six-pack of beer, which he consumed every evening before retiring, while Francine and the children often went hungry.

When she became pregnant with her fourth child, she visited the local welfare office. The social worker told her she had to get a divorce before she could get help and referred her to legal aid. A lawyer drew up divorce papers for her. By then Francine had enough money for an apartment and groceries to feed the children. Mickey, furious with her for ending the marriage, announced that he had another girl and was moving "up north" to live with her. Several weeks later she heard that he was in the hospital in a coma after a near-fatal car crash. He had multiple fractures and possible brain damage. The doctors doubted he would survive. Eventually he awoke and the first person he asked for was Francine. She visited him constantly during his 40-day hospital stay. After his release, she took him home and nursed him back to health.

"I really felt trapped after his accident," Francine told an interviewer. "I don't know why I felt so obligated to that man, but I did. Then the real hell began."[63]

His health improved, but he refused to look for work and sat around the house drinking. He became more violent and oppressive, beating Francine every few days. On some occasions he would force her to sit for long hours in a straight back chair while he berated her, hitting her until she ran and hid. There was talk that the injury to his head had made him more violent and unreasonable and that he should be committed to a psychiatric hospital, but by divorcing him Francine had lost the authority to have him committed.

Francine decided that the only way she would ever achieve independence was by going back to school. She found a secretarial skills program at the local college and obtained a government grant to cover her tuition. She was only 27 at the time, although she believed that her reflection in the mirror resembled a woman of 50. Overcoming considerable resistance from Mickey, she began to take courses. It was a transformative experience for her. She made friends with the other students, completed her homework without Mickey's seeing her, took the children to school, and kept the house clean.

Her description of waiting to be assaulted is repeated here since it seems to be typical of many domestic violence cases.

> First he'd play cat and mouse with me. For two or three hours he'd watch me as though he were daring me to do something wrong. I'd creep around, cold inside with fear. If I sat and watched TV and the chair squeaked I'd look up quickly thinking that might be the thing that would start him. Then I'd look back at the TV so he wouldn't know I was afraid. He might get mad just because I flinched.[64]

Sometimes women who are dealing with this kind of threatening behavior will actually provoke the attack in order to have it over and done with. One woman I know of recalled intentionally breaking a dinner plate to end the suspense and trigger her husband's rage.

> Sometimes when he hit me I'd try to defend myself. It made things worse. If I ran out of the house, Mickey would lock the door with a bolt so I couldn't get back in. I'd have to stay out there freezing, or sitting in my car, for an hour or so. When he calmed down he'd unlock the door. Then, if I was lucky, we could go quietly to bed. In the morning my face would be all puffy and purple. I'd put on makeup and go to school, hoping no one would notice.[65]

She would try to get him arrested but the police were (and continue to be) reluctant to interfere in domestic violence cases. After arrests are made, abused wives seldom bring charges against their husbands, and when they do they often refrain from signing the complaint for fear of driving the family into poverty, becoming victims of retributive violence, or exposing the children to the shame of their father being a convict. While domestic violence "calls for service" are *not* responsible for the most police deaths as is sometimes stated, they still result in 14 percent of all deaths on service calls.[66] Officers are frequently killed by husbands engaged in a family massacre, or during a situation where the husband holds his family hostage or has already killed his family,[67] although such events are not common. While other felons are incarcerated, wife-beaters often go free because wives refuse to sign the complaints, and they abuse again. It is simply not worth the risk and the effort as far as the police are concerned.

During Francine's second term at school she took a psychology course, the theme of which was Socrates' admonition to "Know thyself." For the first paper, she wrote

> My name is Fran Hughes. I am a twenty-nine-year-old female. I Really don't
> know too much about myself . . . One thing I know is that I let people walk all
> over me. I do as I'm told, not as I wish to do. I've been trying to stand up for my
> rights as a person.

By returning to school, Francine was trying to enter a higher status
group, and Mickey feared it would jeopardize their relationship. One evening, after a day of drinking, he ripped up her schoolbooks and made her
burn them in the garbage can. When she told him that would not stop her,
he threatened to take a sledgehammer to her car. He sent the children up
to their rooms without supper, then he spread the dinner she had cooked
on the floor, forced her down on her knees, and made her scrape it up with
her hands. After further humiliations, he raped her, got more drunk, and
fell into a deep sleep. Francine decided that this was the right time to
leave. In the past, her will had failed. How could she make sure that she
would not return to him?

> I got up and walked around the room. Everything I looked at was part of my
> life with Mickey. I hated it. All of it . . . That was when the thought struck
> me: I wasn't going to come back because there wasn't going to be anything
> to come back to—because I was going to burn the house down. What about
> Mickey? Yes! I decided to burn him, too! Then everything would be gone.[68]

Quietly, so as not to wake him, she put the kids in the car, went back to
the house, and got the gasoline can out of the basement.

> I was as calm as though I was doing an ordinary thing . . . I picked up the gas can
> and unscrewed the lid and went into the bedroom. I stood still for a moment,
> hesitating, and a voice urged me on. It whispered, "Do it! Do it! Do it!" I sloshed
> the gasoline on the floor. If I saw Mickey lying there I don't remember it. I don't
> believe I looked at him at all.[69]

Stepping outside the room, she lit a match and tossed it onto the room.
"The fumes of the gas caught with a roar and a rush of air slammed the
door with tremendous force, almost catching my hand. I ran for my life."
She got in the car and started to drive—all this in a kind of fugue state,
unaware of what she was doing. The children looked back, saw their home
in flames, and imagined their father within it. Their screaming voices
brought Francine to her senses. Overcome with horror at what she had
done, she turned around and drove to the police station. By the time the
fire trucks arrived, Mickey was dead and their home had been reduced to
smoldering heap. Francine was placed in a holding cell, and her children

were huddled in the hallway of the police station, waiting for their grand-mother to arrive and take them to her home.

Francine was arrested and charged with first-degree murder. Because of the sordid and sensational details of the case, it was covered in the local press and gradually picked up by the national media, attracting the inter-est of the nascent feminist movement (it was 1977) and advocates for battered women.

After five hours of deliberation, a very short time for a murder case, a jury of 10 women and 2 men found her not guilty by reason of tempo-rary insanity. The cheering crowd outside the courthouse was so dense that her attorney had to clear the way for her. Eighteen days later she appeared as a guest on the Phil Donohue show, a popular national talk show. Faith McNulty's best-selling book on the subject,[70] published three years after the verdict, broadened the audience, but the event that brought it into every American home was a made-for-television film[71] starring Farrah Fawcett Majors, one of the most popular tele-vision actresses of the time. Back in the days before cable and video recorders, people watched a made-for-TV movie when it was broad-cast or missed it, possibly forever, so the audience was vast, 75 million viewers, making it the 17th most widely watched made-for-TV movie in history. It fueled the battered women's movement and changed the laws (aided by the already powerful women's rights movement in the United States) as well as the police response practices for domestic vio-lence complaints.[72]

Today most cities have shelter systems designed to help wives and chil-dren reboot their lives while thwarting the efforts of vindictive husbands. Stalking and menacing have been made a crime in New York and other states. Domestic violence victims can bring charges in civil court or crimi-nal court, or both at once, and orders of protection are relatively easy to obtain. Programs to help abusive husbands (and wives) control their anger without violence are available in many communities as an alternative to incarceration and are sometimes mandated after release from prison.[73] So, in terms of our society, much good came from publicizing the story of Francine Hughes and the Burning Bed.

Nonetheless, the verdict was criticized from several different points of view. Joshua Dressler, a well-known authority on criminal law and procedure, maintained that "the proposition that a battered woman is justified in killing her sleeping abuser, though well meaning, is wrong."[74] Some women's rights groups were unhappy with the temporary insanity abuse because it suggested that it was an insane act for an abused woman to defend herself.[75] Mickey's brother Donovan expressed fear that if Francine got off free, then any woman who had been hit by her husband would be free to kill him.

A TALE OF VENGEANCE?

If we lay out the story itself on the autopsy table, remove the flesh and organs and examine the bones themselves, we see that the Burning Bed is a classic Tale of Vengeance. In a Tale of the Vengeance the hero, a peaceful, vulnerable individual, becomes associated with one or more bullies. They taunt and insult her (usually a man but in this case a woman), but she continues to turn the other cheek. She cannot disengage from the bully because their destinies are bound together in some way (by marriage, by debt, by deed). Eventually the bully pushes her too far, and she snaps, kills the bully or all the bullies in the "gang," and, often through some act of benign fate, suffers no consequences. The Tale of Vengeance is particularly common in movies. *Enter the Dragon, Kill Bill 1 and 2, Gladiator, Straw Dogs, Django Unchained, Last House on the Left, Training Day, Death Wish*, and many other movies are built upon these bones. Many people feel as though they are doing the best they can but are frequently misunderstood, mistreated, and helpless to do anything about it. The vengeance film provides the audience with an opportunity to "get even" through identification with the film's hero. The ancient Greeks labelled this process *catharsis* and valued it highly as a way of providing relief from suppressed emotions.

The problem with the Burning Bed, particularly in the widely watched film version, is this: in the process of being swept along by the story we forget that Mickey Hughes is the victim of a homicide and Francine is the murderer. It is not a question of whether he was a bad man. The moral makeup of the murder victim should not be an issue in a murder trial. The issue is whether the defendant committed the crime and under what circumstances. Was it an accident? an act of uncontrollable rage? self-defense?

The prosecutor's case for temporary insanity was flimsy. In the legal sense, temporary insanity means that the person was briefly insane during the commission of the crime and incapable of understanding the nature of his or her actions. Because it permits a "factually guilty" defendant to avoid punishment, incarceration or institutionalization, courts are understandably reluctant to grant it.

Francine's crime was planned out and executed in a rational manner. She had at least two motives for killing Mickey: he had tormented her, bullied, beaten, raped, and humiliated her for 14 years. Furthermore, she had met another man, George Walkup, while attending community college, and had written him love letters from jail while she was awaiting trial, at least until she learned that he was still married (or so she claimed on the witness stand). The prosecutor also reminded the jury that Francine had brought the can of gasoline upstairs before she had packed the children into the car, during the period while she was still "thinking clearly." So the verdict of the insanity defense seemed like a legalistic ploy. Those who had not been completely swept up by compassion for Francine's ordeal suspected that justice itself was one of the victims. The jury had decided that Mickey Hughes was such a dreadful, worthless wretch that his death was excusable or justified. They wanted to let Francine go unpunished, and they used what was available to achieve that end.

After Mickey Hughes' funeral, one of his brothers dropped by their favorite hangout, a bar in Dansville called the Wooden Nickel, and angrily told a friend, "She's going to get away with murder."[76] A few years later about 50 people gathered at the same bar to watch the TV movie version of the crime. Most of them were personal friends of Mickey and Francine. "People started shaking their heads right away," the owner told an interviewer. "We started with 50 people watching, but pretty soon everyone was just drinking beer, saying, 'This is bullshit.'"[77] The movie had errors of fact—the number of children had been reduced to three—the sequence of events had been changed, and much of the complexities of the relationship had been glossed over, as is often the case with drama adapted from literature. Larry Arnett the current owner of the bar, and an old friend of Mickey's, found it "offensive." The man portrayed in the movie bore little resemblance to the Mickey Hughes he had known, and in real life the violence between Mickey and Francine was nowhere near as one-sided as the movie had depicted it. "He got knocked down as much as she did. I remember one night the two of them got into it right out here," he said, referring to the bar. "She was beating on him. We had to pull them apart. They were both in the wrong."[78]

Betty Phillips, a cousin of Mickey's, interviewed in 2009, said that "the years have been hard" for the Hughes family. Mickey's father, Berlin, and his brother, Donovan, unable to live with their grief and shame, had both committed suicide. It was hard to be part of a family with a "black mark" on its name. Mickey's identity as a wife-beater was common knowledge among 75 million Americans, foreshadowing the kind of momentous shaming that would someday be possible through the Internet. "A lot of things in the movie really did happen," she said, ". . . but did he deserve to die? The system failed both of them."[79]

Francine was last interviewed in 1984. She talked about the nine months she had spent in prison awaiting trial. Since she imagined that she would be spending the rest of her life behind bars, she tried to "block off a lot of emotions toward my children."[80] Then, when she discovered herself to be a free woman, she found it "really hard ... to get close to them again." They may have been reluctant to trust her after seeing her murder their father and burn down their home. During that same period she got a card from Mickey's brothers saying, "You're next,"[81] which kept her looking over her shoulder every time she left the house.

After the trial, Francine worked as a secretary in a real estate office and then as a forklift operator at a factory. Soon she was laid off from that job too. She changed jobs often, having no particular skills. Many thought she was rich because of the success of the book, but in fact she was paid only for the time she spent being interviewed. Faith McNulty, who wrote the book, received the royalties. Francine told an interviewer,

> I went a little crazy. I was partying almost every night trying to escape from something. I drank a lot and was taking speed. It was like I was trying to self-destruct. Then I woke up one day and said, "I've got to quit this or my family is going to fall apart."[82]

Soon afterward Francine married Robert Wilson, who was on parole after serving 10 years of a 30-year sentence for armed robbery. They moved in together after two weeks and were married, at his insistence, within a month. One of the first goals he set for himself was disciplining Francine's children.

The children had reacted in different ways to their father's murder. Although Christy, now 19, had no love for him ("I spit on his grave. He was a rotten son-of-a-bitch," she told an interviewer[83]), the circumstances of his death had left her smoking pot and "running the streets." Jimmy, who was 13, sat around the house smoking and drinking coffee and occasionally beating up his younger brother and knocking down Nicole, Francine's youngest, who was seven. Christie moved out.[84]

At Wilson's request, the family relocated to Tennessee, where his family resided. Francine studied to become a licensed practical nurse and worked briefly in the surgery unit at a local hospital. When Francine's new husband was accused of sexually molesting Nicole, who had just turned 13, Francine left him and took Nicole back to Michigan where they rejoined Christy. Soon Jimmy also joined them, to get away from his stepfather, he told an interviewer.[85] Wilson, dropping by Francine's home (apparently at the request of the interviewer), mentioned that his estranged wife had "beat the tar out of Nicole" a few weeks earlier for misbehaving and had blackened both of Christy's eyes after coming home to find her alone with her boyfriend.[86] Wilson was probably getting back at Francine for divorcing him by offering the interviewer a peek at her violent side, while also justifying his own authoritarian parenting techniques. Having been shamed himself, he was now shaming her.

Had Francine been found guilty and sent to prison, the shame might have been mitigated, but instead, it was being amplified. She was being celebrated as a hero of the women's movement, invited to talk shows, and portrayed by the most popular actress of her day.

NOTES

1. World Health Organization, "Understanding and Addressing Violence against Women: Intimate Partner Violence" (Geneva: World Health Organization, 2012), http://apps.who.int/iris/handle/10665/77432.
2. World Health Organization, "Understanding and Addressing Violence against Women: Femicide,"(Geneva: World Health Organization, 2012), http://apps.who.int/iris/handle/10665/77421.
3. Cynthia Lee, Murder and the Reasonable Man: Passion and Fear in the Criminal Courtroom (New York: New York University Press, 2003).
4. Faith McNulty, The Burning Bed, 1st ed. (New York: Harcourt, 1980).
5. James Gilligan, Violence: Our Deadly Epidemic and Its Causes (New York: Putnam, 1996), 132.
6. Gilligan, Violence.
7. John Gray, Men Are from Mars, Women Are from Venus: The Classic Guide to Understanding the Opposite Sex (New York: Harper Paperbacks, 2012).
8. Ken Burroughs, personal communication, November 23, 2013.
9. Leslie K. Burke and Diane R. Follingstad, "Violence in Lesbian and Gay Relationships Theory, Prevalence, and Correlational Factors," Clinical Psychology Review 19, no. 5 (August 1999): 487–512.
10. M. Lansky, "Shame and Domestic Violence," in The Many Faces of Shame, ed. Donald L. Nathanson (New York: Guilford Press, 1987), 335–362.
11. Del Martin, Battered Wives (San Francisco: Volcano Press, 1981).
12. David Lucas, "World Population Growth and Theories," in An Introduction to Global Studies, ed. Patricia J. Campbell, Aran MacKinnon, and Christy R. Stevens (Hoboken, NJ: Wiley, 2011).
13. Ronald Hutton, The Triumph of the Moon: A History of Modern Pagan Witchcraft (Oxford: Oxford University Press, 2001).
14. Anne L. Barstow, Witchcraze: A New History of the European Witch Hunts, Reprint edition (San Francisco, CA: HarperOne, 1995).
15. Christopher Hitchens, The Portable Atheist: Essential Readings for the Non-Believer (Cambridge, MA: Da Capo Press, 2007).
16. Robert Thurston, The Witch Hunts: A History of the Witch Persecutions in Europe and North America, 2nd ed. (New York: Routledge, 2006).
17. Brian A. Pavlac, Witch Hunts in the Western World: Persecution and Punishment from the Inquisition through the Salem Trials. (Lincoln: Bison Books, 2010).

18. Exodus 13:22, in *The KJV Study Bible* (Nashville: Barbour, 2011).
19. Dan Horn, "To What Extent Was the Protestant Reformation Responsible for the Witch-Hunts in the Years 1520–1650?" (Dorchester, UK: Thomas Hardye School, 2012), 7.
20. Ibid.
21. "The Rule of Thumb," *Woman's Hour* (London: BBC Radio 4, October 15, 2001), http://www.bbc.co.uk/radio4/womanshour/15_10_01/monday/info3.shtml.
22. Ibid.
23. Paul Finkelman, ed., *Encyclopedia of American Civil Liberties* (New York: Routledge, 2006).
24. Dolores J. Trent, "Wife Beating: A Psycho-Legal Analysis," *Women Lawyers Journal* 65 (1979): 9.
25. *Fulgham v. State*, 46 Ala. 143, 145 (Alabama 1871).
26. Ibid.
27. "Flogging for Wife Beaters," *The New York Times*, July 4, 1886.
28. Ibid.
29. Ibid.
30. Violence Policy Center, *When Men Murder Women: An Analysis of 2009 Homicide Data* (Washington, DC: Violence Policy Center, September 2011), http://www.vpc.org/studies/wmmw2011.pdf.
31. K. Starr, M. Hobart, and J. Fawcett, *Every Life Lost Is a Call for Change: Findings and Recommendations From the Washington State Domestic Violence Fatality Review.* (Seattle, Washington: Washington State Coalition Against Domestic Violence, December 2004), http://www.wscadv2.org.
32. Jane Abray, "Feminism in the French Revolution," *The American Historical Review* 80, no. 1 (February 1975): 43.
33. Ibid.
34. M. J. Diamond, "Olympe De Gouges and the French Revolution: The Construction of Gender as Critique," in *Women and Revolution: Global Expressions*, ed. M. J. Diamond (Dordrecht: Springer, 1998), 1–19.
35. Ibid.
36. Jean-Jacques Rousseau, *Émile, Or, Treatise on Education*, trans. William Harold Payne (New York: D. Appleton, 1892).
37. Mauro Cappelletti, John Henry Merryman, and Joseph M. Perillo, *The Italian Legal System* (Stanford, CA: Stanford University Press, 1967).
38. Victoria De Grazia, *How Fascism Ruled Women: Italy, 1922–1945* (Berkeley: University of California Press, 1992), 88.
39. Ibid., 90.
40. Maria Gabriella Bettiga-Boukerbout, "'Crimes of Honor' in the Italian Penal Code: An Analysis of History and Reform," in *Honor*, ed. Lynn Welchman and Sara Hossain (London: Zed Books, 2005), 231.
41. Anup Kaphle, "Pakistani Woman Stoned to Death Because She Married the Man She Loved," *The Washington Post*, May 27, 2014, http://www.washingtonpost.com/blogs/worldviews/wp/2014/05/27/photo-pakistani-woman-stoned-to-death-because-she-married-the-man-she-loved/.
42. Damien Gayle, "Women Stoned to Death in Syria for Adultery," *Daily Mail*, August 9, 2014, http://www.dailymail.co.uk/news/article-2720746/Women-stoned-death-Syria-adultery.html.

43. Rod Nordland, "In Spite of the Law, Afghan 'Honor Killings' of Women Continue," *The New York Times*, May 3, 2014, http://www.nytimes.com/2014/05/04/world/asia/in-spite-of-the-law-afghan-honor-killings-of-women-continue.html.

44. "Jordanian Kills Sister to 'cleanse Family Honor,'" *Al Arabia News*, April 30, 2013, http://english.alarabiya.net/en/News/middle-east/2013/04/30/Jordanian-kills-sister-to-cleanse-family-honor-.html.

45. Honour Based Violence Awareness Network "Statistics & Data," n.d., http://hbv-awareness.com/.

46. Sara Hossain and Lynn Welchman, *"Honour": Crimes, Paradigms and Violence Against Women* (New York: Zed Books, 2005).

47. Kaleef K. Karim, "Quran 4:34, 'Beat Them' (Wife Abuse)?," Discover the Truth, December 4, 2013, http://discover-the-truth.com/2013/12/04/quran-434-beat-them-wife-abuse/.

48. Deuteronomy 21, in *The KJV Study Bible* (Nashville: Barbour, 2011).

49. John L. Esposito, *The Oxford Dictionary of Islam* (Oxford: Oxford University Press, 2003).

50. "Islamic Penal Code of the Islamic Republic of Iran: Book One & Book Two," Iran Human Rights: Documentation Center, April 4, 2013, http://www.iranhrdc.org/english/human-rights-documents/iranian-codes/3200-islamic-penal-code-of-the-islamic-republic-of-iran-book-one-and-book-two.html.

51. McNulty, *The Burning Bed*, 62.

52. Francine Hughes as quoted in ibid., 37.

53. Carol Gilligan, *In a Different Voice: Psychological Theory and Women's Development*, 1st ed. (Cambridge, MA: Harvard University Press, 1993).

54. Judith Himber, "Blood Rituals: Self-Cutting in Female Psychiatric Inpatients," *Psychotherapy: Theory, Research, Practice, Training* 31, no. 4 (1994): 620–631.

55. Alex Crosby et al., *Suicidal Thoughts and Behaviors Among Adults Aged ≥18 Years—United States, 2008–2009*, Surveillance Summaries (Atlanta: Centers for Disease Control and Prevention, October 21, 2011), http://www.cdc.gov/mmwr/preview/mmwrhtml/ss6013a1.htm?s_cid=ss6013a1_eSuicidal.

56. Ibid.

57. "Women CEOs of the Fortune 1000," Catalyst, July 14, 2014, http://www.catalyst.org/knowledge/women-ceos-fortune-1000.

58. Lewis Henry Morgan, *Ancient Society* (Piscataway, NJ: Transaction, 1877).

59. Elizabeth Cady Stanton, "The Matriarchate or Mother-Age: An Address of Mrs. Stanton Before the National Council of Women, February 1891. Voluntary Motherhood : Address of Mrs. Stanton Blatch Before the National Council of Women" (Washington, DC: National Bulletin, 1891).

60. Jill Lepore, "The Last Amazon: Wonder Woman Returns," *The New Yorker*, September 22, 2014.

61. Ibid.

62. Lansky, "Shame and Domestic Violence."

63. Gloria Dillberto, "A Violent Death, a Haunted Life," *People Magazine*, October 8, 1984, http://www.people.com/people/archive/article/0,,20088845,00.html.

64. Francine Hughes as quoted in McNulty, *The Burning Bed*, 164.

65. Francine Hughes as quoted in ibid., 164, 165.

66. Shannon Meyer and Randall H. Carroll, "When Officers Die: Understanding Deadly Domestic Violence Calls for Service," *The Police Chief: The Professional Voice of Law Enforcement* (July 2014).

67. Ibid.
68. McNulty, *The Burning Bed*, 195.
69. Ibid.
70. Ibid.
71. Robert Greenwald, dir. *The Burning Bed* (Culver City, CA: Tisch/Avnet Productions, 1984).
72. Kaavonia Hinton-Johnson, "Hughes, Francine," in *Encyclopedia of Domestic Violence and Abuse*, ed. Laura L. Finley, vol. 2 (Santa Barbara, CA: ABC-CLIO, 2013), 228–231.
73. "New York Domestic Violence Laws," Findlaw, accessed August 8, 2014, http://statelaws.findlaw.com/new-york-law/new-york-domestic-violence-laws.html.
74. J. Dressler, "Battered Women and Sleeping Abusers: Some Reflections," *Ohio State Journal of Criminal Law* 3 (2005): 457–471.
75. Hinton-Johnson, "Hughes, Francine."
76. Louise Knott Ahern, "'The Burning Bed': A Turning Point in Fight against Domestic Violence," *Lansing State Journal*, September 27, 2009, http://www.lansingstatejournal.com/article/99999999/NEWS01/909270304/-Burning-Bed-turning-point-fight-against-domestic-violence.
77. Ibid.
78. Ibid.
79. Ibid.
80. Dillberto, "A Violent Death."
81. Ibid.
82. Ibid.
83. Ibid.
84. Ibid.
85. Ibid.
86. Ibid.

CHAPTER 6

The Bullying of Blacks and Hispanics by Whites

As a number of writers have pointed out, race is a socially constructed concept. That people have different colored skin and different physical characteristics is a biological fact, but the need to assign these factors to arbitrary categories is a social process. It can be a way of enforcing nationalism or tribal identity, or even membership in a family. "The Fasts have such big feet!" my relatives like to exclaim, comparing shoe sizes at family reunions. Biological similarities and differences help us define ourselves and distinguish ourselves from others. As soon as we have defined "others," be it on the basis of gender orientation, sex, or race, we can displace our shame onto them; we can make them our scapegoats. When we do this by skin color and other physiological characteristics, it is called racism.

Some low-status white people, those who inhabit the margins of society, may choose to be open about their racism. They may join groups such as the Ku Klux Klan, the Aryan Nation, or the American Nazi Party, to affirm the value of their racist sentiments. In prison, where life tends to be primitive and elemental, convicts often form tribes by race and make other tribes the targets of their contempt. High-status people, on the other hand, often keep their racism concealed because it is considered such an unattractive behavior in post–civil rights America, because it is illegal, and because it may hurt their business or diminish their popularity. Sometimes under stress high-status people can reveal racist sentiments they did not even know they had, and they may be ruined by it.

DONALD STERLING

Donald Sterling is a billionaire attorney, real estate magnate, and former owner of the Los Angeles Clippers. In April of 2014, a recording of a conversation between Sterling and a female friend known as V. Stiviano, who is black and Mexican, was made public.[1] She had posted a picture of herself on Instagram with basketball great Magic Johnson attending a Clippers' game and Mr. Sterling had responded:

> It bothers me a lot that you want to broadcast that you're associating with black people. Do you have to? [3 minutes, 30 seconds into the tape-recorded message]

> You can sleep with [black people]. You can bring them in, you can do whatever you want. The little I ask you is not to promote it on that . . . and not to bring them to my games . . . [5 minutes, 15 seconds][2]

The tape was made public and widely reported in the media. In situations such as this, where the stakes are high, professional damage control consultants are hired. Their advice is often the same: deliver a sincere and deeply felt apology. The American public, we are told, loves to forgive people who admit having made a terrible mistake. Responding to a public outcry against his statements, Sterling appeared on *Anderson Cooper 360°*, a news show that examines current events in depth and made what seemed to be a spontaneous but well-rehearsed speech:

> I made a terrible, terrible mistake. And I'm here with you today to apologize and to ask for forgiveness for all the people that I have hurt. And I have hurt so many people, so many innocent people . . . when I listen to that tape, I don't even know how I could say words like that . . .

> I'm not a racist. I love people. I always have. But those words came out of my mouth, I guess. And I'm so sorry. And I'm so apologetic.

> My little grandchild goes to a Catholic nursery. And they were passing around candy to everybody. When they got to her, they said, "We don't give candy to racists . . ."

> I hurt my ex-wife. She is a beautiful person. She goes to the hospital, and she's a volunteer at Cedars-Sinai. When I went to law school, she worked at the children's hospital. She's a giver. She works. At this stage in her life, she still works. She didn't need this. Her whole life blew up.[3]

Unfortunately this strategy has been repeated so often that the American public is getting wise to it. Stories about nuns denying candy to a kindergarten child because of her grandfather's sins may strain even the most credulous.

In 2013 76 percent of NBA players were black,[4] more than in any other professional sport. To be a white man who "owns" a group of black men called for sensitivity and respect. Well-known black athletes and activists responded quickly, condemning Sterling's behavior with strong language.

Sterling had recently donated $3 million to the University of California in Los Angeles's (UCLA) Division of Nephrology. UCLA decided to return the gift, stating that Sterling's "divisive and hurtful comments" were at odds with UCLA's core values of "diversity, inclusion, and respect."[5] People who knew that UCLA had taken this position were confused by a garish ad that appeared in the *Los Angeles Times* on the same day, with large color pictures of Mr. Sterling and his wife. The ad thanked the Sterlings for their donation, "the largest gift ever given for basic kidney research at UCLA," and promised to name a laboratory after them, as well as hanging an engraved plaque in the lobby acknowledging the gift.[6] The university was deluged with phone calls and emails. "The ad was placed by Mr. Sterling and not the university,"[7] UCLA responded.

Six years earlier an alternative paper, the *LA Weekly*, had published an exposé of Sterling revealing that he had placed a series of misleading ads in the *Los Angeles Times* describing a "state-of-the-art $50 million dollar [sic] Donald T. Sterling Homeless Center, Medical Center and Courthouse" that he was preparing to build, to provide housing and other services for homeless African American and Latino men. City administrators contacted by the paper had no knowledge of the project. Six years later it was still imaginary. At the time Sterling was under investigation by the Department of Justice for violating the Fair Housing Act because he "refused to rent to African-American prospective tenants . . . and refused to rent to families with children."[8] The Sterlings control thousands of rental units in the Los Angeles area.[9] Regarding race, Mr. Sterling is not the person he would like us to think he is. He exploits people of color (including Ms. V. Stiviano, the members of the football team he once owned, and the homeless blacks and Hispanics of Los Angeles) to elevate his own status and then excludes them from the group of human beings who deserve to be treated with equal respect, regardless of race.

MICHAEL RICHARDS

Michael Richards, the actor who portrayed the immensely popular character Kramer on TV's *Seinfeld*, was a high-status member of the entertainment community. He had co-starred in one of the most successful sit-coms in the history of television. It had run for nine seasons and made its stars wealthy enough that they could live in high style for the rest of their lives without working. After *Seinfeld* went off the air, Richards devoted himself to stand-up comedy. Standing up in front of a live audience and trying to elicit laughter is considered among the riskiest and most demanding of callings in the entertainment industry. It requires nerves of steel, creativity, intelligence, the ability to "read" the audience, and a good sense of what is funny and what is not.

In November of 2006, Richards appeared at the Laugh Factory in West Hollywood, an important stand-up comedy venue. A few minutes into his act, a handsome, well-dressed young black man named Kyle Doss and a group of 15 friends, blacks, whites, and Asians, entered the room, found seats and ordered drinks. They were celebrating a birthday and spirits were high. Richards tried to make them quiet down.[10] "Look at those stupid Mexicans and blacks being loud up there," he said, and then returned to his routine. This level of aggression is not unusual in stand-up and might even be condoned as "edgy."

"My friend doesn't think you're funny," Doss called out a little later, getting back by heckling him.

Richards responded: "He's a nigger! He's a nigger! He's a nigger! A nigger, look, there's a nigger!"[11] He continued by firing demeaning clichés at him for three minutes. By then most of the audience had left.

Some days later Richards appeared on the *Late Show with David Letterman*, alongside his old friend Jerry Seinfeld, to make an apology. "For me to be at a comedy club and to flip out and say this crap, I'm deeply, deeply sorry. I'm not a racist, that's what's so insane about this."

The audience, unsure if this was a "bit," began to laugh. "Stop laughing," Seinfeld said. "It's not funny."

Soon afterward Richards retired from performing stand-up. In 2012 he appeared as himself on *Seinfeld*'s web series of interviews, "Comedians in Cars Getting Coffee," and admitted that the outburst still haunted him and that it was a major reason for his withdrawing from performing. Racism that he was probably unaware of had been revealed.

When an audience member shouts out, "You're not funny," or the audience falls silent following a joke, or some similar incident undermines a comedian's faith in his abilities, he may experience "flop sweat," a kind of panic attack involving cold sweat and a sense of terror.[12] Am I a member of that group of Skilled Comedians? he may ask himself. Or am I another Pathetic Character who Thinks He's Funny? The shame is overwhelming and instantaneous and the body reacts before the brain can make sense out of what is happening. The comedian may strike back against the shamer as though his life was imperiled. If it is a group of minorities, and racial slurs are the only weapon at hand, he will use them. A more experienced comedian, quicker on his feet, might have made something funny out of it. This is not to excuse Richards for his behavior; it is to understand it, and maybe cut him a little slack.

HOW DO WE BECOME RACISTS?

Some pundits have suggested that we are all racists, but it might be both kinder and more accurate to say that we are racists who would rather not be. We are racists "in recovery," meaning that we have identified the demon of racism within ourselves, found it so deeply embedded from such an early age that we cannot rid ourselves of it despite all our efforts. It generates automatic thoughts in response to certain triggers: I see a group of Chicano teens approaching me on a dark street, I feel a flutter of apprehension. I see an Asian student in my class, I assume that he or she will be hard working and good at statistics. As a second-best alternative to ridding ourselves of it, we have learned to recognize our own demon when he raises his head and fight it. We do our best to treat all people equally. We monitor our thoughts, identify ideas of negative (and positive) stereotypes as they appear, and discard them. We live with the discomfort of being divided selves within this issue and try to raise our children so that they will not carry our prejudices into the future.

Assuming we are all racists, where does this racism come from? Thandeka, a Unitarian-Universalist minister, in her book *Being White*,[13] interviewed a number of white people about their early recollections regarding race. One interviewee, Mike, recalled a day in his childhood when, walking down the street with his father and uncle, they passed an interracial couple. His father and uncle began criticizing the man and the kind of woman his companion must be. Mike did not understand exactly what was happening but sensed that this was an important way for grownup men to behave and wondered if he would be capable of imitating it when he grew older.[14]

Jackie, a high school student, talked with such warmth and enthusiasm about one of her teachers that her parents decided to invite him to the house. They were astonished to see that he was black, and their discomfort with the situation was obvious. Jackie sensed that she had done something wrong and swore to herself that she would not make the same mistake in the future.[15]

When she was 16, Sarah brought home a black classmate. Afterward her mother told her never to invite the girl to their home again because she was "colored." That made no sense to Sarah, so she pursued the topic, demanding to know the real reason. Her mother refused to discuss it.

> The indignant look on her mother's face, however, made Sarah realize that if she persisted, she would jeopardize her mother's affection toward her. This awareness startled Sarah because she and her mother were the best of friends. Nothing Sarah had always believed until that moment could jeopardize their closeness. But now, she had glimpsed the unimaginable . . . [It} was not absolutely secure. It could crumble . . . Sarah severed her friendship with the girl.[16]

These are examples of how human culture is passed along through shaming. In each of these cases, the child or teen learned the principle of racism through parental shaming. *This is how we behave (or do not behave) in this family, and if you wish to remain a member in good standing, you will behave this way too.* For Sarah, it was the first encounter with the idea that she was not unconditionally loved by her mother, that certain behaviors might result in her expulsion from the family. Whether this should be considered toxic shaming or healthy shaming depends on the context. If Mike, Jackie, or Sarah was living in the antebellum South and wished to embrace its culture, then it might have been considered healthy shaming. It would have led to an easy way of life and the social acceptance we all crave. In our current existence, at a time when we know better, when we understand the pain of exclusion and the horror of slavery, there can be no justification.

"SCIENTIFIC" RACISM

In 1851 Dr. Samuel A. Cartwright presented a paper at the conference of the Medical Association of Louisiana regarding a disease he had recently identified. He called it Drapetomania (from the Greek δραπετης, *Drapetes*, "a runaway slave" + μανια, *mania*, "madness"), suggesting that the slave who chose to run away did so because he was suffering from a psychiatric disorder. In the opening paragraph Cartwright explained that the black man serves the white by the decree of God (an idea sometimes justified by Genesis 9:20–27) and as long as he is treated well (but not too well), he will stay with his master. But

> If the white man attempts to oppose the Deity's will, by trying to make the negro anything else than "the submissive knee-bender" (which the Almighty declared he should be) . . . or if he abuses the power which God has given him over his fellow-man, by being cruel to him . . . the negro will run away.[17]

If the slave should contract Drapetomania, there was a cure. "The liver, skin and kidneys should be stimulated to maximum activity" by beating the slave with a "broad leather strap" or, in severe cases by amputating the big toes, making running impossible.[18]

A century and a half later, Richard Herrnstein, a Harvard psychologist, and Charles Murray, a political scientist, wrote a book called *The Bell Curve*,[19] which suggests, albeit with several scholarly caveats, that black people score lower on IQ tests than whites because they are less intelligent and that this disparity in intelligence is biological and heritable. Because the gap between the cognitive elite and the less intelligent was supposedly growing ever greater through selective breeding (smart people marry smart people and vice versa), the America of the future would consist of a very large moronic population ruled by a very small ultra-intelligent upper class.

There is so much wrong, scientifically and ideologically, with this premise that it is hard to know where to begin to critique it. It is rare, even in academia, that so much ink has been invested in refuting a single work of "science." A thorough and unbiased discussion of *The Bell Curve*'s shortcomings is available from many sources. Interested readers are directed to a comprehensive article, "Intelligence: Knowns and Unknowns,"[20] by Neisser and colleagues and published in *American Psychologist*, and an excellent book, *The Mismeasure of Man*, by Stephen Jay Gould.[21]

However, there is one particularly intriguing argument that falls within the province of this book. It involves the work of John Ogbu, an African-born educator who taught for many years at the University of California Berkeley. Ogbu had tired of negative comparisons between African Americans and other immigrant groups that were considered better integrated into the dominant culture. He argued that there was a difference between those indigenous low-status ethnic groups who were treated as a caste (he called them "caste-like minorities"[22] or "involuntary minorities"[23]) and those who immigrate voluntarily, seeking political or religious asylum or better economic prospects. The latter group comes with an idealistic vision of their future. Even if they cannot actually achieve it, the possibility remains that their children will. It provides a goal to work toward. Caste-like minorities, on the other hand, "grow up firmly convinced that one's life will eventually be restricted to a small and poorly rewarded set of social roles."[24] This attitude does not inspire academic commitment among children or great ambition among adults. Ogbu hypothesized that this situation could lead to a kind of "cultural inversion," which would involve rejecting behaviors that represent the culture of the dominant group, or "acting white."[25]

Caste-like minorities include African Americans in the United States but also the Maori people of New Zealand, India's "untouchables," the Burakumin in Japan, and Jews of non-European origin in Israel. All these groups tend to score about 15 points, or one standard deviation lower than the dominant culture in the land where they live. Hans Eyesink, a distinguished German psychologist, pointed out many years ago, during a lecture at the London School of Economics, that the same was true for the Irish Protestants—that they scored about 15 IQ points lower than the English—and was punched in the nose by a protester[26] (social science can be a dangerous business). Irish Protestants in America, however, have the same mean IQ score as Americans, validating Eyesink's observation. It is social oppression that lowers IQ scores, not some heritable trait.

EUGENICS

Sir Francis Galton, a half-cousin of Charles Darwin and a distinguished man of science in his own right, developed a theory that appeared to be a logical extension of "survival of the fittest." If those beasts who thrived were those best adapted to changes in the environment, he reasoned, why not promote such changes in the human race through controlled breeding? He called his science "eugenics."

When eugenics reached American shores in the early days of the twentieth century (fads traveled more slowly back then), it was embraced by the academic and intellectual elite, Unitarian theologists, Ivy League College presidents, and professors in the newly emerging fields of anthropology, sociology, and psychology, who wanted to grow their departments. The robber barons of the railroads, the oil fields, and the steel mills also took a lively interest. It offered a vision of the future that they were too ashamed to speak aloud, an opportunity for the upper class to "populate the earth with vastly more of their own socio-economic and biological kind—and less or none of everyone else."[27] As racism and classism combined, it proved irresistible.

In 1901 David Starr Jordan, president of Stanford University, wrote a series of articles promoting eugenics to the nonacademic public. These were published in periodicals such as *Popular Science Monthly* and eventually collected in a book called *The Blood of the Nation: A Study in the Decay of Races by the Survival of the Unfit*. The thesis was introduced, appropriately, with a quote from Rudyard Kipling, the poet laureate of racism followed by a statement Jordan's thesis that war winnows the human race of its finest men (obviously excluding mercenaries) leaving only the chaff:

> "Send forth the best ye breed [when enlisting an army to defend a nation]."
>
> This is Kipling's cynical advice to a nation which happily can never follow it. But could it be accepted literally and completely, the nation in time would breed only second-rate men. By the sacrifice of the best or the emigration of the best, and by such influences alone, have races fallen from first-rate to second-rate in the march of history.[28]

Jordan believed that the throes of civilization at the turn of the twentieth century were the results of the "best bred" having been killed in the Civil War and their widows refusing to remarry and procreate.

Princeton, Yale, Boston University, Smith, and Amherst all did their part to promote the cause, but the epicenter of eugenic excitement was Harvard. Earnest Hooten, head of the university's Department of Anthropology, was among its more outspoken advocates. He wrote that the overpopulation of inferiors was a national emergency.[29] In a speech from 1937, he stated that "Man's achievements have been the work of the intelligent and creative few, whereas the masses have been content with being parasites or slaves."[30] He encouraged his audience, an engineering society gathered for their annual meeting, to direct their considerable intelligence and creativity not so much toward developing new machines but rather toward developing new ways of improving the human being and breeding "better animals by selection and elimination of the inferior."[31] In 1921 the American Eugenics Society came into being; its founders were Madison Grant, a Yale graduate and passionate ecologist; Harry Laughlin, who had a postgraduate degree from Princeton and was "among the most racist and anti-Semitic of early twentieth-century eugenicists";[32] Herbert Fischer, another Yale alum whom Martin Friedman would later characterize as the greatest economist our country has ever produced; Henry Fairfield Osborn, a Princeton graduate who would later become the president of the American Museum of Natural History; and others of high social status and intellectual achievements. By 1926, at least nine members of the organization's advisory council were also on the Harvard faculty, and many more were affiliated with Harvard as students and researchers. The society's vice president, Charles Davenport, was a professor of zoology at Harvard who also founded the Eugenics Records Office, which kept tabs on people's genetic backgrounds. Like Hooton, Davenport believed that increased charity, philanthropy, and medical advances had interfered with the natural survival of the fittest. (This was the 1920s version of *welfare undermines initiative*.) Two of Davenport's Harvard associates, Robert DeCourcey Ward and Prescott Hall, spearheaded the Immigration Restriction League and were instrumental in persuading Congress to curtail the influx of "inferior immigrants" by imposing literacy tests and other restrictions. These laws, while modified in detail, remained in effect until 1965.

The nineteenth-century robber barons were equally smitten with the new science. Their philanthropic foundations were waiting on the dock, wallets open, when eugenics arrived from across the sea. In 1904 the Carnegie Institution began work on a laboratory complex at Cold Spring Harbor, Long Island, (Davenport became director), which would serve as an archive for records containing information on American families and their bloodlines, including which families produced criminals or the feeble-minded, those who seemed destined for poverty, or those with heritable physical disabilities. A Carnegie-supported report published in 1911, the "Preliminary Report of the Committee of the Eugenic Section of the American Breeder's Association to Study and to Report on the Best Practical Means for Cutting Off the Defective Germ-Plasm in the Human Population," presented a list of 18 strategies for improving the quality of the human race. These included identifying the "defective" branches of the family tree and pruning them away by lifelong segregation, sterilization, and finally euthanasia, the most commonly suggested method being a "lethal chamber" or public, locally operated gas chambers.[33]

E. H. Harriman, president of the Union Pacific and Southern Pacific Railroads, donated money so that charities in New York, Chicago, and other big cities could identify Jewish, Italian, and Irish newcomers and examine them closely for possible reasons to deport, incarcerate, or sterilize them.

In 1927 the Rockefeller Foundation funded the Kaiser Wilhelm Institute for Anthropology, Human Heredity, and Eugenics in Berlin. While a German Society of Racial Hygiene had existed since 1905, the interest in eugenics snowballed in Germany following their humiliating defeat in World War I. The terms of the German surrender were unbearably shameful, and eugenics offered a powerful shame-management strategy: what appeared to be weakness was actually the result of the inferior non-Germanic races diluting the "true" German bloodlines. It appeared that American eugenicists had a strong ally across the sea. By 1926, Rockefeller had donated some $410,000 (about $4 million in today's dollars) to German eugenic researchers, among them a little-known enthusiast named Joseph Mengele.

Americans had imagined their eugenic goal as a Nordic stereotype: tall, blond-haired, blue-eyed, and physically fit; the Germans adopted the same type but renamed him the "Aryan Man." During the following decades, Germany goose-stepped headlong into a world where Americans had tread but lightly. In 1934 the Reich passed laws permitting involuntary sterilization of the feebleminded, the mentally ill, epileptics, and alcoholics. Some 400,000 were sterilized prior to World War II. "Marriage laws"—laws prohibiting unions between Aryans and the eugenically unfit, including Jews—were passed in 1935. In 1941 hospitals began exterminating the mentally ill to free up beds for wounded soldiers. More than 70,000 mental patients were poisoned with carbon monoxide. The Final Solution—the killing of all Jews, gypsies, Slavs, and social democrats (deemed as those whose lives were "not worth living") resulted in 11 million deaths, the largest number of human beings ever executed by genocide.

The eugenics movement limped home from World War II crippled and disgraced. It was dismissed from the universities, defunded by the robber barons, and left on life support only so that it might be exhibited in college classrooms as a result of what can happen when shame/rage overwhelms humanity and clarity of thought. Occasional attempts to revive it, such as *The Bell Curve*, have elicited cries to "pull the plug" and rid us of it once and for all.

THE WHITE PROBLEM

In 1808 Congress passed a law barring further importation of slaves, meaning that most African American families have been in the United States for over 200 years, longer than many immigrants of other nationalities. They are *more* American than other immigrant groups but are treated as second class citizens most of the rest of us. While other immigrant groups have become rapidly assimilated, blacks remain on the outside for the obvious reason of skin color. Black teenagers of every social class are frequently stopped and frisked by the police without cause. Worse, they are sometimes shot and killed by police who mistakenly believe that they are carrying or about to use guns. According to the Department of Labor, blacks who are equally qualified to hold a job are hired less frequently than their white counterparts, and when they are hired, they are paid less. Although black men and women constitute only 10 percent of the population, 30 percent of the men and women who occupy cells in our vast prison system (the world's largest) have black skin. African Americans still tend to live in economic ghettoes. They suffer disproportionately from high blood pressure, a medical problem that is often and other stress related medical problems. Why has our dominant culture refused to grant entree to African Americans and instead kept them at the lowest rung of the status ladder?

Here the reader may ask, *Is Dr. Fast justified in blaming the dominant culture for these problems? If African Americans have been in this country so long, and are being treated so poorly, isn't it their own fault? Aren't they hired less often for high-status jobs because they are less motivated and* (the voice drops to a whisper) *less intelligent? Aren't so many of them occupying prison cells because they tend to behave like criminals?*

After World War II, a French journalist asked Richard Wright, a prominent black author, how he felt about the "Negro problem." He replied "There isn't any Negro problem. There is only a White problem."[34] Like Wright, I believe that the problem is not a lack of intelligence, initiative, or honesty among blacks but rather ongoing discrimination against them by whites at every level of society, even after *Brown v. Board of Education*, the courage of Rosa Parks, the sit-ins, the Freedom Riders, affirmative action, the Civil Rights Act, the Voting Rights Act, the Fair Housing Act, the riots in Harlem and Watts, and the assassination of Dr. Martin Luther King. By discrimination, I am referring to actions that favor one racial group over another. Racism is an ideology (a system of beliefs); discrimination is the behavior it inspires.[35]

At the time this book was written, the percentage of unemployed black men was more than twice as high as that of white men. In cases where black men and white men were equally qualified for jobs in terms of education, work experience, certifications, degrees, and commendations, white men were hired for the job at rates ranging from 50 percent (three white men for every two black men) to 240 percent (about five white men for every two black men) more frequently.[36] Most research suggests that this kind of discrimination holds true across occupations and industries, even for businesses that boast of being "equal opportunity employers."[37]

The skeptical reader might ask: *How do we know that they were really equally qualified for the job? Perhaps the black men had a mistakenly high opinion of themselves.*

To answer this question we need to delve a little more deeply into the methods of the researchers. These hiring discrimination statistics were generated by a kind of research called an "audit study." While audit studies vary somewhat in approach, the methodology followed by

Marianne Bertrand, a professor at the University of Chicago, and Sendhil Mullainathan, who teaches at the Massachusetts Institute of Technology, in a study titled "Are Emily and Brendan More Employable Than Latoya and Tyrone?" is exemplary. The professors prepared work resumes for fictitious job candidates. Half of the resumes described highly qualified workers, and half, less qualified workers. Half of the resumes "representing candidates of equal qualifications were randomly assigned White sounding names (such as Emily Walsh or Greg Baker)" and half "African American sounding names (such as Lakisha Washington or Jamal Jones)."[38] Next, groups of four resumes, two pairing a highly qualified "black" candidate and a highly qualified "white" candidate and two pairing a less qualified black candidate and a less qualified white candidate, were individually mailed in response to "help wanted" ads in Chicago and Boston newspapers. In this particular study, nearly 5,000 resumes were submitted in response to 1,300 employment ads, covering a wide range of salaries and occupations. The number of applications versus the number of callbacks for interviews showed that racism was alive and well in post–civil rights America. People with "white sounding names" were given preference over blacks at every level of employment. While no form of research is without flaws, a large-scale, well-conducted audit study such as this must be considered among the most valid ways of measuring discrimination.

When black men were eventually hired for jobs, they were most often in the lower paying "sales" and "service" sectors, and their weekly median pay was 22 percent less than that of white men working in comparable jobs.[39]

Where people can live depends on whether they are employed and, if they are, how much money they are earning. While most of the barriers to black families come in the obvious form of unaffordable rents or sale prices, there are also concealed barriers to integrating neighborhoods. When renting, black applicants receive less information than white applicants about units they were interested in and are given fewer opportunities to view the units. Blacks considering buying homes are redirected into less wealthy communities and neighborhoods with a higher proportion of minority residents. When black and white renters apply for the same property in urban metropolitan areas, landlords favor the white applicants 21.6 percent more often than the black.[40]

When it comes to financing the purchase of a home, blacks are rejected more often than whites when applying for mortgages of comparable value. One study[41] found that the rate of rejection was as high as 82 percent for people of color.[42] When blacks are given mortgages, interest levels are typically more than 0.5 percent higher than whites regardless of income level, date when the mortgage was generated, or age of the buyer. The practice of "redlining" should also be mentioned here. This refers to the reluctance of banks to lend for real estate in minority neighborhoods. While this is illegal, its practice is easily disguised as compliance with obscure banking regulations. All of these hurdles to becoming a homeowner function as a subtle and nefarious barrier to a family's accumulation of wealth. Home equity is the primary source of wealth accumulation for most home-owning families. Many of us have heard members of our parents' generation boasting about the profit they made by reselling their home 30 years after its purchase. This kind of wealth accumulation is denied to most black families. One of the results is that "Whites possess roughly 12 times the wealth of African Americans; in fact, whites near the bottom of the income distribution possess more wealth than blacks near the top of the income distribution"[43]

As communities grow poorer, large chain stores that offer employment to many people move away, complaining of the lack of availability of reliable employees. (Poor families often appear unreliable because they have no backups, no one to watch a sick child who has to stay home from school, no one to drive an hour to post bail for a cousin who has gotten himself arrested, no one to save the furniture when the ancient plumbing has broken and the living room is becoming a swimming pool.) Other merchants are driven away by a lack of customers, vandalism, or even gangs selling "protection."[44] Soon Main Street is a row of boarded-over storefronts, and all that remain are check-cashing stores, a social services office, a clinic, a dentist, a diner and a "dollar" store. Police may stop cruising the streets because the neighborhood poses risks that are out of proportion to rewards. As the housing prices drop, the salaries of the teachers decline and the best teachers look for work elsewhere. Only the burnt-out cases and the idealistic remain. Rankings on best and worst school surveys slide and house prices decline in response, creating a vicious cycle.

This neighborhood has been excluded from the group we might call the American Dream. People who live there are at the bottom of the status ladder. Deprived of a place in the mainstream economy, they must create their own economy. Sudhir Venkatesh, who has written about this subject at length,[45] refers to these systems as "underground economies" or, more poetically, "shadow economies."

> The underground economy is a widespread set of activities, usually scattered and not well integrated, through which people earn money that is not reported to the government and that, in some cases, may entail criminal behavior. In other words, the unreported income can derive from licit exchange, such as

selling homemade food or mowing a neighbor's lawn, and illicit practices, such as advertising sexual favors or selling secondhand guns without a permit.[46]

As much as 17 percent of the labor force may be involved in the underground economy. Although these entrepreneurial individuals rarely make more than $10,000 dollars a year from their efforts, their collective income worldwide may exceed $100 billion annually. They rarely report income or charge a sales tax. Often they are neither licensed nor certified to do what they are doing, and they operate without liability insurance or personal injury insurance.[47]

Many high-status members of the above-ground economy also regularly avoid paying certain taxes. They may have an income stream that generates cash. Four out of five of these above-grounders regularly use cash to employ members of the underground economy to pay for services such as landscaping, childcare, housekeeping, and construction work without ever reporting the transactions to the Internal Revenue Service. This constitutes criminal behavior, but it is commonly ignored because it is an everyday occurrence among well-to-do white people and, when committed on a small scale, appears to be inconsequential: *I already pay enough taxes; what difference will a few dollars make?* In fact, unreported cash/labor exchanges and barters cost the Federal government somewhere between $83 billion and $93 billion per year in lost tax revenue.[48]

In his book, Venkatesh describes some of the more licit occupations in the underground economy, like the car mechanic who operates out of back alleys, a hair-dresser who makes an extra $500 a week by letting the local gang turn her salon into a nightclub on the weekends, a prostitute who rents the backroom of a barbershop at night to ply her trade, a caterer who works out of her home preparing soul food lunches that her children deliver throughout the neighborhood, and gang members who get paid to keep the addicts out of the park across from the elementary school during the hours when the kids are dropped off and picked up. These crimes seem victimless. They provide important services and evoke our admiration in the way overburdened and underresourced people have cobbled them together. But much of the income that drives the underground economy involves the drug trade, gambling, prostitution, loan sharking, and buying and selling guns. These are illegal activities that involve exploitation and violence.

An illegal economy is an unregulated economy. If two people disagree, there are rarely contracts to refer to or rules and regulations to be enforced. There are no police to be called in if tempers get out of hand, no lawyers to hash it out, no civil lawsuits. When the stakes are small, a respected neutral party may be called in to mediate. In fact Venkatesh himself became such a mediator while he was conducting his research because he was precisely the person to play the part, a detached and dispassionate observer with a good sense of what constituted social and economic justice. Such good mediators are not always available.

Money lending, drugs, prostitution, and the selling of weapons occur within nearly all financial ghettoes. They all involve high stakes in terms of investment and profit, risk of incarceration, and possible bodily harm or death.

Since few residents of the economic ghetto can qualify for a bank loan, the loan sharks do a lively business, charging usurious interest rates. If the debtor fails to pay, the lender may threaten violence or take violent action. In Venkatesh's experience, most of the lending in the ghetto where he conducted his research involved loans of less than $1,000 at an interest rate of 30 percent. People borrowed money to

> pay utility bills and the rent; to replace or fix broken equipment; to purchase supplies; to hire a local resident under the table; to pay an official, such as a police officer, precinct captain, or city worker, for a service; to hire a van or truck; and to repay an outstanding debt or loan.[49]

The following story is typical.

> "When my husband died, I was getting a little money [from his street gang], but then they lost [a street war to another gang], so I wasn't getting nothing. That's when my brother [-in-law], Teetie, moved in. Teetie [a drug dealer] was paying half my rent, so you know, I wasn't working and that helped. But he started sleeping with my sister, buying her drugs, and I wasn't having that . . . So I was just trying, for months, to get him to stop beating her, feeding her that bad dope, making her sick. But that's when she ended up in the hospital, so I told him to get out . . . I borrowed money from Otis for rent until I found my job, but I'm still paying that back and he charged 30 percent interest."
> "Did Teetie ever sell drugs in your house?"
> "Well, I won't lie to you. I was so desperate for rent, I let him do it. Big mistake. He was selling out the back and it just made things worse. But I needed the money. So I decided paying a loan shark and getting beaten up [if she didn't make her payments] was better than letting Teetie kill my sister."[50]

Larger amounts are borrowed when business opportunities present themselves. For example, the owner of the hair salon borrowed $2,500 from a loan shark at 30 percent interest to buy lights and a speaker system so that gangs could host weekend parties there. Venkatesh also describes a local merchant who kept borrowing to keep his dollar store afloat. When several of his schemes failed, he declared bankruptcy, an act that resulted in "physical abuse from the creditor, who broke his arms and sent him to the hospital."[51]

DRUGS AND RACE

The escape provided by drugs and alcohol makes them a particularly valuable commodity in places where there is much shame and few sources of worthiness. It is a tool of avoidance, the south pole of the compass of shame. The pleasurable sensation of opiates and cannabinoids overpowers the shame. Alcohol, marijuana, cocaine, and heroin have been features of economic ghettos since the turn of the century. By no coincidence, certain substances have been associated historically with different emigrant groups and come to represent certain clichés about that group.

When the Chinese arrived to build US railroads in 1850, they brought a fierce work ethic and the pastime of smoking opium, a habit promoted in China by the British in the 1870s to increase profits from their poppy plantations in India. Despite the insularity of the Chinese communities in America (the Chinatowns that arose in many urban areas and remain to this day), opium smoking soon became a practice among adventurous and jaded members of the dominant culture. William Randolph Hearst, the newspaper tycoon of the era (the Rupert Murdoch of his day), a racist and promoter of yellow journalism, published a series of lurid articles describing how Chinese men were using opium to seduce American women. This is the common myth of immigrants stealing away the patriarchy's women (who were considered chattel, we should recall) and corrupting their purity. As a result, a series of Federal laws were passed between 1905 and 1919 restricting the import and use of opium.[52]

At about the same time, Mexicans and Mexican Americans began leaving their homes in the Southwest and searching for work in other parts of the country. They brought with them a rich cuture, which included spicy foods, Mariachi music, and marijuana. Once again, Hearst provided his readers with titillating misinformation about the drug. In a story serialized in the *San Francisco Chronicle* in 1923, a private detective and his friends find a strange "weed" secreted below the floorboards of a tramp steamer recently arrived in port.

> The drug is marijuana, said by experts to fasten its grip upon the novice with far greater speed than morphine, cocaine, heroin or opium, and to be more destructive in its effects.

The Marijuana was found while the customs officers were examining the Arroyo at pier No. 15. East River . . . Below [the floorboards] he found several bunches of what seemed to be withered weeds, wrapped in a Costa Rican newspaper of recent date . . .

The chemists say that marijuana is so powerful that a small bit of leaf or twig rolled into a cigarette has such a kick that the traffickers in drugs have no difficulty in getting $1 for such a cigarette. [About $14 in current value.]

In Costa Rica where the plant grows, it is considered so harmful that mere possession of the drug entails a prison sentence.[53]

The border states were quick to pass laws against this "dangerous weed." A Texas legislator argued that "All Mexicans are crazy and marijuana is what makes them crazy," before voting the prohibition of that drug into law in 1919.

Dr. James C. Munch, who frequently appeared as an expert witness in marijuana trials during the 1930s, tried marijuana himself and reported the effects: he believed that he had been transformed into a bat and flitted about his office.[54] Claims of marijuana causing homicidal insanity led to resourceful lawyers using it as a defense for clients accused of homicide, resulting in a number of acquittals.[55] Nathan Luno, an advocate of drug law change, suggests that marijuana prohibition, "beyond being remarkable for the innocuousness of the drug in question, has been equally remarkable for the sheer extent of scientific fraud committed in order to justify its prohibition."[56]

As the Chinese became associated with opium and the Mexicans with marijuana, blacks were depicted in the press as homicidal cocaine fiends. Prior to the passage of Federal prohibition in 1920, Georgia, North and South Carolina, Mississippi, Tennessee, and West Virginia, influenced by temperance groups such as the Prohibition Party, the Anti-Saloon League, and the Woman's Christian Temperance Union, passed laws to abolish the saloon and prevent the sale of whiskey to Negros. Saloons were considered centers of political corruption and were associated with working-class black men who could only afford to buy their liquor by the glass and drink it standing up. The gentry had stocks of alcoholic beverages put away and could drink sitting down (wine at dinner, brandy afterward in the drawing room). Deprived of alcohol, black men became ready targets for cocaine dealers. Cocaine was easily ingested by "sniffing." It provided a euphoric mood and the energy to pass long days in grueling labor. And it was readily available. Many pharmacies sold preparations containing cocaine over the counter, no prescription required. In 1902 the American Pharmaceutical Association estimated that the United States boasted some 200,000 cocaine addicts (1 in 375), "the bulk of whom were genteel, middle-class women."[57] Yet it was the black man who was legislated against. Edward Huntington Williams, MD, offered his expert opinion on the subject in a *New York Times* editorial from 1914:

> For some years there have been rumors about the increase in drug taking in the south . . . rumors that the addiction to such drugs as morphine and cocaine was becoming a veritable curse to the colored race in certain regions . . . Stories of cocaine orgies and "sniffing parties" followed by wholesale murders, seem like lurid journalism . . . But in point of fact there was nothing "yellow" [exaggerated for the sake of sensation] about many of these reports. Nine men killed in Mississippi on one occasion by crazed cocaine takers, five in North Carolina, three in Tennessee—these are facts . . .
>
> The drug [cocaine] may produce the wildest form of insane exaltation, accompanied by fantastic hallucinations and delusions that characterize acute mania.[58]

The article goes on to promote a slew of myths about cocaine: that black men under its influence become homicidal, that they cannot be stopped by bullets of conventional caliber (and consequently the police need larger caliber, more powerful weapons), and that the cocaine users become more lethal marksmen on account of a "temporary steadying of the nervous and muscular system."

At the end of the article, the author admits that the cocaine problem is the result of blacks being denied alcohol, a process he refers to as "class legislation," although I think that "class discrimination" might be a more accurate term. While Williams was no champion of alcoholic beverages, he believed that something "inestimably worse" had been substituted for it.

> This substitute, as I have pointed out, is cocaine; and a trail of blood and disaster has marked the progress of its substitution . . . The evils of alcoholism . . . are not to be compared with the horrors of cocaine. . . . Once the negro has formed the habit, he is irreclaimable. The only method to keep him from taking the drug is imprisoning him. And this is merely palliative treatment, for he returns inevitably to the drug habit when released.
>
> But meanwhile these [politicians] have forced a new and terrible form of slavery upon thousands of colored men—a hideous bondage from which they cannot escape by mere proclamation or civil war.[59]

In each of these three cases, a drug closely associated with an immigrant group had been imbued with the most feared qualities of that same immigrant group: that they would take white people's jobs; have sex with their women, polluting their purity; and, in the case of black men in particular, kill them (perhaps in retribution for the generations during which they were kept as slaves.) The implication was that if the drug could be done away with, the immigrant groups might magically become acculturated and harmless. But as long as they continued to use the drug, they were unacceptable as employees or neighbors.

CRACK COCAINE

In late 1984 and 1985 a new form of cocaine appeared in New York, Los Angeles, and Miami. By processing the cocaine with a chemical base such as baking powder, it could be turned into a "rock" that was cheap and, when smoked, produced a powerful if short-lasting high. Because the substance was addictive, the smoker would crave more crack and soon become a regular customer, often turning to desperate measures to support the habit, such as prostitution, burglary, or robbery. Because crack cocaine was bought one or two doses at a time, the purchaser was far more likely to get arrested than wealthy addicts, who purchased cocaine in large amounts at less frequent intervals. Often the wealthier addicts could avoid the ghetto completely. Because of the size of the transactions, the dealers would assume more of the risk, traveling to visit them in their offices in the better parts of town.[60]

As the crack business flourished, more and more sellers individuals and runners were required to produce and distribute the drug. Juveniles, because they were willing to take the risk and were rarely pulled into court, seemed like a logical choice. The possibility of becoming a drug lord, driving an SUV, wearing expensive jewelry, and drinking champagne held considerable appeal. It was a high-status identity in a neighborhood where few other opportunities existed, and consequently it was worth the risk.

It was assumed that the juveniles would carry guns "because that industry [having no recourse to legal remedies] uses guns as an important instrument for dispute resolution."[61] The juveniles were likely to be carrying thousands of dollars in cash or bags of illegal drugs and were ready targets for competing drug dealers and other predators. During the height of the "crack epidemic, the period between 1985 and 1993, the homicide rate for men over 30 remained unchanged but the rate of gun homicides committed by juveniles quadrupled."[62] The arrest rate for juveniles of color charged with drug-related crimes doubled while that of white juveniles remained the same.

To recap, hiring and wage discrimination leads to unemployment and poor pay; this, combined with housing and loan discrimination, keeps minorities in ghettoes. Because they are shut off from the mainstream economy, ghettoes create their own economy, an underground economy. Because the businesses within these economies function outside the law, disputes are often settled through violence, or the threat of violence. The "Wild West capitalism" of crack cocaine only worsened the situation. The proliferation of handgun violence resulted in a record number of homicides. Discriminatory sentencing laws, overcrowded courtrooms, and overworked public defenders contributed to the mass incarceration of black men.

So, despite the fact that blacks have lived in this country longer than most other ethnicities; despite efforts of civil rights activists, some of whom gave their lives to further the cause; despite the legislation intended to create fairness and equality between the races; despite the millions upon millions of students who pass through social studies classes in schoolrooms across the nation and learn that all people should be treated as equals and recite the pledge of allegiance with the words, "With liberty and justice for all"; despite the lip service paid to racial equality by progressive and conservative adults; and despite the fact that the president of the United States is himself a black man, blacks continue to be discriminated against by almost all white Americans who have any power over hiring and firing people, selling homes to them, lending them money to buy homes or start businesses, enforcing laws, and trying them in courts of law.

Any advancement that takes place in any of the aforementioned areas appears to be tokenism: one black man here, one black woman there. The question is: Why in twenty-first-century America do we continue to cling to our racism despite everything? Are we so deeply ashamed of having excluded blacks from our dominant culture for so many years that we must keep alive the myth of their imagined moral and intellectual deficits simply to justify our own bad behavior?

MEXICANS

As of 2011 Hispanics accounted for 51,927,000[63] (17 percent) of the 310, 500,000[64] Americans living in the United States. The US Census Bureau has estimated that by 2043 whites will no longer constitute a majority of the population.[65] When the Census Bureau made this announcement, many people mistook it to mean that the majority of the population would be Hispanic. In fact, white, non-Hispanics will remain a plurality. In other words, Hispanics will constitute a larger group than other ethnicities in the United States, such as whites, Asians, African Americans, Caribbean islanders, and so on, but they will not be larger than half of all those other groups combined. Within the group of non-whites, Hispanics will become an ever-larger segment, exceeding 30 percent by 2060.[66] Consequently, they seem to pose the greatest threat to the dominant culture and are the targets of much of the shame/rage.

Sixty-five percent (33,539,000) of the US Hispanic population are Mexicans. This number might be considered surprisingly low if we recall that much of the US Southwest was originally part of Mexico. The border shared by Arizona and the Mexican state of Sonora is of particular interest to us because it has come to represent our fear of Hispanic culture swallowing up white Western European culture. It has taken on the properties of an inconsequential birth, ark suddenly revealed as a life-threatening malignancy. People seem to believe that if we can just secure this particular border, we will no longer need to worry about the influx of toxic immigrants.

In November of 2005 the Department of Homeland Security announced the Secure Border Initiative (SBI), a multibillion-dollar program to stop undocumented immigrants from illegally crossing the borders of the United States. One component of the plan was the SBI Tactical Infrastructure, a fancy name for a fence along the parts of the US/Mexico shared border that seemed most vulnerable to smuggling and illegal entry.[67] The cost of the fencing varied because of the difficulties posed by the terrain, the costs of building materials and labor, the price of acquiring privately owned real estate, and the type of fence being constructed (e.g., pedestrian fence or the more robust motor vehicle fence). In areas of frequent border crossings, two rows of fencing were erected for double protection. By October 31, 2008, US Customs and Border Patrol had completed 140 miles of pedestrian fencing at an average cost of $3.9 million a mile, and 75 miles of vehicle fencing at an average cost of $1 million a mile.[68]

In addition to the fencing, more money was invested in a second initiative, SBInet, a system of radars, sensors, and cameras arranged to "detect, identify, and classify the threat level associated with an illegal entry into the United States."[69] These two initiatives combined with other costs such as salaries and training for 18,500 border agents and administration brought the cost to tens of billions of dollars.

In 2011 the SBI apprehended some 327,000 individuals. Of these, 20,000 were smuggling drugs, although the statistics do not reflect the seriousness of the infractions (e.g., whether they involved drug cartels moving massive amounts of methamphetamine across the border in all-terrain-vehicles or an entrepreneurial teenager with a few ounces of marijuana concealed in his backpack. As for terrorists, there were 253 ASICs (Aliens from Special Interest Countries) but no indication that any of them were involved in terrorist activities.[70]

THE WORLD TRADE CENTER

One obvious reason for securing our foreign borders stemmed from the destruction of the World Trade Center in 2001. If a rag-tag team of poorly trained terrorists from distant lands could destroy the World Trade Center, who knew what devastation might be wreaked by the millions with whom we share our borders? A whole "nonfiction" genre of Mexican/US border enforcement literature emerged following 9/11 that seemed driven by this idea. The word "invasion" appears more than 45 times in *Minutemen: The Battle to Secure America's Borders*,[71] 13 times in *Illegals: The Immigrant Threat Posed by our Unsecured U.S. Mexican Borders*,[72] 137 times in *Border War: Invasion USA*,[73] and a whopping 194 times in *Immigration's Unarmed Invasion: Deadly Consequences*,[74] to name only a few. In *Border War*, the image of the Trojan Horse is conjured repeatedly to describe the way the harmless appearance of Mexicans conceals their true ambition to take over the United States.

The tragic loss of life in the destruction of the World Trade Center seemed to have exposed our country's true vulnerability. Were we still a super power? Or had our gradual reduction in military strength following the fall of the Soviet Union made us soft? Had the time come to bypass the government and take matters into our own hands?

In other words, was it time for vigilantism?

THE MINUTEMAN MOVEMENT

On October 1, 2004, Jim Gilchrist, a businessman and accountant, and Chris Simcox, a former actor, rock and roll drummer, elementary school teacher, and newspaper owner, cofounded the Minuteman Project. They were two very different kinds of people, but they had something in common: they both felt that the Federal government was doing an inadequate job of policing US borders, in particular that troublesome stretch separating Cochise County, Arizona, from Sonora, Mexico.

Gilchrist, born in 1949, moved out of the family home when he was 17, after years of abuse by his father and stepfather, and supported himself working at a car wash while he finished high school. He enlisted in the marines and fought in Vietnam, where he was wounded and received a Purple Heart. Afterward he finished college with degrees in journalism and business administration and an MBA in taxation. He qualified as a CPA and pursued a career in business.[75]

Simcox was born in 1961 in rural Illinois, the son of a machinist, a "Goldwater-type conservative" who raised the American flag every morning at 6 AM. His mother, a cardiac care nurse, divorced his father and took Chris to Kentucky. He spent much of his youth bouncing back and forth between the two homes. After graduating high school, he pursued an unsuccessful career as a pro baseball player and a drummer in a band. He moved to New York City, where he claims to have been "mugged twice by people who didn't speak English."[76] He married, had a daughter, and moved to Los Angeles to pursue a career as an actor. In Los Angeles he earned an associate's degree and a bachelor's degree in education from L.A. Pacific Oaks County College. His first teaching job was at "a very bad high school in South Central L.A., in the middle of Bloods and Crips warfare."[77] A job teaching kindergarten through third grade at an affluent private school was more to his liking, and he remained there for 13 years. In 1998 his daughter from his first marriage, turning 14, came to stay with him during the summer. The stay was cut short when she claimed that he had molested her. She did not press charges and the incident was never investigated, but mother and daughter avoided further contact with him.[78]

While September 11 was a seminal event in both men's lives, Simcox's reaction was more histrionic. The following day he changed the message on his answering machine:

> Hi, this is Chris. You have reached a righteous American educational institution. Due to the horrific changes in our society in the last few days, I now must preface that I will accept offers of communication only from people who preface their message with the preamble to the Constitution of the United States of America. If you include that with your message, I look forward to communicating with you, and have a great day. Thanks. Bye.[79]

According to his second wife, Kim Dunbar, he had been prone to sudden violent rages throughout their marriage, once threatening to kill himself with a kitchen knife, but after 9/11 he began to ruminate about stockpiling weapons and apocalyptic premonitions. During a phone call to his son, he gave this advice:

> "You better stop playing baseball, buddy, and you better do something real, 'cause life will never be the same. I'm going to go down to the Mexican border

and sign up for the government for border patrol to protect the borders of the country that I love. You hear how serious I am."

But what, his son inquired, would become of his cat, Moe?

"Moe may end up on the dead pile," Simcox responded.[80]

Fearing that he was suffering a mental breakdown and had become dangerous, Ms. Dunbar filed an emergency appeal for full custody of their son.

By the end of the month, Simcox had fled Los Angeles for good, figuring the city was "doomed." In October, during a 40-day solo camping trip in Arizona's Organ Pipe Cactus National Monument, he reported encountering platoons of illegal aliens and "five paramilitary groups of drug dealers just driving caravans of vehicles right into this country."[81] Following this second "transformative" event, he moved to Tombstone, Arizona, a town of 4 square miles and 1,300 inhabitants, 35 miles from the Mexican border. He initially found work as a performer in the Helldorado Gunfight Theater and Restaurant (with performances every half hour: "You'll cotton to our Cervesa's Cantina, restaurant, shoot'n gallery, pan for gold, mini-golf and more!")[82] and later as an assistant editor at the *Tombstone Tumbleweed*, a local advertising handout and community event calendar. In August of 2002 Simcox bought the paper for $60,000 by cashing in his retirement account or, according to an earlier account, "drain[ing] his son's college fund."[83] Simcox turned the paper into a mouthpiece for his anti-immigrationist views and began organizing border patrols on the weekends. He and a group of four to six volunteers would drive down to the border, set up deck chairs, and spend the weekend keeping watch.[84]

When Gilchrist heard about this, he contacted Simcox and suggested that he had "created a springboard from which they could launch a movement against illegal immigration." It was time to take it "to the next level . . . to take the concept of civilian border guards and make it national. It was time for the Minute Man Project."[85] They agreed to begin the project on April 1, 2005, choosing the date because it was "exactly 230 years after" the beginning of the American Revolution.

Gilchrist writes, in his account of the demonstration that

by the kickoff date of April 1, 2005, almost one thousand volunteers from all over the United States answered Jim Gilchrist's call to defend their nation. Armed with only binoculars, cell phones, and lawn chairs, the silent majority rolled into the southwestern desert to prove to their countrymen that even a large border could indeed be guarded.

For thirty days the Minutemen successfully guarded a twenty-three mile stretch of border from invasion. After stopping all illegal crossings following just ten days on the job, they spent the next twenty days stoically standing watch as television crews and radio hosts broadcast news of their success to the nation.

The question of whether or not America's porous borders could be guarded had been settled. The Minutemen Project had proven that all it required was the will to do so.[86]

Roxanne Doty, a professor of political science at the University of Arizona, visited the office of the *Tombstone Tumbleweed*, ground zero of the Minuteman Project, on that day and recorded her impressions:

> The *Tombstone Tumbleweed* newspaper office is located in a tiny, single-story house with an old-fashioned front porch and a small yard surrounded by a white picket fence ... [A] wanted poster of the 9/11 highjackers is taped to the outside of the door compliments of Veterans for Secure Borders. Next to this poster is another with photos of Pima County, Arizona's most wanted, all burly-looking young men with Hispanic surnames. The intent behind this juxtaposition is clear.
>
> Inside, the office is a bustle of activity and clutter of papers. The phone rings incessantly. A poster with the words "Article IV, Section 4 of the U.S. Constitution—Every State in this Union shall be protected against invasion. Protect U.S. Citizens. Secure Our Borders," printed in large, bold black letters against a white background hangs on the wall.[87]

Concerned about the tidal wave of supporters who would be arriving in their very small town, Simcox had arranged for supporters to stay at RV parks in the area and at the dormitory of a local Bible college. When contacted, the people who ran the facilities in question told a reporter that they had reservations for only 150.[88] Another observer wrote that the volunteers had been "trickling" into the *Tombstone Telegraph* office for their assignments and that most of them were retirees. Walter McCarty, an 82-year-old retired Marine sergeant, said he had come down looking for adventure. "I hope to go out on patrols at night, find some illegals ... I'm restless. I needed something to do before I drove my wife crazy."[89]

McCarty brought a firearm, a .38-caliber pistol, as did many of the other volunteers. Project Minuteman had been promoted as "a citizens' Neighborhood Watch on our border,"[90] an image meant to reassure the public that this was not a violent, militia-type organization that would act outside the law. The tension between merely alerting the official Border Patrol to undocumented immigrants and personally detaining them or taking violent action against them was an ongoing issue on civilian border patrols. President Bush, learning of Project Minuteman, had publically warned them about vigilante actions.

The Southern Poverty Law Center, in their quarterly intelligence report, wrote "Vigilante border patrols are a magnet for violent racists."[91] Indeed, the Aryan Nation had announced the initiative on its website, characterizing it as a "call for action on the part of all Aryan soldiers."[92] J. T. (Jason Todd) Ready, a neo-Nazi, and some of his companions were among those who showed up for the Minutemen Project, but Ready was expelled for handing out white supremacist literature among the volunteers. Ready would be apprehended twice in 2011 for forcibly detaining immigrants in the Sonora desert. He ended his life in 2012 after killing his girlfriend, her daughter, her daughter's boyfriend, and the daughter's 15-month-old baby girl.[93] After his death, the FBI revealed that he had been the subject of a federal domestic terrorism investigation.

Mexicans were understandably offended by Project Minuteman. The mayor of Douglas, a nearby town of 15,000, told *The New York Times*, "We are a proud, mostly Hispanic community. I'm afraid these people who are showing up for the Minuteman Project have a lynch mob attitude."[94]

THE GREAT WALL

Simcox decided he could no longer work with Gilchrist for reasons never made public. He quit the Minuteman Project and, partnering with J. T. Ready, formed a splinter group, the Minuteman Civil Defense Corp (MCDC).[95] The Minuteman Project had attracted the attention of conservative talk radio and cable news shows and opened doors to the offices of important anti-immigrationist politicians.[96] In October, six US Congressmen strapped on their handguns (those with permits) and participated in border patrols to publicize Don Goldwater's run for governor. Simcox met with California Governor Arnold Schwartznegger and Texas Governor Rick Perry, who both publically endorsed the Minuteman patrols.[97] He used his new-found media notoriety to raise money for an "Israeli style" border fence to keep out immigrants. In emails to MCDC members he promised to build 2,000 miles of state-of-the-art border-style fencing at a cost of $55 million dollars.[98] Simcox described the fence as "our high-tech, double-layered gauntlet of deterrent." It would be 14 feet high, with security cameras and sensors, topped with razor wire and flanked by ditches to stop vehicles. Members, excited by his vision (and perhaps unaware that the Federal Strategic Border Initiative was to begin a border fence of similar description, in the same place, at about the same time) began making donations, with one member, Jim Campbell, going so far as to mortgage his home and contribute more than $100,000.

A groundbreaking ceremony was held on Memorial Day of 2006 on the cattle ranch of John Ladd, a wealthy and respected Arizona rancher. His family had owned the property, which spread over 14,000 acres on either side of the Mexican border, for 118 years. Minutemen, who had gathered at the site to be part of what they anticipated as a great event, were stunned to see that the fence they had financed was a conventional cow fence strung with five-strand barbed wire. Members of the MCDC demanded that Simcox meet them in person to address their concerns about how their donations had been spent. Campbell sued Simcox for his $100,000, as well as $1,220,845 in damages. Simcox became difficult to contact, often failing to return phone calls or emails. With little fanfare, he moved to Scottsdale and took a job as an hourly worker at iMemories, a company that converts home movies and photos into digital files.[99]

Gilchrist had meanwhile partnered with Jerome R. Corsi, a right-wing conspiracy theorist, to author a book called *Minutemen: The Battle to Secure America's Borders*,[100] to draw attention to the problem of undocumented immigrants in the United States. While the book attempts to present a balanced picture of the situation, it continually refers to undocumented immigrants as part of an "invasion." The book also presents questionable statistics: for example, that 10 to 20 percent of the undocumented immigrants are criminals and another 10 percent will become criminals once they enter the United States; that open borders would create a welfare state; and that the influx of undereducated Mexicans would dumb down America, undermining its "super power" status.

When House member Christopher Cox, representative for California's 48th congressional district, resigned to become chairman of the Securities and Exchange Commission, Gilchrist ran for the vacated seat as the American Independent Party candidate. He campaigned as a social conservative, keeping immigration reform in the spotlight, but was defeated by Republican state Senator John Campbell.

In 2007 the group's board of directors fired Gilchrist and his executive director over allegations of mismanagement and fraud. They accused him of embezzling $400,000 in Minuteman Project donations and using $13,000 of the organization's money to pay his own legal fees. Gilchrist countered that the board had also mismanaged money. He said he was so busy crisscrossing the country, publicizing the movement that he did not have time to "cross every 'T' and dot every 'I.'"

Simcox returned to the public eye on June 19, 2013, when he was arrested by the Phoenix Police on multiple counts related to molesting three little girls. One was his daughter (from his third marriage; the daughter he had molested previously was from his first marriage) and the other two, her friends. They were all under 10 years old. One girl told her mother that Simcox had told her "secrets" and showed her explicit movies while molesting her. A second girl had revealed, during a forensic interview, that Simcox had bribed her with candy to see her panties and her genitals.

It would be unfair and inaccurate to say that Jim Gilchrist and Chris Simcox were representative of all the men and women who volunteered for the various Minutemen groups that flourished after 9/11, but they are useful for understanding how racism can be hidden and practiced at the same time. The very name of the organization links it to one of the noblest events in American history. It was further fueled by its popularity with conservative political groups and pundits. Gilchrist and Simcox, for example, were guests on the Fox News Channel's program, *Hannity & Colmes* on at least eight occasions (April 5, 7, 8, 11, 13, 18, 2005; April 3, 2006; May 9, 2007).

What was the appeal of being a Minuteman? Minutemen could play the part of an authority figure and dress like a soldier. Because of the nature of their "mission," they felt free to bully and demean Mexicans. Perhaps more than any other ordeal, the process of undocumented boarder crossing strips immigrants of any status they had ever achieved in their homeland. Were they honest men or women? reliable workers? loving parents? skillful artists or artisans? No matter who they had been, by entering the United States without papers, they became legal and social nobodies. Those who had survived mistreatment at the hands of the "coyotes," (the often unscrupulous men hired to lead them to the United States,) and crossed the desolate Sonoran desert, sometimes literally crawling on hands and knees, were physically, emotionally, and economically depleted. They would not fight back and they could not run. They had no advocates to argue their cases. They were perfect victims.

NOTES

1. "Clippers Owner Donald Sterling to GF—Don't Bring Black People to My Games ... Including Magic Johnson," TMZSports, April 25, 2014,

http://www.tmz.com/2014/04/26/donald-sterling-clippers-owner-black-people-racist-audio-magic-johnson/.

2. Ibid.

3. Jack Wang, "Inside the Clippers," *Anderson Cooper 360°* (CNN, May 13, 2014), http://www.insidesocal.com/clippers/2014/05/13/full-transcript-donald-sterlings-interview-with-cnns-anderson-cooper/.

4. Richard Lapchick, *The 2013 Racial and Gender Report Card: National Basketball Association*, Executive Summary (Orlando, FL: Institute for Diversity and Ethics in Sport, June 25, 2013).

5. "UCLA Rejects Donald Sterling Gift," UCLA University News, April 29, 2014, http://newsroom.ucla.edu/releases/ucla-rejects-donald-sterling-gift.

6. "UCLA to Donald Sterling: We Don't Want Your Money!" TMZ Sports, April 29, 2014, http://www.tmz.com/2014/04/29/donald-sterling-ucla-gift-money-racist/.

7. Editors, "UCLA Rejects."

8. Jamie Hais, Department of Justice spokesperson as quoted in Patrick Range McDonald, "Donald T. Sterling Fakes His Philanthropy in a New *Los Angeles Times* Ad," *LA Weekly*, August 20, 2008, http://www.laweekly.com/2008-08-21/news/donald-t-sterling-fakes-his-philanthropy-in-a-new-los-angeles-times-ad/.

9. Ibid.

10. "Kyle Doss Wants Reparations for Kramer Calling Him a Nigger," NBC, 2006, https://www.youtube.com/watch?v=2VFGv0mdckM&feature=youtube_gdata_player.

11. "'Kramer's' Racist Tirade—Caught on Tape," TMZ Sports, November 20, 2006, http://www.tmz.com/2006/11/20/kramers-racist-tirade-caught-on-tape/.

12. There is to my knowledge no academic or medical literature on "flop sweat."

13. Thandeka, *Learning to Be White: Money, Race and God in America* (New York: Continuum, 2000).

14. Ibid., 5–6.

15. Ibid., 6.

16. Ibid., 2.

17. Samuel A. Cartwright, "Diseases and Peculiarities of the Negro Race," *DeBow's Review*, 1851, http://www.pbs.org/wgbh/aia/part4/4h3106t.html.

18. Ibid.

19. Richard J. Herrnstein and Charles Murray, *The Bell Curve: Intelligence and Class Structure in American Life*, 1st Free Press paperback ed. (New York: Free Press, 1996).

20. Ulric Neisser et al., "Intelligence: Knowns and Unknowns," *American Psychologist* 51, no. 2 (1996): 77–101.

21. Stephen Jay Gould, *The Mismeasure of Man*, rev. and exp. ed. (New York: W. W. Norton, 1996).

22. John U. Ogbu, *Minority Education and Caste: The American System in Cross-Cultural Perspective* (New York: Academic Press, 1978).

23. John U. Ogbu, "From Cultural Differences to Differences in Cultural Frame of Reference," in *Cross-Cultural Roots of Minority Child Development*, ed. P. M. Greenfield and R. R. Cocking (Hillsdale, NJ: Lawrence Erlbaum Associates, 1994), 365–391.

24. Neisser et al., "Intelligence," 94.

25. Ogbu, *Minority Education and Caste*.

26. Roger Pearson, *Race, Intelligence and Bias in Academe*, 2nd ed. (Washington, DC: Scott Townsend, 1997), 34–38.

27. Edwin Black, "The Horrifying American Roots of Nazi Eugenics," History News Network, September 2003, http://historynewsnetwork.org/article/1796.

28. David Starr Jordan, *The Blood of the Nation: A Study of the Decay of Races Through Survival of the Unfit* (Boston: American Unitarian Association, 1902), 11.

29. August C. Bolino, *Men of Massachusetts: Bay State Contributors to American Society* (Lincoln, NE: iUniverse, 2012).

30. "Hooten Finds Man Reverting to Ape; Harvard Professor Warns Lag in Biological Development Threatens Civilization; Derides Mechanical Ease; Tells Engineers Genius Like Theirs Must Find Means of Improving Race Calls for Race Improvement Mankind 'Coasting Downhill' Machines Get Better, Man Worse," *The New York Times*, December 9, 1937.

31. Ibid.

32. Paul A. Lombardo, "Nazi Eugenics and the Origins of the Pioneer Fund," *Albany Law Review* 65, no. 3 (n.d.): 822.

33. Edwin Black, *War Against the Weak: Eugenics and America's Campaign to Create a Master Race, Expanded Edition*, exp. ed. (Washington, DC: Dialog Press, 2012).

34. Keneth Kinnamon and Michel Fabre, *Conversations with Richard Wright* (Jackson: University Press of Mississippi, 1993), 99.

35. Lincoln Quillian, "New Approaches to Understanding Racial Prejudice and Discrimination," *Annual Review of Sociology* 32 (2006): 299–328.

36. H. Cross et al., *Differential Treatment of Hispanic and Anglo Job Seekers: Hiring Practices in Two Cities* (Washington, DC: Urban Institute, 1989); Margery Austin Turner, Michael Fix, and Raymond J. Struyk, *Opportunities Denied, Opportunities Diminished: Racial Discrimination in Hiring* (Washington, DC: Urban Institute Press, 1991); Michael Fix and Raymond Struyk, *Clear and Convincing Evidence: Measurement of Discrimination in America* (Washington, DC: Urban Institute Press, 1993; Marc Bendick, Charles W. Jackson, and Victor A. Reinoso, "Measuring Employment Discrimination through Controlled Experiments," *The Review of Black Political Economy* 23, no. 1 (1994): 25–48.

37. M. Bertrand and Mullainathan, "Are Emily and Brendan More Employable than Latoya and Tyrone? Evidence on Racial Discrimination in the Labor Market from a Large Randomized," *American Economic Review* 94, no. 4 (2004): 991–1013.

38. Ibid., 2.

39. $792 for whites, $621 for blacks. US Bureau of Labor Statistics, *Labor Force Characteristics by Race and Ethnicity, 2012* (Washington, DC: US Bureau of Labor Statistics, October 2013), http://www.bls.gov/cps/cpsrace2012.pdf.

40. Margery A. Turner et al., "Discrimination in Metropolitan Housing Markets: National Results from Phase 1 of the Housing Discrimination Study (HDS)," Working paper (Storrs: University of Connecticut, Department of Economics, 2002), http://ideas.repec.org/p/uct/uconnp/2002-16.html.

41. Alicia H. Munnell et al., "Mortgage Lending in Boston: Interpreting HMDA Data," *The American Economic Review* 86, no. 1 (1996): 25–53.

42. For a detailed review of critiques of the study, see Devah Pager and Hana Shepherd, "The Sociology of Discrimination: Racial Discrimination in Employment, Housing, Credit, and Consumer Markets," *Annual Review of Sociology* 34, no. 1 (January 1, 2008): 181–209.

43. Thomas M. Shapiro and Melvin L. Oliver, *Black Wealth/ White Wealth: A New Perspective on Racial Inequality*, 1st ed. (New York: Routledge, 1997), 86.

44. Sudhir Alladi Venkatesh, *Off the Books: The Underground Economy of the Urban Poor* (Cambridge, MA: Harvard University Press, 2006).

45. Ibid.

46. Ibid., 8.

47. Venkatesh, *Off the Books*.

48. Ibid.

49. Ibid., 139.

50. Ibid., 48.

51. Ibid., 140.

52. Nathan Luno, "Prohibition in America: A Brief History," TheDEA.org, June 12, 2003, http://thedea.org/prohibhistory.html.

53. Arthur B. Reeve, "Fortune Hunters (A Serialized Novel): Chapter IV, The Weed of Madness," *The San Francisco Chronicle*, January 17, 1923, 14.

54. Martin A. Lee, *Smoke Signals: A Social History of Marijuana—Medical, Recreational and Scientific* (New York: Simon & Schuster, 2013).

55. Luno, "Prohibition in America."

56. Luno, "Prohibition in America."

57. Jill Jonnes, *Hep-Cats, Narcs, and Pipe Dreams: A History of America's Romance with Illegal Drugs* (Baltimore: Johns Hopkins University Press, 1996), 25.

58. Edward Huntington Williams, "Negro Cocaine 'Fiends' Are a New Southern Menace; Murder and Insanity Increasing Among Lower Class Blacks Because They Have Taken to 'Sniffing' Since Deprived of Whisky by Prohibition," *The New York Times*, February 8, 1914, http://query.nytimes.com/mem/archive-free/pdf?res=9901E5D61F3BE633A2575BC0A9649C946596D6CF.

59. Ibid.

60. Alfred Blumstein, Frederick P. Rivara, and Richard Rosenfeld, "The Rise and Decline of Homicide—and Why," *Annual Review of Public Health* 21, no. 1 (2000): 505–41.

61. Ibid.

62. Ibid.

63. Pew Research: Hispanic Trends Project, *2011 Hispanic Origin Profiles*, Pew Research, July 22, 2014, http://www.pewhispanic.org/.

64. US Census Bureau, "U.S. and World Population Clock," US Census Bureau, n.d., http://www.census.gov/popclock/.

65. Michael Cooper, "U.S. Will Have No Ethnic Majority, Census Finds," *The New York Times*, December 12, 2012, http://www.nytimes.com/2012/12/13/us/us-will-have-no-ethnic-majority-census-finds.html.

66. Ibid.

67. Richard M. Stana, *Secure Border Initiative Fence Construction Costs* (Darby, PA: Diane Publishing, 2009).

68. Ibid.

69. Ibid., 1.

70. US Government Accountability Office, *Border Patrol: Key Elements of New Strategic Plan Not Yet in Place to Inform Border Security Status and Resource Needs* (Washington DC: US Government Accountability Office, December 2012), 21, http://www.gao.gov/assets/660/650730.pdf.

71. Jim Gilchrist and Jerome R. Corsi, *Minutemen: The Battle to Secure America's Borders*, 1st ed. (Los Angeles, CA: World Ahead, 2006).

72. Jon E. Dougherty, *Illegals: The Imminent Threat Posed by Our Unsecured U.S.-Mexico Border* (Nashville: Thomas Nelson, 2004).

73. William W. Johnstone, *Border War (Invasion USA)* (New York: Pinnacle, 2006).

74. Frosty Wooldridge, *Immigration's Unarmed Invasion: Deadly Consequences*, 1st ed. (Bloomington, IN: AuthorHouse, 2004).

75. Gilchrist and Corsi, *Minutemen*.

76. Susy Buchanan and David Holthouse, "Minuteman Civil Defense Corps Leader Chris Simcox Has Troubled Past," Southern Poverty Law Center, *Intelligence Report* (Winter 2005), para. 15, http://www.splcenter.org/get-informed/intelligence-report/browse-all-issues/2005/winter/the-little-prince.

77. Dennis Wagner, "Minuteman's Goal: To Shame Feds into Action," *USA Today*, May 25, 2006, http://usatoday30.usatoday.com/news/nation/2006- 05-24-minuteman-goals_x.htm.

78. Buchanan and Holthouse, "Minuteman Civil Defense Corps Leader," para. 65.

79. Ibid., para. 10.

80. Ibid., para. 41, 42.

81. Ibid.

82. "Helldorado Gunfight Theatre and Restaurant—Tombstone—Reviews of Helldorado Gunfight Theatre and Restaurant," Trip Advisor, accessed October 20, 2014, http://www.tripadvisor.com/ Attraction_Review-g31381-d1382694-Reviews-Helldorado_Gunfight_Theatre_and_Restaurant-Tombstone_ Arizona.html#REVIEWS.

83. Buchanan and Holthouse, "Minuteman Civil Defense Corps Leader."

84. Gilchrist and Corsi, *Minutemen*, 5.

85. Ibid., 6.

86. Ibid., 8.

87. Roxanne Lynn Doty, "States of Exception on the Mexico–U.S. Border: Security, 'Decisions', and Civilian Border Patrols," *International Political Sociology* 1, no. 2 (June 1, 2007): 113–114.

88. Timothy Egan, "Wanted: Border Hoppers. And Some Excitement, Too," *The New York Times*, April 1, 2005, http://www.nytimes.com/2005/04/01/national/01border.html.

89. Ibid.

90. Wagner, "Minuteman's Goal."

91. Buchanan and Holthouse, "Minuteman Civil Defense Corps Leader."

92. Aryan Nation website as quoted in Egan, "Wanted."

93. "J.T. Ready," Southern Poverty Law Center," accessed October 13, 2014, http://www.splcenter.org/get-informed/intelligence-files/profiles/jt-ready.

94. Egan, "Wanted."

95. Hunter Walker, "Minuteman Founder Doesn't Want To Be Confused With Alleged Murderer," *New York Observer*, accessed October 17, 2014, http://observer.com/2012/05/minuteman-founder-doesnt-want-to-be-confused-with-alleged-murderer/.

96. Tim Murphy, "The Meltdown of the Anti-Immigration Minuteman Militia," Mother Jones, accessed August 28, 2014, http://www.motherjones.com/politics/2014/08/minuteman-movement-border-crisis-simcox.

97. Buchanan and Holthouse, "Minuteman Civil Defense Corps Leader," para. 25.

98. Abbie Boudreau and Ken Shiffman, "Minuteman's High-Tech Border Barrier Called 'a Cow Fence,'" CNN, US edition, November 7, 2007, http://www.cnn.com/2007/US/11/07/border.fence/.

99. Stephen Lemons, "Chris Simcox Worked for iMemories, Duties Didn't Include Viewing Kid Pics, Says Company, Arizona Treasurer Doug Ducey Recently Company's Board Chair (w/Update)," Feathered Bastard, June 25, 2013, http://blogs.phoenixnewtimes.com/bastard/2013/06/chris_simcox_worked_for_imemor.php.

100. Gilchrist and Corsi, *Minutemen*.

CHAPTER 7

Failures in Shame Management

School Shootings and Acts of Domestic Terrorism

The history of school violence in modern-day America begins with the Bath, Michigan Consolidated School bombing of 1927,[1] which remains the worst school disaster in history. On May 18, Andrew Kehoe, a 55-year-old farmer, blew up a recently constructed elementary school killing 38 school children and 6 adults and injuring 58 others.

Kehoe was considered a highly intelligent man. He had a degree in electrical engineering from Michigan State University. He was meticulously neat, changing his shirt twice a day, even when it was only lightly soiled. Kehoe seemed to have a Jekyll and Hyde personality, sometimes appearing to be the soul of kindness and at other times quite cruel. Once he beat a horse to death. He spent much of his time trying to increase the efficiency of his tractor by towing more mowers or rollers. According to one neighbor, "He spent so much time tinkering that he didn't prosper."[2] His fascination with mechanical farming may have come from his background in engineering, or it might have been because he had no sons to work the land for him—no children at all in fact, even though he came from a family with 13 brother and sisters—or it might have been because he was very, very cheap and did not want to spend money hiring farm hands.

Kehoe's mother died when he was very young, and his father eventually remarried. He disliked his stepmother intensely. When he was 14, the kitchen stove exploded while his stepmother was trying to light it, dousing her with flaming oil. Young Kehoe threw a bucket of water on her, feeding the flames. A rumor spread that he had tinkered with the stove, altering it in ways that would assure the malfunction. Even if he had intended to kill her, witnessing her incineration was certainly not what he had bargained for. How could he have anticipated the horror of watching a human being burn or the grief it would cause his father and the community?

Kehoe had been school board treasurer and often fought to lower property taxes even though it would impair quality of education. On several occasions he accused Emory Huyck, the superintendent of schools, of financial mismanagement. When the school board began to consider combining the local one-room school houses that dotted the countryside into a big, new, consolidated school building, Kehoe fought it tooth and nail. The local schools were doing well enough, he said, and, furthermore, it would raise taxes. The board approved the consolidation, and Kehoe took it as a personal defeat.

At about the same time he learned that his wife was dying of tuberculosis and that the bank was foreclosing on his farm because he could not meet the mortgage payments. While he was treasurer of the school board he had temporarily taken the position of town clerk and was hoping to be reelected to that office, which paid a small salary an opponent was elected instead.

Kehoe stopped working his farm. He began purchasing dynamite and pyrotol (an incendiary chemical once used by farmers to remove tree stumps and clear brush) and secretly placing explosives around the new school and in his home, in parts of the foundation where they would do the most damage. He used timed detonators so he might synchronize the destruction of both sites.

On May 16 or 17, he killed his wife, and on the 18th, a Wednesday, at 8:45 AM, when the children were all in their classes, he set the detonators and watched the destruction of his home from a safe distance. The ground-shaking *thud* of the dynamite and the sight of a black funnel of smoke rising in the distance assured him that the school had also been destroyed. As the final part of the plan, he drove his truck to the smoldering remains of the school where the superintendent and a dozen other men were already occupied, trying to free children who had been buried under piles of brick and fallen beams. Still sitting in his truck, he rolled down the window and called Emory Huyck over to his truck as if to convey some important message. When Huyck was inches away, Kehoe ignited explosives he had hidden in the truck's chassis, killing both of them and two other adults who had the misfortune to be standing nearby.

Kehoe had experienced early shame by causing or contributing to the death of his stepmother. I call this "distal shame" to distinguish it from the shaming event later in life ("proximal shame") that precipitates an act of suicide, or a rampage killing, or both.[3] Most public acts of suicide or rampage killing seem to follow this pattern.

ROBERT BECHTEL

Another little-known case of school violence occurred at Swarthmore College in 1955. A student named Robert Bechtel, a junior, killed Francis Holmes Strozier, a sophomore, by opening the door to his dorm room, while he was sleeping, identifying him with a flashlight, and then shooting him in the head with a rifle. Bechtel then "ran through the three-story structure, firing the six bullets remaining in the clip of the .22 caliber rifle, and trying to open the doors of other [dorm] rooms"[4] which were, by now, all locked. Had he gained access to these rooms and been in possession of an automatic firearm, this would have qualified as perhaps the first of the school shooting massacres that we have come to dread in recent years.

Bechtel had been bullied since the age of four. He cried easily and often throughout his childhood, and other children provoked him just to see his face distort in misery and the outpouring of tears. Apparently there was something comical about this. In response he trained himself to be stony-faced when bullied or teased. He had a brief psychiatric hospitalization when he was 17 because of feelings of persecution.

When he became an upperclassman at Swarthmore, he was given the job of freshman dormitory proctor in exchange for free room and board. Many of the 25 students in his care found him an irresistible target for pranks and ridicule, even as a young adult. "Last week pranksters tossed Bechtel's bed through his bedroom window and set fire to wastepaper baskets . . . [T]he hazers exploded firecrackers and acetylene 'bombs' in the dormitory building and accused him of being a 'long-hair' without a sense of humor."[5] They tormented him by urinating on his bed, rolling a 16-pound shot-put ball into his door, and taking up obscene chants.[6]

While most Swarthmore students of that era were from wealthy, distinguished families, Bechtel was the son of a single mom, a divorced waitress. He attended a private secondary school and Swarthmore on scholarship. He also worked two hours a night bussing tables at a local restaurant.

Fifty years later, Bechtel was interviewed for a documentary film about the shooting:

> A lot of people have this idea that I must have been angry or enraged or something [during the shootings] . . . Actually, I was just pretty scared, and as soon as I shot . . . I had this feeling of a hand over my heart, and I just gave up on the whole thing right then . . . As far as I was concerned, I would just go to the police, turn myself in and go right to the [electric] chair, get it over with.[7]

But "the chair" would not be his fate. Thanks in part to a letter from Strozier's mother, forgiving Bechtel and asking the court to show mercy, he was referred to a psychiatric hospital where he spent almost five years prior to his trial. He was found not guilty for reasons of insanity. After his release he earned a doctorate, started a family, and began a successful teaching career.[8]

"Children are traumatized by bullying, and I was traumatized many times," Bechtel told an interviewer (these would be the distal shame events). "And it's not the bullying at Swarthmore (the proximal shame events) that really caused it [the murder]; it's that whole history of bullying that I brought to Swarthmore, and that's what triggered it off".[9] Acts of extreme violence such as this are not simply the result of bullying but rather of later shaming re-evoking earlier shame. Under such circumstances, the emotion in question becomes so intense that the rational mind no longer works clearly. The shooter experiences a kind of transient psychoses. It seems to his confused mind that the only solution is to remove the bully by killing him and perhaps others who may symbolize him.

The relatively small number of victims of these early shootings compared with more recent rampage shootings was not a benefit of the superior morals of the day, or more dutiful church attendance, or the absence of violence in films and the yet-to-be invented video games, but rather the limits of gun technology, production, and distribution. In order for a shooter to exterminate many people quickly, he (or, on rare occasions, she) needs a weapon that is easily obtained, inexpensive, and semiautomatic (it fires rapidly each time the trigger is depressed without having to manually move a new cartridge into the firing chamber). Although a number of semi-automatic rifles existed in the early years of the twentieth century, they were neither inexpensive nor readily available. It was not until the 1960s that cheap, foreign-made "assault" rifles flooded the American market as a result of improvements in manufacturing and revolutions abroad.[10]

By the 1980s school shooters, enchanted by the film Rambo, were able to equip themselves with scary-looking AK-47 type weapons. While these rifles were semi-automatic (they were not *fully* automatic; they could not fire a stream of bullets, like a machine gun), they had a powerful psychological effect, empowering the shooter and terrifying the victims. Every planned-out act of public violence is part theater.

In January of 1989 perhaps the first of these pseudo-commandos,[11] a 24-year-old named Patrick Edward Purdy, parked his old Chevy station wagon in front of Cleveland Elementary School in Stockton, California. He was wearing military fatigues and a flak jacket, covered by a camouflage shirt with "P.L.O.," "Libya," and "Death to the Great Satin (*sic*)" emblazoned on it. "Freedom," "Victory," and "Hezbollah" were carved into the stock of his Chinese-made military-style semi-automatic rifle.[12] Purdy had been raised in Stockton and had attended this very same elementary school from kindergarten through third grade. He had quit school at 16 to wander back and forth across the country, trying to find some direction to his life. Most of his classmates had been Caucasian back then, but by 1989 families from Asia and the Pacific Rim, the latest emigrant group in that part of the country, accounted for almost 70 percent of Stockton's population. Cleveland Elementary had been specially designated as a haven for Southeast Asian refugee children.

Purdy set his car on fire with a Molotov cocktail in a Budweiser bottle and proceeded to the schoolyard.

> Lori Mackey [a teacher] ... ran to her classroom window when she heard what she thought were firecrackers, and saw a man standing in the schoolyard, spraying gunfire from what turned out to be a Russian-designed AK-47 rifle [*sic*]. There were 400 to 500 pupils from the first to third grades playing at the noontime recess.
>
> "He was not talking, he was not yelling, he was very straight-faced," she said of the gunman, whom she described as about 5 feet 10, with short blonde hair. "It did not look like he was really angry; it was just matter-of-factly."[13]

Purdy killed five children between the ages of six and nine. One was Vietnamese, the others, Cambodian. He wounded 29 other children and a 37-year-old teacher before taking his own life.

Later, when the police searched his room at the El Rancho Motel on the edge of town, they found more than 100 toy soldiers, tanks, jeeps, and weapons, displayed on every shelf, grate, radiator, and "even in the refrigerator"[14] (possibly playing out some Arctic expedition).

Purdy had lived a brief and tumultuous life. He was born in 1964 in Fort Lewis, Washington, to a father who had been honorably discharged from the Army for psychiatric problems. At some point his parents were divorced. Details of Purdy's life are known mostly through his police record, which began when he was 16, while soliciting sex from a police officer. He was arrested two years later for drug possession, then again in 1983, in Beverly Hills, for possession of a dangerous weapon, and later that year on charges of receiving stolen property. In October of 1984, he was jailed 30 days for attempted robbery and criminal conspiracy and in April of 1987 for firing a 9-millimeter pistol in Eldorado National Forest and then resisting arrest. He kicked the deputies and announced that it was his duty "to overthrow the suppressors" (*sic*). During his 45 days in the county jail, he tried to hang himself and cut his wrists with his fingernails and toenails. He was taken to a county health center for a psychiatric assessment, the results of which were withheld because of his age. His probation officer described him as a danger to himself and others.[15]

In 1988, at the age of 24, he managed to complete a course in welding. He got a job at a machine shop, which lasted less than a month. Then he roamed the country, working at a nursery in Key West, Florida; as a security officer in Glendale, California; at a DuPont chemical plant in Memphis, Tennessee; and at a power plant in Connecticut.

When asked by a reporter if Purdy had staged his massacre out of hatred for Asians, the chief investigator, Capitan Dennis Perry of the Stockton Police Department, told *The New York Times* that interviews with family members and co-workers suggested that he "disliked everybody," particularly authority figures like police officers.[16] "He did not leave us a message," Perry continued. "Without that we'll never know exactly why he did what he did. In a way, he beat us because we'll never know."[17]

But we know more about Purdy than Captain Perry thought. We know that playing with toy soldiers suggests an emotional age of six to eight. We know that he was utterly alone in his life, could not hold a job, and could not even function as a criminal or a male prostitute without getting immediately arrested. Cleveland Elementary School, his alma mater, may have been the only group in which he could ever claim membership. But the school was no longer *his* school. It now belonged to Asians, Vietnamese, and Cambodians. His choice of weapons and military fatigues suggested the role of a soldier. Did he massacre them to win it back, the way he imagined his father might have taken a Vietnamese village?

School shootings occurred sporadically throughout the following decade but failed to capture the interest of the general public until 1997, when the incidents began to follow one another on a bimonthly basis: Bethel, Alaska; Pearl, Mississippi; West Paducah, Kentucky; Jonesboro, Arkansas; Edinboro, Pennsylvania; Springfield, Oregon; and finally, on April 20, 1999, Littleton, Colorado.[18] Even today the mention of these place names evokes a frisson of terror and disgust at the waste of young lives.

The Columbine High School shootings became the most closely followed news stories of the year and one of the three most closely followed stories of the decade.[19] This interest was attributed to the number of fatalities, the fact that it took place in a well-to-do suburb of Denver rather than a rural town, and that it played out on television in real time. Dylan Klebold and Eric Harris were both from intact, well-educated, middle-class families and were able to keep their plans for murder and mayhem secret for over a year before the shootings; parents started to wonder about their own teenage children, what rage and resentment might be harbored in their hearts, waiting to find an opportunity for violent expression.

Many people believe that school shootings became less frequent following Columbine. In fact, the opposite is true, but, with the exception of the horrifying massacres at Virginia Tech and Sandy Hook Elementary School and a few other isolated cases, the media approached them more tentatively and covered them in less detail, with less fanfare. Unwittingly, the media had raised the bar, creating a competitive atmosphere. *How many people do I need to kill to get somebody's attention around here?* Seung-Hui Cho, the Virginia Tech shooter, killed 32 people, occasionally shooting bodies multiple times to be sure his victims were not simply wounded.

ACTS OF DOMESTIC TERRORISM

The US Department of Defense has defined domestic terrorism as the "calculated use of unlawful violence to inculcate fear; intended to coerce or intimidate governments or societies in pursuit of goals that are generally political, religious, or ideological."[21] For the current discussion, I concentrate on incidents involving "lone wolf" terrorists, rather than those instigated by hate groups, where the motives become more difficult to disentangle.

Domestic terrorism is said to have begun with the invention of dynamite in 1867. On Tuesday May 4, 1886, Haymarket Square in Chicago was the scene of one of the most violent riots in American history. The previous day the police had killed several laborers who had been striking for an eight-hour workday. The next day, while the police were attempting to disperse a peaceful protest, a dynamite bomb thrown by person or persons unknown turned the afternoon into a chaotic nightmare. Seven officers and at least four civilians were killed. The Chicago police, trying to restore order, fired into the crowd, killing 12 more civilians. We know little about the perpetrators of these early events since bombers hid within the crowds or concealed their bombs within suitcases and carpetbags and forensic science was in its infancy. While a group of anarchists was eventually rounded up, tried, and convicted, the degree of their participation in the bombing remained in question.

On July 22, 1916, a Preparedness Day Parade, the largest parade ever held in San Francisco (over 51,000 marchers), was organized by the chamber of commerce to demonstrate support for the United States entering World War I. The movement toward pacifism was strong at that time, supported by the labor unions and members of Industrial Workers of the World (the Wobblies). About a half hour into the parade, a bomb made of a length of steel pipe filled with TNT and shrapnel was detonated, killing 10 and injuring 40. A young girl had her legs blown off. Some said the bomb was hurled from the crowd and others, that it had been dropped from the roof of a nearby building or left on the street, concealed in a suitcase. Four radical labor leaders were arrested and prosecuted for the murders, although there was little evidence of their involvement in the bombing. Those in power had managed their shame by killing four who were symbolic of the he who had actually brought the bomb.

The Bath Michigan Consolidated School bombing of 1927, described at the beginning of this chapter, might well be included here as an act of domestic terrorism, in that Andrew Kehoe used dynamite to forward his agenda and express his frustrations with local government.

THE MAD BOMBER

George Metesky became better known to the public as the "Mad Bomber." He dropped out of high school in his sophomore year to join the Marines, where he worked as a specialist electrician. Following his discharge, he moved in with his two unmarried sisters in Waterbury, Connecticut, and took a job as a mechanic at a local Con Edison subsidiary. In 1931, the blast from a boiler backfire knocked him on his back and filled his lungs with noxious fumes. In his own words:

> [I had my accident] on September 5th, 1931. There were over 12,000 "Danger Signs" in the plant, yet not even "First Aid" was available or rendered to me. I had to lay on cold concrete. Later pneumonia. Three months later T.B. [tuberculosis.] Mr. F. W. Smith [the president of Con Gas] was riding around on the soft cushions of a 16 cylinder Cadillac. Me, laying on concrete.[22]

After 26 weeks of sick pay, he was dismissed from his job. He tried to collect worker's compensation to cover his formidable medical bills, but Con Ed claimed he had waited too long and no longer qualified. He filed two more appeals that were denied. He remained at the home of his devoted, unmarried sisters, who nursed him and provided him with an allowance, supplemented by money left to him by his father, a night watchman. He lived a solitary and eccentric life, following a regular schedule, putting on a suit, driving his car 80 feet down the driveway to the garage where he had his workshop, then changing into his coveralls, reversing the process at the end of his work day. On many days he was bedridden because of his tuberculosis.

In November 1940, having exhausted all his options for collecting workman's compensation, including the sending of some 900 letters to the mayor, the police commissioner and the newspapers without any response, he began to build bombs. He fashioned them out of sections of pipe and filled them with gunpowder taken from rifle bullets. He had been the victim of injustice and the world appeared deaf to his protests. It is one thing if people acknowledge the wrongdoing even if it is not corrected but something else entirely if it is ignored. When we listen to people's stories, we show them respect. We enhance their status. In the words of the French Philosopher, Simone Weil, *Attention is the rarest and purest form of generosity.* When we ignore their stories, we exclude them from our world.

Metesky, voiceless and lacking any other recourse, resorted to violence. Later he explained that he had been careful to make the bombs small so that no one would be harmed. He often called in warnings or sent notes beforehand, describing when and where a bomb would explode so that the area could be evacuated but also to "own" his acts.

The first bomb was placed on a windowsill of a Con Ed power plant and the second nearby. Metesky stopped his random bombings at the onset of World War II, explaining, in a note to the New York Police Department that he was doing so out of "patriotic feelings." It was enough that the country had to worry about aggression from outside its borders without also worrying about destruction from within. By 1951 the nation was getting back on its feet, and Metesky was back in his workshop, creating bombs of an "improved design," which he planted in many of the better-known buildings in Manhattan, as well as movie theaters, phone booths, and the subway. He continued to rail against Con Ed in his notes and phone calls. In 1952 for the first time one of his bombs caused an injury, and two years later another bomb injured three bystanders. Remarkably, no one was ever killed, but the public grew understandably more agitated, never knowing when or where a bomb might be detonated. In December of 1956, following an explosion in the Brooklyn Paramount Theater, Police Chief Stephen P. Kennedy ordered, in his own immodest words, "the greatest manhunt in the history of the police department."[23] The *Journal American*, a now-defunct New York City newspaper, offered the bomber space to voice his complaint (in other words, they allowed him to tell his story to the world that was now willing to listen) and a psychiatrist/criminologist named James Brussel, "profiled" him (the first use of profiling to identify a criminal). The person ultimately responsible for his capture, however, was a woman named Alice Kelly, an industrious clerk at Con Ed, who carefully reviewed the files of workers injured in plant accidents and came up with Metesky's name and address.

Metesky was judged unfit to stand trial, "hopeless and incurable, both physically [his tuberculosis] and mentally,"[24] and transferred to a hospital for the criminally insane. Metesky made a surprising recovery from tuberculosis but remained diagnosed as "paranoid schizophrenic" until his release in 1973.[25] He died in 1993 at the age of 90. In his last letter to the *Journal American*, composed prior to his arrest, he wrote:

> You say my compensation case can be reopened. What about the price on my head? What about my people who housed me, fed me, clothed me, and did everything they could, and still do, to sustain my life? I would not sell my people out for all the money in N.Y.C. Society and the authorities will have to carry their full burden of the blame for what they forced me to do. Why was I robbed of my earning capacity, then dumped onto my people, a burden to support for 25 years?[26]

Ted Kaczynski

Not all "set and run" bombers are similarly motivated.

When Ted Kaczynski was nine months old, his body became covered with hives. Doctors, unable to find the cause, hospitalized him repeatedly over an eight-month period. He was pinned down spread-eagled during examinations and submitted to many tests. His parents were allowed only brief visits, as was the policy in hospitals in 1943. While he had seemed a normal, affectionate baby prior to the hospitalizations, on his return home home, his mother wrote in her baby book, "Baby home healthy but quite unresponsive after his experience." The entree was dated March 12, 1943. In an interview, she described the "unresponsiveness" growing like a cancer that consumed her son's soul. His mother was very well read, and popularized accounts of John Bowlby's new research on the importance of the maternal bond were appearing in magazines and newspapers of the time. As Teddy got older, his mother grew sufficiently concerned about him, in particular his lack of interest playing with other children, that she considered enrolling him in a study being conducted by Bruno Bettelheim on autistic children.[27]

Leo Kanner, a Hungarian psychiatrist, had been the first to recognize and describe autism in a paper[28] published the year Teddy was born. Because Kanner could find no medical cause for the disorder, and his initial group of subjects had mothers who were cold and distant, he suggested that these qualities might be a cause of the disorder, an idea he discarded soon afterward. Bettelheim, however, hung onto the "icebox mother" idea and used his "expert" status to create a successful business treating autism in the 1950s.

Ted's IQ was measured at 167 when he was in fifth grade, with particular strengths in science and mathematics. He was passionate about his hobbies, which included coin collecting and playing the trombone. He composed music, which he performed with his father, an amateur pianist, and his brother, a trumpeter. He skipped sixth grade, an event he recalled during his court-ordered psychological evaluation as pivotal in his life. He did not fit in with the older children, he told a forensic psychiatrist, and became the target of teasing and verbal abuse.[29] When seventh-grade math remained bored him, he was moved to eleventh grade. He was accepted at Harvard in the fall of 1958 at the age of 16 and graduated at 20, attracting little attention to himself in general but alienating a number of roommates[30] with passive aggressive behaviors such as ignoring them, slamming doors, and blasting his trombone in the dead of night.[31]

During his days at Harvard, he participated as a subject in the infamous MKUltra experiments secretly sponsored by the CIA and locally overseen by Harvard psychology professor Henry Murry. The MKUltra testing was conducted at many sites, including some 44 colleges and universities, as well as hospitals, prisons, and pharmaceutical companies. Its aim was "the research and development of chemical, biological, and radiological materials capable of employment in clandestine operations to control human behavior." Kaczynski and others were subjected to a "purposely brutalizing psychological experiment."[32] Kaczynski later stated that this experience had been instrumental in his decision to kill people.

Kaczynski went on to complete his master's and doctoral degrees at the University of Michigan in five years, winning an award for best dissertation in mathematics. He considered his time at the University of Michigan as another pivotal point in his development. He began having dreams about "organized society," which continued for several years. According to Kaczynski, in these dreams people, often psychologists, were trying to "capture my mind" and/or "tie me down."[33] They, and sometimes parents or other authority figures, would try to

> convince me that I was "sick" or would be trying to control my mind through psychological techniques. I would be on the dodge, trying to escape or avoid the psychologist either physically or in other ways. But I would grow angrier and finally I would break out in physical violence against the psychologist and his allies.

At that moment,

> I experienced a great feeling of relief and liberation. Unfortunately, however, the people I killed usually would spring back to life again very quickly. They just wouldn't stay dead. I would awake with a pleasurable sense of liberation at having broken into violence, but at the same time with some frustration at the fact that my victims would not stay dead. However, in the course of some dreams, by making a strong effort of will in my sleep, I was able to make my victims stay dead. I think that, as the years went by, the frequency with which I was able to make my victims stay dead through exertion of will increased.[34]

In the summer of his fourth year at Michigan, Kaczynski experienced several weeks of continual sexual arousal while fantasizing himself as a woman. He decided to get a sex-change operation and, knowing that a psychiatrist's letter was necessary for the operation, made an appointment with a psychiatrist. While he was in the waiting room, he was overwhelmed with shame at his planned duplicity. When he saw the doctor, he said that he had made an appointment because he was depressed about the possibility of being drafted.

> As I walked away from the building afterwards, I felt disgusted about what my uncontrolled sexual cravings had almost led me to do and I felt—humiliated, and I violently hated the psychiatrist. Just then there came a major turning point in my life. Like a Phoenix, I burst from the ashes of my despair to a glorious new hope.
>
> I thought I wanted to kill that psychiatrist because the future looked utterly empty to me. I felt I wouldn't care if I died. And so I said to myself why not really kill the psychiatrist and anyone else whom I hate. What is important is not the words that ran through my mind but the way I felt about them. What was entirely new was the fact that I really felt I could kill someone. My very hopelessness had liberated me because I no longer cared about death. I no longer cared about consequences and I said to myself that I really could break out of my rut in life and do things that were daring, irresponsible or criminal.[35]

Initially he decided to kill someone and then kill himself, but he did not want to "relinquish his rights so easily."

> I will kill but I will make at least some effort to avoid detection so that I can kill again . . . If it doesn't work and if I can get back to civilization before I starve then I will come back here and kill someone I hate.

The University of California at Berkeley offered Kaczynski an assistant professorship. The year was 1967; he was 25 years old. He quit after two years; neither the protests of the department nor the extremely negative teaching evaluations from his students were a factor. He told his family that he had left because his students planned to become engineers and their work would destroy the environment. Ted's father had raised him and his brother to love nature and often took them wilderness camping.

He spent the next two years working at menial jobs while waiting to learn about some wilderness land he and his brother had applied for purchase in Canada. When their application was refused, Ted and his brother purchased 1.5 acres in Lincoln, Montana, and built a cabin without plumbing or electricity. There Kaczynski tried to live off the land, spending about $400 a year and riding into Lincoln on his bicycle when he needed supplies. Eventually he broke off all contact with his brother and his parents and lived in nearly total isolation. (This illustrates the shame-management strategy of hiding.)

His first mail bomb, a primitive explosive device in a finely finished wooden box, was mailed to a professor who had rejected the manuscript that later became the *Unabomber Manifesto*. This project may have marked Kaczynski's transcendence of conventional morality, a subject very much on his mind at the time. He believed that most of society was a victim of "oversocialization," a term coined by sociologist Dennis H. Wrong[36] in the late 1950s. In the *Unabomber Manifesto*, Kaczynski wrote:

> The moral code of our society is so demanding that no one can think, feel and act in a completely moral way . . . In order to avoid feelings of guilt, they continually have to deceive themselves about their own motives and find moral explanations for feelings and actions that in reality have a non-moral origin. We use the term oversocialized to describe such people.
>
> Oversocialization can lead to low self-esteem, a sense of powerlessness, defeatism, guilt, etc. One of the most important means by which our society socializes children is by making them feel ashamed of behavior or speech that is contrary to society's expectations. If this is overdone, or if a particular child is especially susceptible to such feelings, he ends by feeling ashamed of HIMSELF . . . The majority of people engage in a significant amount of naughty behavior. They lie, they commit petty thefts, they break traffic laws, they goof off at work, they hate someone, they say spiteful things or they use some underhanded trick to get ahead of the other guy. The oversocialized person cannot do these things, or if he does do them he generates in himself a sense of shame and self-hatred . . . Thus the oversocialized person is kept on a psychological leash

and spends his life running on rails that society has laid down for him. In many oversocialized people this results in a sense of constraint and powerlessness that can be a severe hardship. We suggest that oversocialization is among the more serious cruelties that human beings inflict on one another.[37]

Kaczynski used his manifesto to justify murder. He accomplished this logical legerdemain by equating trivial moral misconduct such as lying, committing petty thefts, breaking traffic laws, and "goofing off at work" with serial killing. He used specious arguments about oversocialization to displace his own shame onto those whom he believed were responsible for shaping (or, more accurately, misshaping) society into its current form and then he tried to kill them. He created a false dichotomy by positioning wildlife and wilderness as the antithesis of oversocialization and sought vengeance on those whom he perceived as having acted against nature. Thomas J. Moser, a Burson-Marsteller executive, was killed by a Kaczynski mail bomb because "Burston-Marsteller (sic) helped Exxon clean up its public image after the Exxon Valdez incident" and because "its business is the development of techniques for manipulating people's attitudes." He killed Gilbert Murray with a mail bomb because Murray was president of the timber industry lobbying group and defended logging. He targeted academics whom he believed had rejected the early version of the manuscript that later became the *Unabomber Manifesto*, as well as academics whom he perceived as anti-nature. Between the period of 1978 and 1995 he set at least 16 bombs, killed 3 innocent people, and wounded 11 others.

Jim David Adkisson

While domestic terrorists continued to make bombs, many post-Columbine cases involved rampage shootings. One might say that the influence of Columbine was so great that it changed the fashion in mass violence. The following two cases are less known to the public and demonstrate very clearly the connection between shame, suicidality, and homicidal violence.

On Sunday, July 27, 2008, Jim David Adkisson, a 58-year-old out-of-work mechanic with a serious drinking problem, entered the Tennessee Valley Unitarian Universalist Church carrying a guitar case. Some 200 congregants were seated in the chapel that morning, watching their children perform the musical *Annie*. Although Adkisson was a talented guitar player, the case contained not a guitar but a shotgun, and he proceeded to shoot and kill two congregants, wound six others, and leave a series of images in the minds of the adults and children who were present that day that will probably haunt them for years to come. A handwritten manifesto, found in his pickup truck after the shootings, explained his "political" motives.

> Over the years I've had some good jobs, but I was always laid off. Now I'm 58 years old and I can't get a decent job.
>
> I always wondered why I was put on this earth. For years I thought I was put here to die as cannon fodder in Vietnam but somehow cheated the devil out of it. Lately I've been feeling helpless in our war on Terrorism. But I realized I could engage the terrorists' allies here in America, the best allies they've got.
>
> The Democrats!
>
> The Democrats have done everything they can do to tie our hands in this War on Terror. They're all a bunch of traitors. They want America to lose the War on Terror for reasons I can not understand. It makes me soooo mad!

He chose to target the Unitarian Universalist Church because

> This isn't a church, it's a cult . . . a collection of sickos, weirdoes & homos. The UU church is the Fountainhead . . . of anti-American organizations like Moveon. org, code pink, . . . These people embrace every weirdo that comes down the pike, but if they find out you are a conservative, they absolutely hate you. I know, I experienced it.

Unitarian Universalism is a liberal faith, which was brought to the United States by the founding fathers, Thomas Jefferson, John Quincey Adams, Benjamin Rush, Ethan Allen, and others during the time of the American Revolution. It has attracted many artists and intellectuals through the decades, and played a seminal role in passing civil rights and gay marriage legislation.[38]

Not only could he not find work, but he had recently learned that his food stamps were being cut off. He had five failed marriages. On March 17, 2000, is fifth wife, Liza Alexander Adkisson, had filed for a restraining order and started divorce proceedings. She wrote:

> On Feb 22, my husband, Jim David Adkisson told a friend of mine that one of his options is to blow my brains out & then blow his own brains out . . . I told him [Adkisson] that I felt a strong need for separation and he yelled, 'Well then, leave!' I went and stayed in a hotel that night. I am in fear for my life and what he might do.[39]
>
> In the end of his manifesto/ suicide note, he explains, in the words that might have been taken from a country-western song, that he has nothing left to live for. He may have imagined that the killing of these good people could

alleviate his shame/rage toward his ex-wife. His emotions had reached a point where he was no longer thinking clearly.

No one gets out of this world alive so I've decided to skip the bad years of poverty. I know my life is going downhill fast from here. The future looks bleak. I'm sick and tired of being sick and tired. I'm absolutely fed up. So I thought I'd do something good for the country. Kill Democrats till the cops kill me.

I have no next of kin, no living relatives. If you would take my sorry carcass to the body farm, or donate it to science, or just throw me in the Tennessee River.

Sincerely, Jim Adkisson[40]

George Sodini

The inability to enjoy intimacy with a woman plagues male school shooters and domestic terrorists. Almost all heterosexual men would like to be one of those who seem naturally comfortable with women and easily engage them in relations, both social and sexual. To be excluded from this group is a special kind of shame as it implies something inferior or damaged in men's maleness and goes to the core of their being.

In August of 2009, George Sodini, a 48-year-old systems analyst at a Pittsburgh law firm, barged into a women's aerobics class at an LA Fitness gym, turned off the lights, and began shooting. He killed three women and wounded nine others before committing suicide. Part of this planned "project" was an online blog that he kept for 10 months prior to the shooting. He wrote about his double life: the happy self he projected at work and the sad and lonely reality of his life. He wrote about a lifetime of being bullied by an older brother (who now was his employer and boss), a domineering mother, and a father who totally ignored him.

It is difficult to live almost continuously feeling an undercurrent of fear, worry, discontentment (sic) and helplessness. I can talk and joke around and sound happy but under it all is something different that seems unchangeable and a permanent part of my being.[41]

But mostly he wrote about his inability to have intimate relationships with women.

Who knows why? I am not ugly or too weird. No sex since July 1990 either (I was 29 . . .) Last time I slept all night with a girlfriend it was 1982. Girls and women don't even give me a second look ANYWHERE . . .

Women just don't like me. There are 30 million desirable women in the US (my estimate) and I cannot find one . . . Looking at The List [of reasons why he should commit suicide] makes me realize how TOTALLY ALONE, a deeper word is ISOLATED.

It seemed to him as though all women, as a group, had rejected him, and there was no fixing it: "I have no options because I cannot work toward and achieve even the smallest goals. That is, ABOVE ALL, what bothers me the most."[42]

Sodini left $225,000 to the University of Pittsburg, but the university said it had "no interest" in Sodini's bequest and was considering distributing the money among the victims of the shooting as an act of restorative justice.[43] To associate itself in any way with a shameful misogynistic event such as this would be to lower the status of a fine university.

ACTIVE SHOOTER AND MASS CASUALTY INCIDENTS

While writing a book on school shooters some years ago,[44] I noticed the similarity between these events and many acts of domestic terrorism. The motivations for these crimes can be better understood, and consequently better prevented, if their similarities are acknowledged.

Each of the perpetrators described in this chapter, regardless of whether they were labeled school shooters or domestic terrorists, attempted to manage their proximal shame by committing a "calculated use of unlawful violence intended to intimidate societies in pursuit of a goal[45] (that is the definition of domestic terrorism used by the Department of Defense). In the lives of those perpetrators—those about whom we have sufficient biographical information—we can identify distal shame with some certainty. Kehoe contributed to the death of his stepmother, a crime made more grievous by going unacknowledged and unpunished by the community. Bechtel was bullied throughout his childhood.[46] The loss of the ability to work and the refusal of Con Edison to take responsibility was one distal shame event for Metesky, but there may have been other, earlier events. He was diagnosed as having schizophrenia, and people in the prodromal phase of that disease are often odd enough and vulnerable enough to satisfy any bully's need for a victim. Kaczynski's autistic behavior, plus being placed in classes with children three or four years older than he was, made him a ready victim for abuse. Who knows what the results of the MKUltra experiments were? It was, after all, a program designed to test interventions that would make a person behave counter to society's norms.

In each case, some act of fate had prevented the shooter (or bomber) from managing his shame in a healthy, nonviolent manner. Attempts were made. Purdy, the drifter, tried to settle down by taking a course in welding and getting a job at a machine shop. Metesky sent letters seeking justice for the denial of his worker's compensation. Sodini struggled to be pleasant and popular and learn how he could make himself appealing to women. Other hindrances to managing their shame might have included masculine role expectations, denial of feelings, and problems with communication. It is no coincidence that some of these cases involved men with special gifts in mathematics and engineering and deficits in communication skills, a profile we currently place somewhere on the autism spectrum.

Women, as keepers of the social network, are trained from an early age to talk about their feelings. If they have shame, they often share it with their friends, sometimes repeatedly, often for periods of time so lengthy that they elicit spousal disbelief. Men are expected to compete, to keep their problems to themselves, and deny their vulnerability all qualities that interfere with the admission and management of shame.

THE CATATHYMIC CRISES

The kind of phenomenon we are talking about in this chapter has been recognized as pathological in the psychiatric literature, but not often. It is always associated with an emotion but never specifically with shame. It has not found its way into the mental health jargon nor any edition of the American Psychiatric Association's *Diagnostic and Statistical Manual of Mental Disorders*. The specific diagnosis remains unknown to the majority of mental health workers and criminologists, as well as the public.

The diagnosis is *catathymic crises* (from the Greek *kata*, meaning "according to" and *thymos*, meaning "spirit" or "temper"), a term coined in 1912 by Hans W. Maier, a highly regarded Swiss psychiatrist and director of the Zurich Psychiatric Hospital Burghölzli. He conceived of catathymia as

> a psychological process or reaction activated by a strong and tenacious affect [emotion] connected to an underlying complex of ideas. The affect, when stimulated, overwhelms the individual's psychological homeostasis [his mental stability] and disrupts logical thinking.[47]

In shame theory, the "strong and tenacious affect" is shame/rage and the "underlying complex of ideas" involves resentment against the person or persons who are imagined to have excluded the individual from whatever groups would have given him or her a sense of belonging. Catathymia has been used over the decades to describe otherwise inexplicable acts of extreme violence.[48] Frederic Wertham has broken down the onset of catathymia into phases:

1. An initial thinking disorder, which follows an original precipitating (or traumatic) circumstance.
2. Crystallization of a plan, when the idea of a violent act emerges into consciousness. The violent act is seen as the only way out. Emotional tension becomes extreme, and thinking becomes more and more egocentric.
3. Extreme emotional tension culminating in the violent crisis, in which a violent act against one's self or others is attempted or carried out.
4. Superficial normality, beginning with a period of lifting of tension and calmness immediately after the violent act. This period is of varying length, usually several months.
5. Insight and recovery, with the reestablishment of an inner equilibrium.[49]

AMOK

The existence of the catathymic crises as a "clinical entity" is reinforced by its occurrence in other cultures.

"Amok" was first described by Captain James Cook, in 1770, when he visited Malaysia during his first voyage of discovery in the *H. M. Bark Endeavor*. During an episode of Amok, the Malaysians explained to Cook, a young warrior would fall into a period of brooding. Eventually he would emerge from his hut, a machete in hand, and go on a killing spree, hacking to death whomever he chanced to meet. Afterward, his mood would be restored to normal and his thinking, to its previous clarity. Often he would have amnesia for the harm he had done. Because the Malays considered amok a disease, they did not punish the offender.

It was called "amok" because early Malaysian warriors used to scream the word when engaging in battle. In the Malay language, the act of running amok was described as *mengamok,* and the man doing the killing (usually with a machete) was called the *pengamok.* This event was considered common enough, and dangerous enough that Cook appointed an officer whose sole responsibility was to capture the pengamok, should a mengamok occur. Later explorers found occurrences of amok in Sumatra, Papua New Guinea, Singapore, Indonesia, the Philippines, Laos, and other Southeast Asian countries.

The first Western doctor to publish a paper on the subject was J. D. Gimlette in 1901.[50] The four stages that he described were prodromal brooding, homicidal outburst, persistence in homicide without an apparent motive, and a claim of amnesia.[51] (Note the similarity with Wertham's five phases of catathymic crises.) A number of school shooters reported amnesia or the sensation of coming out of a trance after committing their shootings.[52] Regarding prevalence, Malaysia's leading newspaper reported 190 cases of amok between 1935 and 1970 and 45 cases between 1965 and 1970.[53] An article from 1967 identifies amok as a problem of shame.

> A common psychodynamic hypothesis explains amok as a projection of rage onto one's reference group, a form of suicide in a culture that forbids suicide. Because the pengamok comes from a culture that uses shame rather than guilt to maintain conformity, he is prone to display distraught behavior by acting against society rather than against himself.[54]

A diagnosis very much like amok had been included in the *Diagnostic and Statistical Manual of Mental Disorders*, third edition, published in 1980, but was removed from the revised edition in 1987 for fear that if it was recognized as a legitimate psychiatric disorder, it might be used as a defense for mass murderers. This was a pressing concern because in 1981, the year after the book's committees began preparing the revised edition (a process that was to occupy them for the next five years), John Hinckley, Jr., who had tried to assassinate President Reagan and critically wounded James Brady, Reagan's press secretary, was found not guilty for reasons of insanity. Brady died in August of 2014 as the result of wounds inflicted by Hinckley.

AGE IS THE DIFFERENCE

The most significant difference between school shooters and the domestic terrorists is age. "Perpetrators are usually young or middle-aged men living away from home who have recently suffered a loss or an insult or have otherwise 'lost face,'" as Gaw and Bernsten[55] point out in a comprehensive study of amok. (Notice how they use the archaic "lost face" in order to avoid the word "shame.") Adolescents, as we have discussed in a previous chapter, are dealing with the developmental task of creating the foundations of their adult identity.[56] If they have been convinced that they have no future, no family, no vocation, no friends and that they will be excluded from every group that might provide them status in life, they might as well not be alive. If not being alive provides an opportunity to live out their dream of vengeance, of playing commando or hit man, with only the positive consequence of being killed (gloriously, one hopes) in the process, all the better. Young domestic terrorists such as James Eagon Holmes, who appeared during the midnight screening of a new *Batman* movie in Aurora, Colorado dressed as the Joker and fired randomly into the audience, is an exemplar.

The middle-aged shooter has a different developmental task: Erik Erikson considers the primary developmental task of this age group as "generation versus stagnation."[57] Their mindset, while similar in other aspects to that of their younger counterparts, differs in this regard. They have run out of solutions for making something of their lives. They may be unable to form an intimate relationship with any woman in order to create a family or have started a family over and over, only to find it unraveling—wives suing for divorce, children moving out at an early age without leaving a forwarding address. They may be skilled laborers or mathematical geniuses but are fired from every job or find themselves unable to tolerate the stress and sociability of the workplace. They may lose their homes to foreclosures or misfortune. They might suffer from a psychiatric disorder that will not go away no matter how hard they try to dispel it through medication, home remedies, or sheer will. They have few or no friends. All that remains is the rage at having a good life denied to them, displaced on a population that symbolizes a culpable entity, be it the Con Edison Company, women who attend exercise classes, immigrant children from Vietnam and Cambodia, or journal editors who refuse to publish their manuscripts.

Recall from Chapter 1 that "shame is a necessary but not a sufficient cause of violence"[58] There must be no available means of prosocial shame management, such as a trustworthy, nonjudgmental listener, or a group of listeners, and no factors, such as shame denial, communication diffi- culties, or preconceptions regarding male behavior, stopping the offender from seeking such help. In addition, there may be other factors, physi- ological or neurological, that exacerbate or inhibit these reactions that we acknowledge but the etiology of which we do not yet understand.

The similarities between school rampage shootings and domestic ter- rorist attacks have not gone unnoticed by the FBI. As mentioned ear- lier, the two categories appear to have been combined under the rubric of "active shooter" incidents (known as ASIs, or ASEs [active shooter events).[59] These are defined as "violent acts and shootings occurring in a place of public use." Note that the FBI is solely concerned with the most effective way of countering the violence and protecting people and only in theoretical, psychological, and emotional aspects of offenders insofar that their understanding aids them in accomplishing this end.

A total of 160 ASIs took place between 2000 (the year after Columbine) and 2013,[60] the number of incidents increasing annually: six shootings in 2001, 11 in 2003, 14 in 2007, 19 in 2009, and so on. Were this a graph of a business's yearly growth, the shareholders would be standing up and applauding. But it is not; rather it represents incidents of innocent people being killed for no apparent reason, of children being traumatized, and of whole communities being steeped in grief and fear. The number of casualties (1,043), including 486 killed and 557 wounded, also increased at a similar rate. A quarter of the incidents (39) occurred in schools; slightly less than a third (50) in malls and "businesses open to pedestrian traffic"; and the rest in government offices, churches, residences, health-care facilities, and open spaces.[61]

This is disturbing news. Why should these kinds of shootings be on the increase when the Department of Education, the Attorney General's Office, the Secret Service, the FBI, and police departments across the nation have made a concerted effort to reduce their number?

Income Inequality

If I am a citizen of a Scandinavian country—Sweden is a good example—my neighbor and I will probably be earning more or less the same number of kronas. Janitors, nannies, cleaning ladies, and gardeners—those jobs usually lobbed off on undocumented immigrants—are much better paid in Sweden, while middle and upper management are paid much less, creating relative income equality.[62] Everyone's labor is highly valued. I may hate my neighbor because his dog pees on my flowers, or he plays death metal music at 3 AM, but I do not feel envious or cheated because he earns so much more than I do.

On the other hand, if I am living in the United States, my neighbor's salary may be 10 times my own. He may have worked hard to earn that money and be deserving of it. It still makes me wonder if I am worth less than he, or even if I am worthless. Part of my male identity is "being a good provider" and my membership in that group seems in jeopardy when I compare myself with him and the way he can provide for his family. Salary disparity is a form of background shame, ubiquitous, inescapable, and largely invisible, like the noise of an old refrigerator that is only noticed when it shuts off.

> [W]hen people are made to feel worthless then there are more fights, more brawls, more scuffles, more bottles smashed and more knives brandished, and more young men die. The lives of young men have polarised (*sic*) and this inequality has curtailed opportunities; hopelessness appears to have bred fear, violence and murder.[63]

The greater the inequality, be it within a community, state, or country, the higher the incidence of homicide and assault (See figure 7.1).[64] This is a particularly robust correlation supported by more than 50 studies.[65] Japan and the Scandinavian countries have the lowest number of homicides and assaults and the smallest income inequality. Portugal, Israel, and the United States have the highest number of homicides and assaults and the largest income inequality.[66] But there are outliers. Finland has relative income equality but a high homicide rate, possibly related to long, dark winters and excessive alcohol consumption. While the United States has extreme income inequality, the homicide rate is disproportionately high. It might be considered "off the charts." Singapore has extreme income

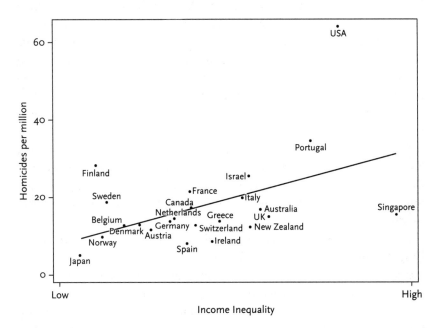

Figure 7.1:
Homicide and income inequality worldwide.

inequality with a very low homicide rate because of a unique combination of historical, cultural, political and economic factors.

This relationship holds true not simply for nations but also for many states and cities. Utah, New Hampshire, Iowa, Wyoming, and Alaska have the lowest income inequality and homicide rate, while Louisiana, New Mexico, Illinois, Tennessee, Alabama, and Mississippi have high inequality and the highest homicide rates.[67] The same correlation has been demonstrated between Canadian provinces and even between different neighborhoods in Chicago.[68]

Frank Elgar and Nicole Aitken demonstrated in a study of 33 countries that the relationship between income inequality and homicide rates "are difficult to attribute to geographic proximity or to cultural, political or historical similarities."[69] Prior to World War II, Japan had high income inequality and a high homicide rate. After World War II, Japan's economy was reorganized in a way that decreased wealth disparity. The homicide rate declined sharply, leaving Japan with the lowest homicide rate of any country.[70] A researcher might say that this example controls for the variables of "culture" and "geographic location."

As we saw in chapter 4, the suicide rates of men tend to *rise and fall* along with the economy. During a recession, a man feels ashamed to be less wealthy than he once was (attack self), particularly if he can no longer support his family. In a similar way, the homicide rate follows the *inequality* of wealth. It makes a man feel ashamed to be less wealthy than his neighbor (attack other). I have no doubt that as women continue to join the workforce in numbers comparable to those of men and become the primary breadwinners for their families, they will experience similar levels of shame, but I cannot predict how they will manage the emotional consequences.

The inequality of wealth reached a high point in 1928 among those men known as the robber barons. It became more democratized during the Great Depression. Around 1978 it began to rise again, reaching the current level in 2015. Today 1 percent of families control more than 20 percent of the nation's wealth.

All the evidence suggests that the reduction of income inequality in the United States would reduce the homicide rate, as well as the number of incarcerated individuals, and have many other beneficial effects, such as improving mortality among the poor[71] and reducing bullying.[72]

Income equality can be achieved through reinstating the inheritance tax, increasing the minimum wage, and capping individual wealth. Twenty-two percent of the children in the United States live in poverty.[74]

The fact that those who fashion our laws allow this to occur should be a source of the deepest shame to them.

NOTES

1. Arnie Bernstein, *Bath Massacre: America's First School Bombing* (Ann Arbor: University of Michigan Press, 2009); Monty J. Ellsworth, *The Bath School Disaster: Text & Pictures*, 1st ed. (Bath, MI: Self-published, 1928), http://daggy. name/tbsd/tbsd-x.htm.
2. Ellsworth, *Bath School Disaster.*
3. Jonathan Fast, "Gary Scott Pennington: Distal and Proximal Shame in a School Rampage Shooting," *Violence and Gender* 1, no. 3 (2014): 134–142.
4. "Swarthmore Man Slain as a Hazer; Proctor, Infuriated by Pranks, Shoots Sleeping Student in Dormitory Rampage," *The New York Times*, January 12, 1955, http://query.nytimes.com/gst/abstract.html?res=9A06E4D9123AE53BBC4A52 DFB766838E649EDE.
5. Ibid.
6. Mathew P. Blanchard, "A Killer's Past and Present Collide He Wants to Tell Why He Shot a Swarthmore Classmate in '55: Not Everyone Cares to Hear It," *Philadelphia Inquirer*, February 13, 2005.
7. Steven Rea, "'55 School Killer: A Life Taken, Lived Film Spotlights Swarthmore, Forgiveness," *Philadelphia Inquirer*, April 13, 2007, http://articles.philly. com/2007-04-13/news/25241455_1_forgiveness-daughters-psychology.
8. Ibid.
9. Ibid.
10. Jonathan Fast, *Ceremonial Violence: A Psychological Explanation of School Shootings* (New York: Overlook Press, 2008).
11. James L. Knoll IV, "The 'Pseudocommando' Mass Murderer: Part I, the Psychology of Revenge and Obliteration," *The Journal of the American Academy of Psychiatry and the Law* 38, no. 1 (2010): 87–94.
12. Robert Reinhold, "After Shooting, Horror but Few Answers," *The New York Times*, January 19, 1989, http://www.nytimes.com/1989/01/19/us/ after-shooting-horror-but-few-answers.html.
13. "Five Children Killed as Gunman Attacks a California School," *The New York Times*, January 18, 1989, http://www.nytimes.com/1989/01/18/us/ five-children-killed-as-gunman-attacks-a-california-school.html.
14. Reinhold, "After Shooting."
15. Robert Reinhold, "Killer Depicted as Loner Full of Hate," *The New York Times*, January 20, 1989, http://www.nytimes.com/1989/01/20/us/killer-depicted-as- loner-full-of-hate.html.
16. Ibid.
17. Ibid., para. 3.
18. Fast, *Ceremonial Violence.*
19. Pew Research Center for the People and the Press, "Columbine Shooting Biggest News Draw of 1999," May 1, 2000, www.people-press.org/yearendrpt.htm.
20. "Gun Rhetoric vs. Gun Facts," FactCheck.org, December 20, 2012, http://www. factcheck.org/2012/12/gun-rhetoric-vs-gun-facts/.

21. Cary Stacy Smith, *The Patriot Act: Issues and Controversies* (Springfield, IL: Charles C. Thomas, 2009), 64.

22. "The Bomber's Grievances Came to Light in a Series of Letters; Paper Received Notes; Text of His Correspondence to Journal-American Tells of Bitterness Over Injury Suspect's First Letter Sent From Westchester Final Communications," *The New York Times*, January 23, 1957, http://select.nytimes.com/gst/abstract.html?res=F60A11F63C5F147B93C1AB178AD85F438585F9.

23. Emanuel Perlmutter, "Kennedy Orders Wide Manhunt For Movie Bombing Perpetrator," *The New York Times*, December 4, 1956, http://query.nytimes.com/gst/abstract.html?res=9F02EEDE163AE23ABC4C53DFB467838D649EDE.

24. "'Bomber' Ordered to State Hospital; Leibowitz Commits Metesky to Matteawan as 'Hopeless and Incurable Man' Mental Factor Decisive," *The New York Times*, April 19, 1957, http://query.nytimes.com/gst/abstract.html?res=9C04E6DC173 0E23BBC4152DFB266838C649EDE.

25. Michael T. Kaufman, "Mad Bomber,' Now 70, Goes Free Today; Mad Bomber,' Now 70, Goes Free Today 37 Blasts Set Initials 'F.P.' Explained Institute Assailed," *The New York Times*, December 13, 1973, http://query.nytimes.com/gst/abstract.html?res=9B02E4DE1339E73ABC4B52DFB4678388669EDE.

26. "The Bomber's Grievances." Note the punctuation in this passage has been corrected.

27. Sally C. Johnson, "Forensic Evaluation of Theodor Kaczynski" (Ninth Circuit Court of Appeals, January 16, 1998), http://www.paulcooijmans.com/psychology/unabombreport.html.

28. L. Kanner, "Autistic Disturbances of Affective Contact," *Acta Paedopsychiatrica* 35, no. 4 (1968): 100–136.

29. Johnson, "Forensic Evaluation."

30. Alston Chase, *Harvard and the Unabomber: The Education of an American Terrorist*, 1st ed (New York: W. W. Norton, 2003).

31. Robert D. Mcfadden, "Prisoner of Rage—A Special Report; From a Child of Promise to the Unabom Suspect," *The New York Times*, May 26, 1996, http://www.nytimes.com/1996/05/26/us/prisoner-of-rage-a-special-report-from-a-child-of-promise-to-the-unabom-suspect.html.

32. Chase, *Harvard and the Unabomber*.

33. Johnson, "Forensic Evaluation."

34. Ibid.

35. Ibid.

36. Dennis H. Wrong, "The Oversocialized Conception of Man in Modern Sociology," *American Sociological Review* 26, no. 2 (1961): 183–193.

37. Theodore Kaczynski, *The Unabomber Manifesto: Industrial Society and Its Future* (Filiquarian Publishing, 2005), para. 25–26.

38. Jone Johnson Lewis, Sue Bennett, and Dan Hotchkiss, "American Politics: Who Were Some Famous Unitarian Universalists?" Famous UUs.com, n.d., http://www.famousuus.com/american.htm.

39. Lisa Adkisson, "Petition for Order of Protection" (Chancery Court, Anderson County, TN, March 17, 2000).

40. James Adkisson, "I Guess You're Wondering Why I Did This," July 27, 2008.

41. Sean D. Hamill, "Blog Details Shooter's Frustration," *The New York Times*, August 6, 2009, http://www.nytimes.com/2009/08/06/us/06shoot.html?_r=1&scp=1&sq=George+Sodini&st=nyt.

42. Ibid.

43. Bobby Kerlik, "Pitt Says 'No' to LA Fitness Killer's Bequest of $225,000," *Pittsburg Tribune–Review*, August 18, 2009, http://triblive.com/x/pittsburghtrib/news/tribpm/s_638749.html.

44. Fast, *Ceremonial Violence*.

45. J. D. Brake, "Terrorism and the Military's Role in Domestic Crisis Management: Background and Issues for Congress" (Washington, DC: Congressional Research Service, 2001).

46. Rea, "'55 School Killer."

47. Louis B. Schlesinger, "The Catathymic Crisis, 1912–Present: A Review and Clinical Study," *Aggression and Violent Behavior* 1, no. 4 (1996): 307.

48. Schlesinger, "The Catathymic Crisis."

49. Frederic Wertham, "The Catathymic Crises," in *Violence: Perspectives on Murder and Aggression*, ed. I. L. Kutash, S. B. Kutash, and Louis B. Schlesinger (San Francisco, CA: Jossey-Bass, 1978), 165–170, as quoted in Schlesinger, "The Catathymic Crisis."

50. John D. Gimlette, "Notes on a Case of Amok," *The American Journal of Tropical Medicine and Hygiene* 4 (1901): 195–199.

51. B. G. Burton-Bradley, "The Amok Syndrome in Papua and New Guinea," in *The Culture-Bound Syndromes*, ed. Ronald C. Simons and Charles C. Hughes (Dordrecht: Springer, 1985), 237–249.

52. Fast, *Ceremonial Violence*.

53. Jin-Inn Teoh, "The Changing Psychopathology of Amok," *Psychiatry* 35, no. 4 (1972): 345.

54. Pow Meng Yap, "Classification of the Culture-Bound Reactive Syndromes," *Australasian Psychiatry* 1, no. 4 (1967): 172–179.

55. Gaw, Albert C., and Ruth L. Bernstein. "Classification of Amok in DSM-IV." *Psychiatric Services* 43, no. 8 (August 1, 1992): 789–793.

56. Eric H. Erikson, *Childhood and Society* (New York: W.W. Norton, 1950).

57. Ibid.

58. James Gilligan, *Violence: Reflections on a National Epidemic*, 1st ed. (New York: Vintage, 1997), 111.

59. Pete J. Blair and Katherine W. Schweit, "A Study of Active Shooter Incidents in the United States between 2000 and 2013" (San Marcos and Washington, DC: Texas State University and Federal Bureau of Investigation, US Department of Justice, 2014), http://www.fbi.gov/news/stories/2014/september/fbi-releases-study-on-active-shooter-incidents/pdfs/a-study-of-active-shooter-incidents-in-the-u.s.-between-2000-and-2013.

60. Ibid.

61. Ibid.

62. In all examples in this chapter, income inequality is calculated using the Gini coefficient. This is universally considered the most accurate measure and is employed in all academic studies of the topic that I have seen

63. Mary Shaw, Helena Tunstall, and Danny Dorling, "Increasing Inequalities in Risk of Murder in Britain: Trends in the Demographic and Spatial Distribution of Murder, 1981–2000," *Health & Place* 11, no. 1 (2005): 52.

64. Kate Pickett and Richard Wilkinson, *The Spirit Level: Why Greater Equality Makes Societies Stronger*, Reprint edition (New York: Bloomsbury, 2011).

65. Ibid.

66. Ching-Chi Hsieh and M. D. Pugh, "Poverty, Income Inequality, and Violent Crime: A Meta-Analysis of Recent Aggregate Data Studies," *Criminal Justice Review*

18, no. 2 (September 1, 1993): 182–202; Matthew R. Lee and William B. Bankston, "Political Structure, Economic Inequality, and Homicide: A Cross-National Analysis," *Deviant Behavior* 20, no. 1 (January 1999): 27–55.

67. Pickett and Wilkinson, *The Spirit Level*, 135.

68. Ibid., 136.

69. Martin Daly, Margo Wilson, and Shawn Vasdev, "Income Inequality and Homicide Rates in Canada and the United States," *Canadian Journal of Criminology* 43 (2001): 219.

70. Frank J. Elgar and Nicole Aitken, "Income Inequality, Trust and Homicide in 33 Countries," *The European Journal of Public Health* 21, no. 2 (April 1, 2011): 244.

71. David T. Johnson, "The Homicide Drop in Postwar Japan," *Homicide Studies* 12, no. 1 (February 1, 2008): 146–160.

72. I. Kawachi and B. P. Kennedy, "Income Inequality and Health: Pathways and Mechanisms," *Health Services Research* 34, no. 1 Pt 2 (April 1999): 215–227.

73. Frank J. Elgar et al., "Income Inequality and School Bullying: Multilevel Study of Adolescents in 37 Countries," *Journal of Adolescent Health* 45, no. 4 (October 2009): 351–359.

74. Mailman School of Public health, Columbia University. "Child Poverty." National Center for Children in Poverty, 2015. http://www.nccp.org/topics/childpoverty. html.]

CHAPTER 8

Restorative Justice and Restorative Processes

RETRIBUTIVE JUSTICE

The United States practices retributive justice, "a system by which offenders are punished in proportion to the moral magnitude of their intentionally committed harms."[1]

People appear to have an inborn inclination toward retributive justice, probably as the result of centuries of Judeo-Christian culture. The Old Testament says in at least three places that if a person intentionally takes the life of another human being, he or she must then be put to death.[2] It also insists that the punishment be appropriate to the crime. "And thine eye shall not pity; *but* life *shall go* for life, eye for eye, tooth for tooth, hand for hand, foot for foot,"[3] a message so important that it is repeated four times in the Old and New Testaments. In the practice of retributive justice, punishment must be fair and consistent and never vengeful or vindictive. "Vengeance *is* mine; I will repay, saith the Lord,"[4] a passage that is repeated in various forms no less than 13 times in the Bible.[5] However, this is easier said than done, particularly in cases where the victim has our sympathies, the offender is vile, and the crime is horrifying, as was the case with Francine Hughes who was acquitted after immolating her husband (see chapter 5). In the most controversial cases, the community of people who have an emotional connection to the case can become so large and so passionate in their belief of what constitutes a just outcome that the judge and jury may worry that to punish the offender too lightly might put themselves at risk of social exclusion or the unleashing of violence in the community.

Early American justice, the justice of the Puritans, was vengeful, vindictive, and shaming, as is sometimes the tendency in primitive societies composed of religious extremists. Because religion was at the center of their lives, punishments abounded for missing church services, misbehaving in the pews, or committing sexual transgressions. Justice was autocratic, theocratic, and patriarchal, with the magistrates, who were often also the religious leaders, making the laws and meting out the punishments.[6] The most common punishment was the stocks, an American invention modeled after the British bilboe, an iron bar with sliding manacles and a padlock at one end. The American version featured heavy slabs of wood, with half-moon cutouts to immobilize an offender in the sitting position by restraining him or her at the ankles and wrists. One might be placed in the stocks for a few hours for a minor offense such as missing church or for days for more serious offenses. The pillory or "stretch neck" was another popular form of punishment. It consisted of a crosspiece of two notched boards, hinged like the stocks, but rather than restricting the wrists and ankles, these closed about the neck and usually also the wrists. The crosspiece was set on a vertical post (like the crosspiece on a crucifix) high enough so that the offender's feet just touched the ground. Onlookers were encouraged to taunt the offenders, tickle or paddle them, or throw food or offal. Sometimes offenders died from the pelting before they could be taken down.

> Punishments were almost always public, for the aim was to humiliate the wayward sheep and teach him a lesson so that he would repent and be eager to find his way back to the flock. Nothing made a colonial magistrate happier than public confessions of guilt and open expressions of remorse.[7]

In the larger settlements, the stocks, whipping post, pillory, and gallows were all permanent features of the town square, so punishment would also serve to edify (and perhaps entertain) the public.

Puritanism was all about shame. The pillory was a device constructed around the principle of maximizing shame. The prosecutors would even nail the offender's ears to the crosspiece, to prohibit the lowering of the head. It was "so fashioned," Nathaniel Hawthorne wrote in *The Scarlet Letter*,

> as to confine the human head in its tight grasp, and thus hold it up to public gaze. The very ideal of ignominy was embodied and made manifest in this

contrivance of wood and iron. There can be no outrage, methinks ... more flagrant than to forbid the culprit to hide his face for shame.[8]

Delaware had the dubious honor of being the last state to abandon the pillory in March of 1905.

In Hawthorne's previously mentioned historical fiction, the heroine is forced to wear a red cloth letter "A" stitched to the breast of her garment so that everyone will know that she is an adulteress. More often, our Puritan forefathers burned letters into the flesh. The burglar was branded with a letter "B" on his right hand for his first offense, on the left hand for the second, and, were he caught stealing on the Sabbath, the brand would be on his forehead. In Maryland, every county had to have a set of branding irons, including an "SL" for seditious libel, which could be burned on either cheek, an "M" for manslaughter, a "T" for thief, a "R" for rogue, and an "F" for forger. In Maryland and Virginia, one who had stolen hogs more than one time wore the letter "H" on his forehead.[9] Once branded, the letter became a lifelong companion and a reminder of one's transgression every time the offender gazed in a mirror.

Flogging was a popular practice of the Puritans and many other cultures and was endured in US prisons until 1940, although some states retained it even later as a punishment for wife-beating, because it seemed exceptionally appropriate in such cases. The last flogging in the United States occurred in Delaware in 1952, when a wife-beater was given 20 lashes. Flogging was officially condemned by Federal courts in 1968, although it remained in the Delaware Criminal Code as a vestige until 1972.[10] Echoes of flogging endure in 19 states, where teachers are still allowed to hit children in the schoolroom as long as they do not raise bruises.[11]

Rainey Bethea, "a farmhand and sometimes criminal," was the last man publicly hanged in the United States. Bethea, a 26-year-old black man, had been convicted of raping and strangling a 70-year-old widow. The jury was so certain of his guilt that they deliberated over it for less than 5 minutes.[12] The event took place in Owensboro, Kentucky, on the banks of the Ohio River, in 1936 in front of a crowd estimated at 20,000. In a photograph, the gallows rise like the wheelhouse of a ship riding the crest of an ocean of upraised heads.[13] Newspapers of the time described a carnival atmosphere with vendors selling hot dogs, popcorn, and cold drinks. Kentucky outlawed hangings in 1938, the last state to do so. Thirty-two states still execute people, all by lethal injection. Thirty-five people were executed in 2014: 10 in Texas, 10 in Missouri, and the rest in Arizona, Ohio, Florida, Oklahoma, and Georgia.

In recent years attempts have been made to resurrect public shame as a means of rehabilitating offenders. In 2004 the Ninth Circuit Court of Appeals upheld a lower court's decision to make a convicted San Francisco mail thief stand in front of a local post office wearing a sandwich board that said, "I stole mail. This is my punishment."[14] A&E, a basic cable network, produces a TV show called *Beyond Scared Straight*, currently in its eighth season and based on the discredited Scared Straight intervention.[15] Teens considered "at risk" are locked up in a prison cell with violent felons and forced to listen to stories about murders and prison rapes. (There is currently a wealth of research showing that Scared Straight results in increasing criminal behavior in adolescents, the very opposite of its intended result. Young lives are being put at risk in the name of entertainment.)[16] The sheriff of a jail in Mason County, Texas, makes offenders wear pink jumpsuits and pink slippers to reduce their violent behavior by unmanning them.[17]

Military-style boot camps for teen offenders, based on the Paris Island basic training regimen for new Marines, became popular in the 1990s as an alternative to prison overcrowding and a means of cost cutting. While they were not open to the public, they derived much of their popularity from video clips where men dressed in paramilitary attire screamed at adolescents loudly enough to occasionally break an ear drum, made them wake at 5 AM, stand like statues in the rain, and "drop and do 50" (pushups) on demand. Parents of disobedient teens may have imagined that their children would emerge with spit and polish and the manners of West Point grads.

Boot camps for adolescent offenders were suspect from their inception. They did not reduce recidivism, and they raised questions about which offenders would benefit from the program. One flaw that seems to have escaped critics was that the original boot-camp program after which the penal variant was copied was designed to train willing enlistees to be good Marines, to follow orders, to suppress their own needs and desires, and occasionally to kill people, none of which necessarily creates good citizens. Boot camps became less popular after the death in 2006 of 14-year-old Martin Lee Anderson as the result of staff trying to force him to complete a mile run.[18] Despite this and other deaths and injuries, and evidence suggesting that recidivism rates are no better than traditional incarceration, many boot camps are still in service, run by states and private organizations. The appeal of these interventions, like the punishments of the Puritans, is manifold: first, they seem intuitively helpful, both in correcting the offender's behavior and deterring others; second, they are satisfying to observe because they suggest that something "powerful" is being done to end bad behavior; and third, we can displace our shame on the offender and watch it be sweated or shouted out of him.

Benjamin Rush, whose signature can be found on the constitution of the United States, was a doctor, a humanitarian, an abolitionist, an advocate of prison reform, and an outspoken critic of public punishment. In an influential pamphlet published in 1787, he wrote,

> all public punishments tend to make bad men worse, and to increase crimes by their influence upon society . . . THE reformation of a criminal can never be effected by a public punishment . . .
>
> EXPERIENCE proves that public punishments have increased propensities to crimes. A man who has lost his character at a whipping-post has nothing valuable left to lose in society. Pain has begotten insensibility to the whip, and shame to infamy.
>
> Added to his old habits of vice, he probably feels a spirit of revenge against the whole community whose laws have inflicted his punishment upon him; and hence he is stimulated to add to the number and enormity of his outrages upon society.[19]

THE UNITED STATES IS OVERINCARCERATED

Most modern punishments involve incarceration. According to a recent report of the US Department of Justice,[20] 6,899,000 people are "under the supervision of adult correctional systems at year-end 2013" meaning that they are incarcerated, on parole, on probation, under the jurisdiction of state or federal prisons, or being held in local jails. The United States' is the largest prison system in the world.[21] One of every 110 American adults is incarcerated in prison or jail, and one of every 51 adults is on probation or parole.

The cost is staggering—more than $39 billion in total, with an average annual cost of $31,286 per inmate.[22] Of all the states, New York spends the most, with an average annual cost of $60,000 per inmate. New York City spent an astonishing $167,731 per inmate in 2012.[23] Parents of teenage children will note that this is enough for several years at the best Ivy League college.

"Recidivism" is a term used to describe a person who, after being released from prison, violates probation or parole or commits another crime. According to the Bureau of Justice Statistics, 76.6 percent, or about three-quarters, of those incarcerated by the states were rearrested within five years of being given their freedom.[24] More than half of them had been rearrested within a year of their release.[25] There is very little rehabilitation going on here.

When we strip away a person's clothes and possessions, isolate them from their family and employment, cage them for years in the company of other criminals (or worse, in complete isolation) then release them into society in this deeply damaged state without vocational training and careful preparation for reintegration into society, only the most fortunate and resilient will survive.

RESTORATIVE JUSTICE

Restorative justice is a way of restoring rightness after an offense has disrupted a community. The disruption might be a schoolyard fight, a white-collar crime, a riot, or a war. The best-known example of restorative justice is South Africa's Truth and Reconciliation Commission established by President Nelson Mandela and presided over by Desmond Tutu, a program created to heal the social wounds of apartheid. Similar commissions have been established in Argentina to resolve human rights violations involving the disappearance of persons; in Canada to reconcile the human rights abuses of the Indian residential school system; in El Salvador, as part of the peace treaty to end the Salvadorean Civil War; and in many other countries that still bear the open wounds of civil wars and the abuses of colonialism. The principles of restorative justice can also be applied to small groups and individuals and are referred to by other names, such as "family group conferencing" and "restorative circles." We do not hear much about this topic in the United States, but it is of great interest in other countries, particularly parts of England, Canada, New Zealand, and Australia.

The goal of restorative justice is to bring peace and a sense of resolution to all the stakeholders, not only the victims, their friends, families, and representatives of the community but also the perpetrators—in other words, *all* those whose lives may have been derailed by the offense. Rather than the crime being considered an offense against the state, prosecuted by the state, as in retributive justice, the victim and the community are considered the harmed parties; it is they who decide on what is required to make things right. Restorative justice discourages the kind of shame that makes offenders devalue and disdain themselves and strengthens their self-identification as criminals. They have done something wrong, but they do not embody this wrongness. They are welcomed back into the dominant culture (the group that might be known as Law-Abiding

Citizens) under the condition that they have provided the restitution (and possibly performed the penance) required by the victim or victims and the community.

The offender must confront the victim and hear about the loss and grief he or she has suffered as a result of the crime. Similarly, members of the victim's family describe how the crime has affected their lives, and representatives of the community also join in this process. We can understand the importance of this when we consider the effect of a school shootings or terroristic event on a community.

Rather than having a judge at the head of the room, raised on a platform, dressed in a symbolic robe, and wielding a gavel, restorative justice participants often meet at a site representative of the community where the offense occurred: a school in the case of bullying, a company conference room if a white-collar crime has occurred there.[26] They sit in a circle to indicate the equality of their participation in the process, a custom among some native peoples that dates back to antiquity. Police and other representatives of the state may be present, but everyone has an equal status in making decisions about the offender's fate. They must agree to keep in mind the key values of restorative justice: to focus on healing rather than hurting; engage in respectful dialogue; make amends; take responsibility; and express remorse, apology, and forgiveness. Restorative justice can take place only when all participants agree to its principles.[27]

The restorative justice circles or conferences continue to meet until everyone has had his or her say. A consensus must be reached, recorded in a written contract, and signed by the offender, the victim, and a police officer or another official. If the matter is truly settled, then there is no need to go to court. These contracts can include compensatory payments to victims, formal apologies, community work, the agreement to enter rehab, "surrender of weapons or ownership of a motor vehicle, moving from living on the street to living with an aunt, and so on."[28] It might even include some form of incarceration.

In my experience Americans, hearing about restorative justice for the first time, typically worry that punishments will not be sufficient to "teach the criminal a lesson." In fact, criminals rarely learn any lessons from being demeaned in the courtroom, confined in a prison cell, and disenfranchised upon release, except that American society is cruel and unforgiving and the word "felon" is the true mark of Cain in assuring that getting a decent job, owning a home, and starting or maintaining a family will become monumentally difficult if not impossible tasks.

Restorative justice is not the opposite of retributive justice, and it cannot always be implemented in its purist form. Rather, restorative and retributive justice should be considered two points on a gradient. The offender may still be punished. Those who have been harmed may agree that a prison sentence or a fine is necessary.[29] Restoration of capitol or property may be one outcome of the process. It is generally agreed that pure restorative justice is countermanded in certain types of cases, such as domestic violence.[30] Containment remains an issue for persistent violent offenders and those with extreme sociopathic tendencies, although these groups constitute only one-quarter of the current US prison population.[31]

RESTORATIVE JUSTICE IN COUNTRIES THAT HAVE SUFFERED INTERNAL STRIFE

Restorative justice has shown its efficacy in righting injustices done to a large community of people, as exemplified by the Truth and Reconciliation Commission in South Africa. The objective of the commission was

> to promote national unity and reconciliation in a spirit of understanding which transcends the conflicts and divisions of the past by—
> (a) establishing as complete a picture as possible of the causes, nature and extent of the gross violations of human rights which were committed . . . as well as the perspectives of the victims and the motives and perspectives of the persons responsible for the commission of the violations, by conducting investigations and holding hearings;
> (b) facilitating the granting of amnesty to persons who make full disclosure of all the relevant facts relating to acts associated with a political objective and comply with the requirements of this Act;
> (c) establishing and making known the fate or whereabouts of victims and by restoring the human and civil dignity of such victims by granting them an opportunity to relate their own accounts of the violations of which they are the victims, and by recommending reparation measures in respect of them.[32]

Obviously one reason for the success of the commission was that, in return for participation, it granted amnesty, both to whites who had committed crimes against blacks and equally heinous crimes—murder, kidnapping, beatings, and mutilations—committed by blacks against whites. This amnesty does not diminish the power of the restorative justice process in healing the wounds and uniting black and white South Africa. Those who had been carrying crippling shame could unburden themselves publically, before a group representative of the entire country, and be forgiven. The missing bodies of loved ones could be located, as well as those who had gone into hiding because of threats of retribution. Reparations could be made.

The example set by South Africa inspired similar commissions to seek resolution for states emerging from periods of governance by dictators, civil war, or internal unrest and problems created by colonialism (a form of bullying). A recent list included no fewer than 28 countries around the world.

It is interesting to imagine what our country might be like today had President Lincoln established a Truth and Reconciliation Commission on this model following the Civil War (the Reconstruction Acts, while well-intended, were directed at implementing the emancipation and restoring order to the country, and did not take into consideration compensating blacks for the centuries of slavery preceding the Civil War). This is not a new idea. Attempts have been made to provide such reparations. In 1999 the African World Reparations and Repatriation Truth Commission demanded $777 trillion be paid to Africa to right the wrongs of slavery. The number was calculated on the basis of the number of human lives lost to Africa during the slave trade and the value of the gold, diamonds, and other minerals looted during the period of British rule. Debra Kofie, one of the individuals behind the proposal, said, "[Africans] are the only group that have not received reparations. The Jewish people have received reparations. The Native Americans have received reparations. The Korean comfort women and so-on and so forth."[33] Five years later, in 2004, Lloyds of London was sued billions of dollars by the descendants of African slaves who claimed that by insuring slave ships they were a party to the crime of slavery. The claim was dismissed by a New York court.[34]

The very large sums of cash may have made the demands seem unrealistic. In fact reparations to the descendants of slaves could be made simply and painlessly through tax relief. This would represent an important step that is both actual and symbolic in righting a grievous wrong. To provide incremental tax breaks for companies based on the number of slave descendants hired might even undo the current corporate discriminatory practices described in chapter 6. Affirmative action might be reconsidered as reparation rather than an undeserved gift, as some conservative politicians have implied.

REINTEGRATIVE SHAMING

John Braithwaite is a criminologist and a Distinguished Professor at the Australian National University, the author of many books on restorative justice, and the recipient of many honors and awards. For the past 25 years he has devoted his life to a project called Peacebuilding Compared, which studies conflicts and wars that have occurred around the world, the causes of these conflicts, and the efforts to resolve them in a lasting manner, with emphasis on peace-building as a form of restorative justice.

Braithwaite recounts successful restorative conferences, using kind and careful shame to create prosocial behavior, in a variety of settings. He calls this "reintegrative shaming" because it is a way of inviting offenders to rejoin the dominant culture and instilling in them (or perhaps reawakening) the moral fiber needed to accomplish this. It also demonstrates that people are willing to invest their time and effort into helping offenders and have the respect to hear out their stories. Finally, learning how a crime has affected a victim, the victim's family, and the community may plant a seed for or revive a sense of empathy in the offender.[35] This is similar to the use of healthy shaming to teach children acceptable behavior, as described in chapter 1, but it is considered a *return* to healthy behavior. No blaming is permitted because blaming is destructive shaming of the self and is counterproductive.

THE CHURCH BURNING—TWO VERSIONS

It is enlightening to imagine how the same crime might play out under retributive justice and restorative justice. The following story is presented in two versions, both of them loosely based on several real-life cases.

Andy dropped out of high school when he was 17. Shortly before graduation he got into a fight in the cafeteria with a black teenager named Montrose, whom he had known since grade school. Montrose received a week's detention, but Andy was suspended because he was carrying a knife. Because he had never taken out of his pocket during the fight, he considered himself the victim of a gross miscarriage of justice and declared that he would never go back to high school and get his diploma, just to teach them all a lesson.

Andy worked as a stock boy, a sales assistant, and a van driver for a dry cleaning store but could never hold a job long because of his drinking and surly attitude. On the afternoon of his 18th birthday he learned that he had not been hired for a job as a plumber's assistant. Later that evening he got a message from his girlfriend, who was supposed to be celebrating with them. Instead, she and her cousin had decided to drive down to Nashville to hear a singer they liked. Determined to celebrate, he and his buddy, Eddy, visited at a local bar, finished an entire bottle of bourbon and tried to write a song about life's injustices.

Around 2 AM they decided to burn down the Mt. Zion Baptist Church where the black community of their town worshipped. It seemed to Andy, now that he was quite drunk, that because the black teenagers had started the fight and ruined his future by making him quit school, burning down the church would be a good way of getting even. Eddy was unsure about this but agreed to go along. They stole a handful of matchbooks from the bar, filled some five-gallon cans with gasoline, and drove the pickup truck to the north end of town. As they were weaving down the street, Andy recalled that he had a can of spray paint left over from a job that afternoon. He could write a message on the church wall expressing his indignancy.

They were too drunk to set a proper fire and made enough noise banging the gasoline cans to wake the sexton, who photographed them with his new cell phone before calling the fire department. In the first light of dawn the boys found themselves cuffed and being booked for arson. In Tennessee, where we imagine this all taking place, that constitutes a Class B felony, which calls for a prison sentence of 8 to 30 years and a fine not to exceed $25,000. However, the next day members of the congregation pointed out that someone had spray painted *Niggers Die!* on the church wall prior to setting the fire, leaving little doubt that this was a hate crime, which bumped it up to a Class A felony, punishable by a minimum of 15 to 60 years in prison and a fine not to exceed $50,000.

In the world of retributive justice, Andy's attorney, realizing he had no case, urged him to accept a plea bargain. In return for saving the county the time and expense of a trial, his sentence would be reduced to a Class B felony and he would serve eight years in a state prison with possibility of parole for good behavior and pay a fine of $5,000 to the state.

This had different repercussions for everyone involved. Members of the Mt. Zion Church were upset, not so much because they had to worship at the Episcopal Church around the corner until repairs were done but because for the older members the event reawoke terrible memories of the pre–civil rights era when the Ku Klux Klan and church burnings were a fact of life. They desperately wanted to talk to the boys and find out why they had committed the act. A sense of incompleteness seemed to hang over everything that was said and done following the fire.

Andy's family, overwhelmed by the shame of their son's behavior, wrote a letter of apology to the church and sent a check of $100. They would have liked to send more, but they were pressed for cash. They had taken out a second mortgage to pay Andy's legal fees and fine.

In prison, Andy discovered that the population was divided into tribes: the blacks had a tribe, as did the Hispanics. Andy was warmly accepted into the white tribe, the Aryan Brotherhood, particularly after he shaved his head and had some swastikas tattooed on his chest and arms. As the members of the brotherhood came to trust him, he learned about the racketeering and drug trade that they ran in collaboration with members outside the prison. It was a network of people who seemed to possess wealth, respect, and power (admittedly achieved through violence and extortion). Upon his release, Andy became part of a drug trade infrastructure that stretched throughout the South-East. He had a few years of glory before he was shot and killed during a dispute with a rival gang of drug dealers.

THE CHURCH BURNING—VERSION II

Prior to the trial, Reverend Brown, the minister of the Mt. Zion Church, arranged to meet with the judge, the prosecutor, and the sheriff. He suggested that rather than charging Andy for the crime, he and his friend might be put to work rebuilding the church. They would also become church members, with attendance every Sunday being compulsory. That way they would get to know some black people personally and see that, under the skin, people are people. The judge and the prosecutor agreed, and a second meeting was scheduled, this to include Andy and Eddy, their parents, a facilitator trained in restorative justice, and six members of the church. Working together they began to craft an agreement.

Andy had been agreeable to anything that kept him out of prison, but when he heard about giving up his Sundays to sit in the hot church and listen to old ladies sing, he became furious and stomped out of the session. Reverend Brown's patience was endless. He met with Andy's parents, and Andy's dad had a long talk with him. Eventually he agreed to all the terms of the contract.

Andy was good with tools. A member of the congregation who was an experienced carpenter guided him in his work, showing him the proper way to cut away the burned siding and replace the studs and joists. On Sundays Andy sat through the church meetings stony-faced. After a few months of this, he got to know a few of the congregants personally and began to enjoy the chorus and the sermons. When the repairs of the church were done, the carpenter began taking Andy on other jobs as an assistant. Two years after setting the fire he was scarcely recognizable to his old friends. He was kinder, wiser, and more tolerant. He earned his

GED, enlisted in the Army, and learned to program in Python. When he came home on leave, he always spent Sunday mornings at the Mt. Zion Baptist Church.

He had successfully managed a great deal of shame thanks to the patience and support of the church community. The wrong that had been done was made right for all involved. While this sounds a little like a Hallmark TV movie, it is not an uncommon outcome. People want to manage their shame in a healthy way. Everyone would rather be a member of the dominant culture than the criminal underclass. A community of people who understood hard luck was, in accordance with their faith and ideology, determined to help him. These factors all contributed to a positive outcome.

Some crime victims and families of victims have no interest in restorative justice. In the 13 cases I wrote of in my book about school shootings,[36] nearly all of the parents of the deceased, as well as members of the school communities who spoke publically, wished to see the perpetrators executed or incarcerated for the rest of their lives. Although I am a determined believer in the value of restorative practices, if I lost a child or grandchild in a school shooting, I might feel the same way.

RESTORATIVE JUSTICE WITH INDIVIDUALS AND SMALL GROUPS

The practice of restorative justice with individuals began in 1974 when Mark Yantzi, a probation officer, arranged a meeting of two teens who had gone on a vandalism spree, slashing car tires and throwing bricks through windows.[37] Yantzi, a young man from Kitchener, Ontario, had volunteered with the Mennonite Central Committee to work in probation in Elmira, New York, where the offense occurred. During a regular meeting with volunteers from other churches, he suggested that his young vandals might benefit by talking to their victims. The group supported him in this decision but voiced doubts about whether the court would allow it. Yantzi decided to include the idea as an addendum to a presentencing report. The judge was reluctant to proceed and questioned whether there was a precedent. After reflecting on it, he agreed, and a meeting was arranged between the vandals and the victims.[38]

In the initial meeting, the victims calculated their copays after insurance reimbursement and asked the young men to compensate them for the difference. The vandals were defensive and made excuses for their bad behavior. In the second meeting, they brought checks and talked.

One victim recognized that he had played hockey with one of the vandal's uncles. He told the boy that if they met on the street, he should say, "'Hi', because we are square now" (no hiding in shame). A woman whose husband had died a year earlier told the vandals that she had no longer felt safe after they threw a brick through her window. She asked her grandchildren to come and stay with her. "Now I sit across from you and see that I have no reason to be afraid. You remind me of my grandson. If he did something like this, I'd like him to be responsible the way you are."[39]

The success of this meeting for the victims, the offenders, and the community was such that it led to the first victim–offender reconciliation program, which was established in Kitchener, Ontario, Canada, with the support of the Mennonite Central Committee in collaboration with the local probation department.[40]

RESTORATIVE JUSTICE AND BULLYING

The success of restorative practices in elementary and high schools seems to rest on how it is implemented. In a trial implementation in 20 high schools and six primary schools in England,[41] results were mixed. Some teachers thought they were implementing restorative justice but had merely adopted the vocabulary. Restorative conferencing was time consuming, and parents were often excluded at the request of the students or because of logistical problems. The lack of a clearly defined one-size-fits-all protocol became a handicap, particularly for teachers who had been using traditional school punishments for many years and were set in their ways. If a teacher has a limited amount of time and needs to get through a "unit," the most efficacious solution is to expel the troublemaker from the classroom. Unfortunately, this is Shaming 101.

The SaferSanerSchools program had better results. SaferSanerSchools is a program run by the International Institute for Restorative Practices, a nonprofit graduate school located in Bethlehem, Pennsylvania, with a dual mission: to provide graduate education to people with a passionate interest in the subject and to conduct research evaluations to test whether restorative practices result in more content and productive communities. The SaferSanerSchools training covers a range of school-related restorative practices, such as making affirmative statements, leading a proactive circle conference, using reintegrative shame management, and a restorative approach in family conferencing, to name just a few.[42] The entire school staff is trained in restorative practices, and it is implemented with ongoing guidance and support from the Institute. This immersive reeducation is necessary to change the culture of an institution. It is worth remembering that the American "common school," as public schools were once called, pioneered the practice of making a poor student sit on a stool in the corner wearing the "dunce's cap."

Schools that participated in the SaferSanerSchools program demonstrated a dramatic transformation of culture. In Palisades High School, a small high school (616 students) in rural Bucks County, a restorative practices program was begun in 1998. By 2002 disciplinary referrals had dropped from 1,752 to 1,154; administrative detentions from 716 to 282; incidents of disruptive behavior from 273 to 153; and out-of-school suspensions from 105 to 65.[43] In 2013 Palisades was recognized as one of America's best high schools by *Newsweek* and received a Governor's School of Academic Excellence award.[44] These awards may or may not directly reflect the implementation of restorative processes, as schools are also affected by the economy, the changing demographics of the community, changes in administration and goals set by the school board, and so forth. Another pilot program in Palisades Middle School that started two years later showed similar improvements, including a reduction in disciplinary referrals from 913 to 516 and a reduction in incidents of fighting from 27 to 16. A third pilot study, also begun in 2000, at Springfield Township High School in Erdenheim, Pennsylvania, another small rural school, showed a reduction of over 60 percent in incidents of classroom disruption.[45]

A second series of evaluations was launched in 2006 in three inner-city schools. In the following two-year period, West Philadelphia High School, with a student body of 803 students (97 percent black and 100 percent economically disadvantaged), reported that assaults on students decreased from 46 to 18, assaults on teachers and administrators from 25 to 5, and incidents of disorderly conduct from 43 to 12.[46] In City Springs Elementary/Middle School, a large inner-city school in Baltimore, suspensions dropped from 86 to 10; and in Kosciuszko Middle School, a large, racially diverse inner-city school in Hamtramck, Michigan, referrals dropped from 1,024 to 380.[47] Qualitative data describing the transformation from a punitive, disciplinary approach to restorative practices support a causative hypothesis. One teacher said,

> When we were using a traditional punitive discipline approach, certain kids were spending more time out of school than in, and student achievement was very low. With restorative practices, discipline referrals have been cut

in half; suspensions, expulsions and office referrals all are much improved and the amount of recurring offenders and fights has been greatly reduced. The processes are so powerful in helping kids reflect on their decisions and behavior and how they affect others.[48]

My guess is that academic achievement also improved during the periods in question, but I was not privy to that data.

NAMES DAY

Many dedicated antibullying programs are currently available from faith-based organizations, educational consultants, nonprofits, and even the Federal government.[49] The Olweus Bullying Prevention Program remains popular despite mediocre results in the United States. While I am not familiar with every program or approach, I am acquainted with some. One that seems to best incorporate restorative justice and reintegrative principles into a yearly inoculation is called Names Can Really Hurt Us, which many schools shorten to "Names Day."

The Names Can Really Hurt Us High School Assembly program[50] was created under the auspices of the Anti-Defamation League in 1995 by Marji Lipshez-Shapiro, and the program has evolved over the years according to the needs of the students. Lipshez-Shapiro told me that she was unaware of the principles of restorative processes or reintegrative shame under that nomenclature when she created the program but that the ideas were consistent with her own philosophy. Restorative processes under any name are effective, as demonstrated by the First Nations people of the United States and Canada and the Maori of New Zealand, who created these practices long before the arrival of European settlers.[51]

Names Day is currently an event ("The most important day of your school year," according to one high school principal[52]) implemented in rural, urban, and suburban schools across the country, with most of the programs taking place in Connecticut, where the program was created. It is run by the Anti-Defamation League with assistance from a Names Day team comprised of staff and students from the host school, who participate in two three-hour training sessions prior to the assembly. Lipshez-Shapiro believes that the thorough nature of the training is one reason for its efficacy. It is not an assembly featuring some visiting lecturer; it is a program by and for the students. It provides an opportunity for adults and teens together to reshape a school into a civil community.

During the Names Day assembly, students gather in the auditorium where they are welcomed by the Names Day team. Team members establish the norms and expectations for the assembly and provide terms to facilitate the discussion. The bully is the "perpetrator." "Bystanders" are those who watch the bullying, uncertain about what action to take. "Allies" are the bystanders who take the side of the "target" and put a halt to the bullying. The labels suggest a course of action.

The next part of the program is a short film produced by a Connecticut high school student that features real high school students relating the experiences of bias and bullying from their own lives. Following the video, Names Day team members share their own experiences of being bullied and how they came to terms with them. Recently a Filipino-American girl talked openly and shamelessly about a study group she was in when she was a freshman. A boy sitting across from her

> broke one of the silences by poking me in the eye and saying "How do you see out of these eyes?" and then rolling the skin around his eyes so his eyes looked like mine . . . The worst thing he did, though, was at the end of the study session, when he looked at me and said "I don't know if it's possible for an Asian to be stupid, but here you are. I guess you're not really Asian. You're one of those Asians that wants to be American, but isn't."
>
> The boy probably doesn't remember half of what he said, but I remember all of it, and it still hurts. However, what hurts even more is the lack of [supportive] response from my friends.[53]

Although she considered members of the study group her friends, none of them showed the courage or the peace of mind to move from being a bystander to an ally.

By telling the story, this student was managing her own shame, but she was also creating an atmosphere of anticipatory reintegrative shame. In other words, everyone in the audience was imagining how they would have intervened on her behalf had they been in the study group that day and witnessed her abuse.

Another panel member, a Hispanic student, was picked on in middle school for being fat. When he got to high school he had lost some weight and gained some height, and he "looked pretty good,"—by his own account—but he remained embittered.

> The teasing had stopped, and I was in such a good place. I figured why not give people a taste of their own medicine now. I knew that this was not in any way, shape or form the right thing to do, but it seemed like something I wanted to

do. I started making fun of people the way it was done to me. I went from being the fatass to the jackass.[54]

The need to displace his shame was contrary to what he knew was right, but the impulse was so powerful that he became a victim to it. By confessing it to the entire school, he was walking the path of shame management.

By this point the program has established a climate of honest personal expression, nonjudgmental acceptance, and openness to self-revelation among members of the audience. It is then time for the "open mic."

At a Names Day event I attended, the silence at this point in the program was so intense that we could almost hear the clock ticking off the seconds. I began to worry. *What if nobody came forward to speak?* I didn't realize it at the time but the real question was, *Who would open the floodgate?* Finally one boy rose from his seat in the back of the auditorium and walked down the aisle. By the time he had reached the microphone, another boy was following close behind. Then another. Then two girls. Soon there was the kind of line one might expect at the opening of a *Twilight* sequel.

The speeches were extraordinary. The kids laid bare their adolescent souls.

So, um, I've got ADHD, I was finally diagnosed. At least I don't think I'm a freak anymore. I'm on medication now and working really hard. People remember me the way I was, but I'm not like that anymore. I'm not. I'm just asking—give me a second chance, OK? Just come up and say, Hi. Please.[55]

Another student spoke on behalf of his sister:

My sister is autistic. You see her in the hallway but you don't know her. She's the sweetest, most wonderful person. But no one will talk to her to find out. Why does she have to hear the words *retard* and *spaz*? Why does she have to come home crying every day?[56]

"What really impressed me," a Names team member said afterward, "was how many people truly apologized for being bullies and admitting that they were really sorry. This year, we really affected the student body, and they became one class."[57]

A small boy arrived at the microphone and talked about how another boy had bullied him throughout middle school. Then the bully himself, who was in the auditorium that morning, ran up to the microphone and apologized. Then and there, in front of everyone, they hugged it out.

NOTES

1. Kevin M. Carlsmith and John M. Darley, "Psychological Aspects of Retributive Justice," *Advances in Experimental Social Psychology* 40 (2008): 194.
2. Deuteronomy, 15:12, Leviticus, 24:17, and Exodus 21:12 in *The KJV Study Bible* (Newburyport: Barbour, 2011).
3. Mathew, 5:38. The message appears earlier, in Deuteronomy 19:21, Leviticus 24:20; and Exodus 21:24, *KJV Study Bible*.
4. Romans 12:19, *KJV Study Bible*.
5. Leviticus 19:18; Deuteronomy 32:35; 1 Samuel 26:10, 1 Samuel 26:11; Psalms 94:1; Proverbs 20:22, 24:29; Jeremiah 51:36; and others, *KJV Study Bible*.
6. James A. Cox, "Bilboes, Brands and Branks," *Colonial Williamsburg Journal* (Spring 2003) http://www.history.org/Foundation/journal/spring03/branks.cfm.
7. Ibid.
8. Nathaniel Hawthorne, *The Scarlet Letter* (Boston: Ticknor, Reed and Fields 1850).
9. Lawrence M. Friedman, *A History of American Law*, 3rd ed. (New York: Touchstone, 2005).
10. Kelly R. Webb, "Flogging," in *Encyclopedia of Prisons and Correctional Facilities*, ed. Mary Bosworth (Thousand Oaks, CA: SAGE, 2004), 326–328.
11. Valerie Strauss, "19 States Still Allow Corporal Punishment in School," *The Washington Post*, September 18, 2014, http://www.washington-post.com/blogs/answer-sheet/wp/2014/09/18/19-states-still-allow-corporal-punishment-in-school/.
12. Brett Barrouquere, "Nation's Last Public Execution, 75 Years Ago, Still Haunts Town," *Boston Globe*, August 14, 2011, http://www.boston.com/news/nation/articles/2011/08/14/after_75_years_last_public_hanging_haunts_city/.
13. Ibid.
14. Benjamin Bycel, "Sandwich Boards of Shame for Convicted Execs," *Los Angeles Times*, August 13, 2004, http://articles.latimes.com/2004/aug/13/opinion/oe-bycel13.
15. Anthony Petrosino, Carolyn Turpin-Petrosino, and John Buehler, "Scared Straight and Other Juvenile Awareness Programs for Preventing Juvenile Delinquency: A Systematic Review of the Randomized Experimental Evidence," *The Annals of the American Academy of Political and Social Science* 589, no. 1 (September 1, 2003): 41–62.
16. J. O. Finckenauer, *Scared Straight and the Panacea Phenomenon* (Englewood Cliffs, NJ: Prentice-Hall, 1982); Petrosino, Turpin-Petrosino, and Buehler, "Scared Straight"; J. O. Finckenauer et al., *Scared Straight: The Panacea Phenomenon Revisited* (Prospect Heights, IL: Waveland Press, 1999), 256.
17. Dan Glaister, "Pink Prison Makes Texan Inmates Blush," *The Guardian*, October 10, 2006, US edition, http://www.theguardian.com/world/2006/oct/11/usa.danglaister.
18. Jim Avila and Sarah Koch, "Boot Camp Death—Caught on Tape," ABC News, April 28, 2007, http://abcnews.go.com/2020/story?id=2751785&page=1.
19. Benjamin Rush, *An Inquiry into the Effects of Public Punishment Upon Criminals and Upon Society* (Philadelphia, PA: Joseph James, 1787).
20. Lauren E. Glaze and Danielle Kaeble, *Correctional Populations in the United States, 2013* (Washington, DC: US Department of Justice, Office of Justice Programs, Bureau of Justice Statistics, December 2014).

21. Ibid.
22. Vera's Center on Sentencing and Public Safety Performance Project of the Pew Center on the States, *The Price of Prisons: What Incarceration Costs Tax Payers* (New York: Vera Institute of Justice, January 2012), http://www.vera.org/sites/default/files/resources/downloads/the-price-of-prisons-40-fact-sheets-updated-072012.pdf.
23. New York City Independent Budget Office, "New York City by the Numbers," August 22, 2013, http://ibo.nyc.ny.us/cgi-park2/?p=516.
24. Mathew R. Durose, Alexia D. Cooper, and Howard N. Snyder, *Recidivism of Prisoners Released in 30 States in 2005: Patterns from 2005 to 2010* (Washington, DC: US Department of Justice, April 2014).
25. Ibid.
26. John Braithwaite, "Shame and Criminal Justice," *Canadian J. Criminology* 42, no. 3 (2000): 281.
27. Ibid.
28. Ibid., 293.
29. Howard Zehr, *The Little Book of Restorative Justice* (Intercourse, PA: Good Books, 2002).
30. J. Stubbs, "Beyond Apology?: Domestic Violence and Critical Questions for Restorative Justice," *Criminology and Criminal Justice* 7, no. 2 (May 1, 2007): 169–187.
31. The Sentencing Project, "The Federal Prison Population: A Statistical Analysis" (Washington, DC: The Sentencing Project, 2004), http://www.sentencingproject.org/doc/publications/inc_federalprisonpop.pdf.
32. Truth and Reconciliation Commission, *Promotion of National Unity and Reconciliation Act 34 of 1995*, 1995, ch. 2, para. 3, "Objectives of Commission," http://www.justice.gov.za/legislation/acts/1995-034.pdf.
33. "Trillions Demanded in Slavery Reparations," BBC News, August 20, 1999, http://news.bbc.co.uk/2/hi/africa/424984.stm.
34. Gavin Stamp, "Counting the Cost of the Slave Trade," BBC News, March 20, 2007, http://news.bbc.co.uk/2/hi/business/6422721.stm.
35. Braithwaite, "Shame and Criminal Justice."
36. Jonathan Fast, *Ceremonial Violence: A Psychological Explanation of School Shootings* (New York: Overlook Press, 2008).
37. Ted Wachtel, "Defining Restorative" (Bethlehem, PA: International Institute for Restorative Practices, 2013), http://djci4vzeaw44g.cloudfront.net/wp-content/uploads/sites/13/2014/04/A4_IIRP_Europe_Defining_Restorative.pdf.
38. "Mark Yantzi Talks About First Case Where Offenders Met Victims," Restorative Works Learning Network, 2012), http://restorativeworks.net/2012/03/mark-yantzi-talks-about-first-case-where-offenders-met-victims/.
39. Ibid.
40. McCold 1999; Peachey, 1989.
41. "National Evaluation of the Restorative Justice in Schools Programme" (London: Youth Justice Board for England and Wales, 2004); "SaferSanerSchools: Transforming School Culture with Restorative Practices" (Bethlehem, PA: International Institute for Restorative Practices, 2003).
42. "SaferSanerSchools: Whole-School Change Through Restorative Practices" (Bethlehem, PA: International Institute of Restorative Practices, 2011), http://www.iirp.edu/pdf/WSC-Overview.pdf.

43. Laura Mirsky, "SaferSanerSchools: Transforming School Cultures with Restorative Practices," *Reclaiming Children and Youth* 16, no. 2 (2007): 5.
44. Palisades School District, "School Profiles 2014–2015:Palisades High School" (Kintnersville, PA: Palisades School District, 2014), http://www.palisadessd.org/cms/lib03/PA01000106/Centricity/Domain/167/2014-2015%20-school%20profile.pdf.
45. Mirsky, "SaferSanerSchools."
46. "SaferSanerSchools: Whole-School."
47. Ibid.
48. Sharalene Charns, Director of Federal Programs, K-12 Instruction and Bilingual Education, Hamtramck [MI] School District, as quoted in ibid.
49. StopBullying.gov.
50. "Names Can Really Hurt Us," Anti-Defamation League, 2012, http://regions.adl.org/connecticut/programs/names-can-really-hurt-us.html.
51. Zehr, *The Little Book.*
52. Gerri Hirshey, "Pushing Back at Bullying," *The New York Times*, January 28, 2007, http://www.nytimes.com/2007/01/28/nyregion/nyregionspecial2/28rbully.html.
53. Paul Schott, "Names Day Program Targets Bullying," GreenwichTime.com, November 23, 2013, http://www.greenwichtime.com/news/article/Names-Day-program-targets-bullying-5003120.php.
54. Ibid.
55. Hirshey, "Pushing Back." This and the following excerpt are from a 2007 Greenwich High School Names Day but are pretty typical of what I heard in 2013. Again, I chose to quote them for accuracy and confidentiality.
56. Ibid.
57. Schott, "Names Day Program."

REFERENCES

"4 Policemen Hurt in 'Village' Raid; Melee Near Sheridan Square Follows Action at Bar." *The New York Times*, June 29, 1969.

"About Us." Lambda Legal. Accessed January 3, 2014. http://www.lambdalegal.org/about-us.

Abray, Jane. "Feminism in the French Revolution." *The American Historical Review* 80, no. 1 (February 1975): 43.

Adam, Barry D. *The Rise of a Gay and Lesbian Movement*. Social Movements Past and Present. Boston: Twayne, 1987.

Adkisson, James. "I Guess You're Wondering Why I Did This." July 27, 2008.

Adkisson, Lisa. "Petition for Order of Protection." Chancery Court, Anderson County, TN, March 17, 2000.

"AFTAH Interview with Barb Anderson—Discusses Radical Sex Ed and School Promotion of Homosexuality." Americans for Truth About Homosexuality, November 27, 2010. http://americansfortruth.com/2010/12/01/112710-aftah-interview-with-barb-anderson/.

Ahern, Louise Knott. "'The Burning Bed': A Turning Point in Fight against Domestic Violence." *Lansing State Journal*, September 27, 2009. http://www.lansingstate-journal.com/article/99999999/NEWS01/909270304/-Burning-Bed-turning-point-fight-against-domestic-violence.

Alcoholics Anonymous: The Story of How Many Thousands of Men and Women Have Recovered from Alcoholism. 4th ed. New York: Alcoholics Anonymous World Services, 2001.

Ali, Russlynn. "Dear Colleague Letter." Office of the Assistant Secretary for Civil Rights, US Department of Education, October 26, 2010. http://www2.ed.gov/about/offices/list/ocr/letters/colleague-201010.html.

American Association of Suicidology. "Youth Suicide Fact Sheet." American Association of Suicidology, 2006. http://www.suicidology.org/.

American Psychiatric Association. *Diagnostic and Statistical Manual of Mental Disorders*. 1st ed. Washington, DC: American Psychiatric Association, 1952.

"Anoka-Hennepin Disputes Bullying-Suicide Connection." MPR News, December 7, 2010. http://www.mprnews.org/story/2010/12/17/anoka-hennepin-bullying-suicides.

Athens, Lonnie H. *The Creation of Dangerous Violent Criminals*. Urbana: University of Illinois Press, 1992.

Avidor, Ken, Karl Bremer, and Eva Young. *The Madness of Michele Bachmann: A Broad-Minded Survey of a Small-Minded Candidate.* Hoboken, NJ: Wiley, 2011.

Avila, Jim, and Sarah Koch. "Boot Camp Death—Caught on Tape." ABC News, April 28, 2007. http://abcnews.go.com/2020/story?id=2751785&page=1.

Babington, Charles, and Jonathan Weisman. "Rep. Foley Quits in Page Scandal." *The Washington Post*, September 30, 2006, http://www.washingtonpost.com/wp-dyn/content/article/2006/09/29/AR2006092901574.html.

"Bad Teacher Cast Discusses Bad Nicknames." Young Hollywood, 2011. http://www.younghollywood.com/videos/yhstudio/june/bad-teacher-cast-discusses-bad-nicknames.html.

Barrouquere, Brett. "Nation's Last Public Execution, 75 Years Ago, Still Haunts Town." *Boston Globe*, August 14, 2011. http://www.boston.com/news/nation/articles/2011/08/14/after_75_years_last_public_hanging_haunts_city/.

Barstow, Anne L. *Witchcraze: A New History of the European Witch Hunts.* Reprint ed. San Francisco, CA: HarperOne, 1995.

Bendick, Marc, Charles W. Jackson, and Victor A. Reinoso. "Measuring Employment Discrimination through Controlled Experiments." *The Review of Black Political Economy* 23, no. 1 (1994): 25–48.

Bernstein, Arnie. *Bath Massacre: America's First School Bombing.* Ann Arbor: University of Michigan Press, 2009.

Bertrand, M., and Mullainathan. "Are Emily and Brendan More Employable than Latoya and Tyrone? Evidence on Racial Discrimination in the Labor Market from a Large Randomized." *American Economic Review* 94, no. 4 (2004): 991–1013.

Bettiga-Boukerbout, Maria Gabriella. "'Crimes of Honor' in the Italian Penal Code: An Analysis of History and Reform." In *Honor*, edited by Lynn Welchman and Sara Hossain. London: Zed Books, 2005.

Bion, W. R. *Experiences in Groups: And Other Papers.* 1st ed. New York: Routledge, 1991.

Birkey, Andy. "Conservative Christian Parents Fight for Right to Discriminate Against LGBT Students at Anoka Hennepin." *Twin Cities Daily Planet*, January 13, 2012. http://www.tcdailyplanet.net/news/2012/01/13/conservative-christian-parents-fight-right-discriminate-against-lgbt-students-anoka-.

Blachman, Dara R., and Stephen P. Hinshaw. "Patterns of Friendship Among Girls With and Without Attention-Deficit/Hyperactivity Disorder." *Journal of Abnormal Child Psychology* 30, no. 6 (2002): 625–640.

Black, Edwin. "The Horrifying American Roots of Nazi Eugenics." History News Network, September 2003. http://historynewsnetwork.org/article/1796.

Black, Edwin. *War Against the Weak: Eugenics and America's Campaign to Create a Master Race*, Exp. ed. Washington, DC: Dialog Press, 2012.

Blair, Pete J., and Katherine W. Schweit. "A Study of Active Shooter Incidents in the United States between 2000 and 2013." San Marcos and Washington, DC: Texas State University and Federal Bureau of Investigation, US Department of Justice, 2014. http://www.fbi.gov/news/stories/2014/september/fbi-releases-study-on-active-shooter-incidents/pdfs/a-study-of-active-shooter-incidents-in-the-u.s.-between-2000-and-2013.

Blanchard, Mathew P. "A Killer's Past and Present Collide He Wants to Tell Why He Shot a Swarthmore Classmate in '55: Not Everyone Cares to Hear It." *Philadelphia Inquirer*, February 13, 2005.

Blumstein, Alfred, Frederick P. Rivara, and Richard Rosenfeld. "The Rise and Decline of Homicide—and Why." *Annual Review of Public Health* 21, no. 1 (2000): 505–541.

Bolino, August C. *Men of Massachusetts: Bay State Contributors to American Society*. Lincoln, NE: iUniverse, 2012.

"'Bomber' Ordered to State Hospital; Leibowitz Commits Metesky to Matteawan as 'Hopeless and Incurable Man' Mental Factor Decisive." *The New York Times*, April 19, 1957. http://query.nytimes.com/gst/abstract.html?res=9C04E6DC17 30E23BBC4152DFB266838C649EDE.

Boudreau, Abbie, and Ken Shiffman. "Minuteman's High-Tech Border Barrier Called 'a Cow Fence.'" CNN, US edition, November 7, 2007. http://www.cnn.com/2007/US/11/07/border.fence/.

Bowlby, John. "Forty-Four Juvenile Thieves: Their Characters and Home-Life." *International Journal of Psycho-Analysis* 25 (1944): 19–53.

Bowlby, John. *Attachment*: Vol. 1, *Attachment & Loss*. 2nd ed. New York: Basic Books, 1983.

"Boy Suicide Had Death Song." *The New York Times*, April 6, 1936.

Bradshaw, John. *Healing the Shame That Binds You*. 1st ed. New York: HCI, 1988.

Braithwaite, John. *Crime, Shame and Reintegration*. Cambridge, UK: Cambridge University Press, 1989.

Braithwaite, John. "Shame and Criminal Justice." *Canadian Journal of Criminology* 42, no. 3 (2000): 281–298.

Brake, J. D. "Terrorism and the Military's Role in Domestic Crisis Management: Background and Issues for Congress." Washington, DC: Congressional Research Service, 2001.

Bretherton, I, and K. A. Munholland. "Internal Working Models in Attachment Relationships: A Construct Revisited." In *Handbook of Attachment: Theory, Research, and Clinical Applications*, edited by Jude Cassidy and Phillip R. Shaver. New York: Guilford Press, 1999.

Briggs, Bill. "One Every 18 Hours: Military Suicide Rate Still High despite Hard Fight to Stem Deaths." NBC News, May 23, 2013. http://usnews.nbcnews.com/_news/2013/05/23/18447439-one-every-18-hours-military-suicide-rate-still-high-despite-hard-fight-to-stem-deaths.

Brummel, Bill, and Geoffrey Sharp. *Bullied: The Jamie Nabozny Story*. 2010. http://vimeo.com/30915646.

Buchanan, Susy, and David Holthouse. "Minuteman Civil Defense Corps Leader Chris Simcox Has Troubled Past." Southern Poverty Law Center, *Intelligence Report* (Winter 2005). http://www.splcenter.org/get-informed/intelligence-report/browse-all-issues/2005/winter/the-little-prince.

Burke, Leslie K., and Diane R. Follingstad. "Violence in Lesbian and Gay Relationships Theory, Prevalence, and Correlational Factors." *Clinical Psychology Review* 19, no. 5 (August 1999): 487–512.

Burton-Bradley, B. G. "The Amok Syndrome in Papua and New Guinea." In *The Culture-Bound Syndromes*, edited by Ronald C. Simons and Charles C. Hughes, 237–249. Netherlands: Springer, 1985.

Bycel, Benjamin. "Sandwich Boards of Shame for Convicted Execs." *Los Angeles Times*, August 13, 2004. http://articles.latimes.com/2004/aug/13/opinion/oe-bycel13.

Byrne, John. "Anti-Gay Congressman David Dreier, Said to Be Gay, 'Lived with Male Chief of Staff.'" *The Raw Story*, n.d. http://www.rawstory.com/exclusives/byrne/david_dreier_outed_brad_smith_gay_920.htm.

Cady, Paul H. "Memorandum Re: Department of Justice Investigation of Complaint." US Department of Justice, Office of Civil Rights, April 25, 2011. http://i2.cdn. turner.com/cnn/2011/images/07/18/doj.investigation.pdf.

Cappelletti, Mauro, John Henry Merryman, and Joseph M. Perillo. *The Italian Legal System*. Stanford, CA: Stanford University Press, 1967.

Carlsmith, Kevin M., and John M. Darley. "Psychological Aspects of Retributive Justice." *Advances in Experimental Social Psychology* 40 (2008): 193–236.

Carlson, Dennis. "Anoka-Hennepin Policy Aims to Respect All Families and Students." MPR News, June 8, 2011. http://www.mprnews.org/story/2011/06/08/carlson.

Cartwright, Samuel A. "Diseases and Peculiarities of the Negro Race." *DeBow's Review*, 1851. http://www.pbs.org/wgbh/aia/part4/4h3106t.html.

Caruthers, Osgood. "Canadian Envoy Ends Life; Named in U.S. Red Inquiry; E. Herbert Norman Jumps From Building in Cairo—Case Angers Ottawa." *The New York Times*, April 5, 1957, sec. A.

Centers for Disease Control. "Youth Risk Surveillance Survey—United States, 2013." *Morbidity and Mortality Weekly Report*, Surveillance Summaries 63, no. 4 (June 13, 2014).

Centers for Disease Control and Prevention. "Trends in Suicide Rates Among Persons Ages 10 and Older, by Sex, United States, 1991–2009." Accessed April 8, 2014. http://www.cdc.gov/violenceprevention/suicide/statistics/trends01.html.

Chase, Alston. *Harvard and the Unabomber: The Education of an American Terrorist*. 1st ed. New York: W. W. Norton, 2003.

"Civil Rights Division Educational Opportunities Case Summaries." US Department of Justice. Accessed March 25, 2014. http://www.justice.gov/crt/about/edu/ documents/casesummary.php.

Cleckley, Hervey M. *The Mask of Sanity: An Attempt to Clarify Some Issues about the so-Called Psychopathic Personality*. Augusta, GA: E. S. Cleckley, 1988.

"Clippers Owner Donald Sterling to GF—Don't Bring Black People to My Games ... Including Magic Johnson." TMZ Sports, April 25, 2014. http://www.tmz.com/2014/04/26/donald-sterling-clippers-owner-black-people-racist-audio-magic-johnson/.

Coleman, Loren. *Suicide Clusters*. Boston: Faber & Faber, 1987.

Collins, Lauren. "Friend Game." *The New Yorker*, January 21, 2008. http://www.newyorker.com/reporting/2008/01/21/080121fa_fact_collins.

Cooper, Michael. "U.S. Will Have No Ethnic Majority, Census Finds." *The New York Times*, December 12, 2012, http://www.nytimes.com/2012/12/13/us/us-will-have-no-ethnic-majority-census-finds.html.

Cox, James A. "Bilboes, Brands and Branks." *Colonial Williamsburg Journal* (Spring 2003). http://www.history.org/Foundation/journal/spring03/branks.cfm.

Crosby, Alex, Beth Han, LaVonne A. G. Ortega, Sharyn E. Parks, and Joseph Gfroerer. *Suicidal Thoughts and Behaviors Among Adults Aged ≥18 Years—United States, 2008-2009*. Surveillance Summaries. Atlanta: Centers for Disease Control and Prevention, October 21, 2011. http://www.cdc.gov/mmwr/preview/mmwrhtml/ss6013a1.htm?s_cid=ss6013a1_eSuicidal.

Cross, H., G. Kenney, J. Mell, and W. Zimmerman. *Differential Treatment of Hispanic and Anglo Job Seekers: Hiring Practices in Two Cities*. Washington, DC: Urban Institute Press, 1989.

Daly, Martin, Margo Wilson, and Shawn Vasdev. "Income Inequality and Homicide Rates in Canada and the United States." *Canadian Journal of Criminology* 43 (2001): 219–236.

Darwin, Charles. *On the Origin of Species by Means of Natural Selection: Or the Preservation of Favoured Races in the Struggle for Life.* New York: D. Appleton, 1869.

Darwin, Charles. *The Expression of the Emotions in Man and Animals.* London: John Murray, 1872. http://darwin-online.org.uk/content/frameset?itemID=F1142&viewtype=text&pageseq=1.

D'Augelli, Anthony R., Arnold H. Grossman, Nicholas P. Salter, Joseph J. Vasey, Michael T. Starks, and Katerina O. Sinclair. "Predicting the Suicide Attempts of Lesbian, Gay, and Bisexual Youth." *Suicide and Life-Threatening Behavior* 35, no. 6 (2005): 646–660.

De Grazia, Victoria. *How Fascism Ruled Women: Italy, 1922–1945.* Berkeley: University of California Press, 1992.

Dempsey, Cleta L. "Health and Social Issues of Gay, Lesbian, and Bisexual Adolescents." *Families in Society* 75, no. 3 (1994): 160–167.

Desiree Shelton & Sarah Lindstrom v. Anoka-Hennepin School District, Champlain Park High School et al., n.d.

Diamond, M. J. "Olympe De Gouges and the French Revolution: The Construction of Gender as Critique." In *Women and Revolution: Global Expressions*, edited by M. J. Diamond, 1–19. Dordrecht: Springer, 1998.

Dillberto, Gloria. "A Violent Death, a Haunted Life." *People Magazine*, October 8, 1984. http://www.people.com/people/archive/article/0,,20088845,00.html.

"Donald Trump Biography: Reality Television Star." Biography.com, 2015. http://www.biography.com/people/donald-trump-9511238#synopsis.

Doty, Robert C. "Growth of Overt Homosexuality In City Provokes Wide Concern." *New York Times*, December 17, 1963.

Doty, Roxanne Lynn. "States of Exception on the Mexico–U.S. Border: Security, 'Decisions,' and Civilian Border Patrols." *International Political Sociology* 1, no. 2 (June 1, 2007): 113–137.

Dougherty, Jon E. *Illegals: The Imminent Threat Posed by Our Unsecured U.S.-Mexico Border.* Nashville: Thomas Nelson, 2004.

Dressler, J. "Battered Women and Sleeping Abusers: Some Reflections." *Ohio State Journal of Criminal Law* 3 (2005): 457–471.

Durkheim, Emil. *Suicide: A Study in Sociology.* London: Routledge, 1897.

Durose, Mathew R., Alexia D. Cooper, and Howard N. Snyder. *Recidivism of Prisoners Released in 30 States in 2005: Patterns from 2005 to 2010.* Washington, DC: US Department of Justice, April 2014.

Eckholm, Erik. "In Efforts to End Bullying, Some See Agenda." *The New York Times*, November 6, 2010, http://www.nytimes.com/2010/11/07/us/07bully.html.

Egan, Luke A., and Natasha Todorov. "Forgiveness as a Coping Strategy to Allow School Students to Deal with the Effects of Being Bullied: Theoretical and Empirical Discussion." *Journal of Social and Clinical Psychology* 28, no. 2 (2009): 198–222.

Egan, Timothy. "Wanted: Border Hoppers. And Some Excitement, Too." *The New York Times*, April 1, 2005, http://www.nytimes.com/2005/04/01/national/01border.html.

Ekman, P., and W. V. Friesen. "Constants Across Cultures in the Face and Emotion." *Journal of Personality and Social Psychology* 17, no. 2 (1971): 124–129.

Ekman, Paul. "Basic Emotions." In *Handbook of Cognition and Emotion*, edited by Tim Dalgleish and Mick Power. New York: Wiley, 2000.

Elgar, Frank J., and Nicole Aitken. "Income Inequality, Trust and Homicide in 33 Countries." *The European Journal of Public Health* 21, no. 2 (April 1, 2011): 241–246.

Elgar, Frank J., Wendy Craig, William Boyce, Antony Morgan, and Rachel Vella-Zarb. "Income Inequality and School Bullying: Multilevel Study of Adolescents in 37 Countries." *Journal of Adolescent Health* 45, no. 4 (October 2009): 351–359.

Elison, J., R. Lennon, and S. Pulos. "Investigating the Compass of Shame: The Development of the Compass of Shame Scale." *Social Behavior and Personality: An International Journal* 34, no. 3 (2006): 221–238.

Ellsworth, Monty J. *The Bath School Disaster: Text & Pictures*. 1st ed. Bath, Michigan: Self-published, 1928. http://daggy.name/tbsd/tbsd-x.htm.

Erdely, Sabrina. "One Town's War on Gay Teens." *Rolling Stone* 2, no. 2 (2012). http://www.rollingstone.com/politics/news/one-towns-war-on-gay-teens-20120202.

Ericson, Steve. "District 11 Deals With Another Student Suicide." CTN News, Channel 15, May 20, 2011. http://www.ctnstudios.com/index.php?option=com_content&view=article&id=553:district-11-deals-with-another-student-suicide&Itemid=100.

Erikson, Eric H. *Childhood and Society*. New York: W.W. Norton, 1950.

Esposito, John L. *The Oxford Dictionary of Islam*. Oxford: Oxford University Press, 2003.

Falk, William. "That Wasn't the Week That Was." *The New York Times*, September 5, 2004, http://www.nytimes.com/2004/09/05/opinion/05falk.html.

Fast, Jonathan. *Ceremonial Violence: A Psychological Explanation of School Shootings*. New York: Overlook Press, 2008.

Fast, Jonathan. "Gary Scott Pennington: Distal and Proximal Shame in a School Rampage Shooting." *Violence and Gender* 1, no. 3 (2014): 134–142.

Favazza, Armando R. *Bodies Under Siege: Self-Mutilation and Body Modification in Culture and Psychiatry*. Baltimore: Johns Hopkins University Press, 1996.

Finckenauer, J. O. *Scared Straight and the Panacea Phenomenon*. Englewood Cliffs, NJ: Prentice-Hall, 1982.

Finckenauer, J. O., P. W. Gavin, A. Hovland, and E. Storvoll. *Scared Straight: The Panacea Phenomenon Revisited*. Prospect Heights, IL: Waveland Press, 1999.

Finkelman, Paul, ed. *Encyclopedia of American Civil Liberties*. New York: Routledge, 2006.

"Five Children Killed as Gunman Attacks a California School." *The New York Times*, January 18, 1989, http://www.nytimes.com/1989/01/18/us/five-children-killed-as-gunman-attacks-a-california-school.html.

Fix, Michael, and Raymond Struyk. *Clear and Convincing Evidence: Measurement of Discrimination in America*. Washington, DC: Urban Institute Press, 1993.

Flanigan, Beverly J. "Shame and Forgiving in Alcoholism." *Alcoholism Treatment Quarterly* 4, no. 2 (March 7, 1988): 181–195.

"Flogging for Wife Beaters." *The New York Times*, July 4, 1886.

Frazer, Sir James George. *The Golden Bough: A Study of Magic and Religion*. New Delhi: Cosmo Publications, 2005.

Freud, Sigmund. "The Interpretation of Dreams." *Psychology Today*, 1899.

Freud, Sigmund. *Three Essays on the Theory of Sexuality*. Translated by James Strachey. Mansfield Centre, CT: Martino Publishing, 2011.

Friedman, Lawrence M. *A History of American Law*. 3rd ed. New York: Touchstone, 2005.

Fulgham v. State, 46 Ala. 143 (Alabama 1871).

Garbarino, James. *Lost Boys; Why Our Sons Turn Violent and How We Can Save Them*. New York: Free Press, 1999.

Gaw, Albert C., and Ruth L. Bernstein. "Classification of Amok in DSM-IV." *Psychiatric Services* 43, no. 8 (August 1, 1992): 789–793.

Gayle, Damien. "Women Stoned to Death in Syria for Adultery." *Daily Mail*, August 9, 2014. http://www.dailymail.co.uk/news/article-2720746/Women-stoned-death-Syria-adultery.html.

Gibson, P. "Gay Male and Lesbian Youth Suicide." In *Alcohol, Drug Abuse, and Mental Health Administration. Report of the Secretary's Task Force on Youth Suicide: Vol. 3, Prevention and Interventions in Youth Suicide.* Washington, DC: US Department of Health & Human Services, Public Health Service, Alcohol, Drug Abuse, and Mental Health Administration, 1989.

Gilchrist, Jim, and Jerome R. Corsi. *Minutemen: The Battle to Secure America's Borders.* 1st ed. Los Angeles, CA: World Ahead, 2006.

Gilligan, Carol. *In a Different Voice: Psychological Theory and Women's Development.* 1st ed. Cambridge, MA: Harvard University Press, 1993.

Gilligan, James. *Violence: Our Deadly Epidemic and Its Causes.* New York: Putnam, 1996.

Gilligan, James. *Violence: Reflections on a National Epidemic.* 1st ed. New York: Vintage, 1997.

Gilligan, James. *Preventing Violence: Prospects for Tomorrow.* New York: Thames & Hudson, 2001.

Gimlette, John D. "Notes on a Case of Amok." *The American Journal of Tropical Medicine and Hygiene* 4 (1901): 195–199.

Glaister, Dan. "Pink Prison Makes Texan Inmates Blush." *The Guardian*, US edition, October 10, 2006, http://www.theguardian.com/world/2006/oct/11/usa.danglaister.

Glaze, Lauren E., and Danielle Kaeble. *Correctional Populations in the United States, 2013.* Washington, DC: US Department of Justice, Office of Justice Programs, Bureau of Justice Statistics, December 2014.

"Gloomy Sunday Lyrics." Lyricsfreak.com. Accessed September 17, 2008. http://www.lyricsfreak.com/b/billie+holiday/gloomy+sunday_20017999.html.

Gould, Stephen Jay. *The Mismeasure of Man.* Rev. and exp. ed. New York: W. W. Norton, 1996.

Government Accountability Office. *Border Patrol: Key Elements of New Strategic Plan Not Yet in Place to Inform Border Security Status and Resource Needs.* Washington, DC: Government Accountability Office, December 2012. http://www.gao.gov/assets/660/650730.pdf.

Gray, John. *Men Are from Mars, Women Are from Venus: The Classic Guide to Understanding the Opposite Sex.* New York: Harper Paperbacks, 2012.

Greenwald, Robert, dir. *The Burning Bed.* Culver City, CA: Tisch/Avnet Productions, 1984.

"Gun Rhetoric vs. Gun Facts." FactCheck.org, December 20, 2012. http://www.factcheck.org/2012/12/gun-rhetoric-vs-gun-facts/.

Guyer, Amanda E., Erin B. McClure-Tone, Nina D. Shiffrin, Daniel S. Pine, and Eric E. Nelson. "Probing the Neural Correlates of Anticipated Peer Evaluation in Adolescence." *Child Development* 80, no. 4 (2009): 1000–1015.

Hamill, Sean D. "Blog Details Shooter's Frustration." *The New York Times*, August 6, 2009, http://www.nytimes.com/2009/08/06/us/06shoot.html?_r=1&scp=1&sq=George+Sodini&st=nyt.

Hare, Robert D. *Without Conscience: The Disturbing World of the Psychopaths Among Us.* 1st ed. New York: Guilford Press, 1999.

Hawkins, Beth. "Bullying Gay and Lesbian Kids: How a School District Became a Suicide Contagion Area." *Minnesota Post*, December 7, 2011. http://www.minnpost.com/politics-policy/2011/12/bullying-gay-and-lesbian-kids-how-school-district-became-suicide-contagion-a.

Hawthorne, Nathaniel. *The Scarlet Letter*. Boston: Ticknor, Reed and Fields, 1850.

"Helldorado Gunfight Theatre and Restaurant—Tombstone—Reviews of Helldorado Gunfight Theatre and Restaurant." Trip Advisor. Accessed October 20, 2014. http://www.tripadvisor.com/ Attraction_Review-g31381-d1382694-Reviews-Helldorado_Gunfight_Theatre_and_Restaurant-Tombstone_Arizona.html#REVIEWS.

Herek, Gregory M. *Hate Crimes: Confronting Violence Against Lesbians and Gay Men*. Thousand Oaks, CA: SAGE, 1992.

Herman, Judith Lewis. "Shattered Shame States and Their Repair." Paper presented at the John Bowlby Memorial Lecture, Cambridge, MA, March 10, 2007.

Herrnstein, Richard J., and Charles Murray. *The Bell Curve: Intelligence and Class Structure in American Life*. 1st Free Press pbk. ed. New York: Free Press, 1996.

Hetrick, Emery S., and A. Damien Martin. "Developmental Issues and Their Resolution for Gay and Lesbian Adolescents." *Journal of Homosexuality* 14, no. 1–2 (1987): 25–43.

Himber, Judith. "Blood Rituals: Self-Cutting in Female Psychiatric Inpatients." *Psychotherapy: Theory, Research, Practice, Training* 31, no. 4 (1994): 620–631.

Hinton-Johnson, Kaavonia. "Hughes, Francine." In *Encyclopedia of Domestic Violence and Abuse*, edited by Laura L. Finley, 2:228–231. New York: ABC-CLIO, 2013.

Hirshey, Gerri. "Pushing Back at Bullying." *The New York Times*, January 28, 2007, http://www.nytimes.com/2007/01/28/nyregion/nyregionspecial2/28rbully.html.

Hitchens, Christopher. *The Portable Atheist: Essential Readings for the Non-Believer*. Cambridge, MA: Da Capo Press, 2007.

Holland, Barbara. *Gentlemen's Blood: A History of Dueling*. New York: Bloomsbury, 2004.

"Hooten Finds Man Reverting to Ape; Harvard Professor Warns Lag in Biological Development Threatens Civilization; Derides Mechanical Ease; Tells Engineers Genius Like Theirs Must Find Means of Improving Race Calls for Race Improvement Mankind 'Coasting Downhill' Machines Get Better, Man Worse." *The New York Times*, December 9, 1937.

Horn, Dan. "To What Extent Was the Protestant Reformation Responsible for the Witch-Hunts in the Years 1520–1650?" Dorchester, UK: Thomas Hardye School, 2012.

Hossain, Sara, and Lynn Welchman. *"Honour": Crimes, Paradigms and Violence Against Women*. New York: Zed Books, 2005.

Hsieh, Ching-Chi, and M. D. Pugh. "Poverty, Income Inequality, and Violent Crime: A Meta-Analysis of Recent Aggregate Data Studies." *Criminal Justice Review* 18, no. 2 (September 1, 1993): 182–202.

Huddleston, Scott. "Wounded Soldier Heals With Comedy." *San Antonio Express-News*, August 13, 2010. http://www.mysanantonio.com/entertainment/stage/article/Wounded-soldier-heals-with-comedy-848017.php#src=fb.

Huesmann, L. Rowell, Leonard D. Eron, Monroe M. Lefkowitz, and Leopold O. Walder. "Stability of Aggression Over Time and Generations." *Developmental Psychology* 20, no. 6 (November 1984): 1120–1134.

"Hunted as Slayer, Brooks Ends Life." *The New York Times*, August 28, 1948, sec. A.

Hunter, Mic. *The Twelve Steps and Shame*. Hazeldem Classics for Continuing Care. Center City, MN: Hazelden, 1988.

Hutton, Ronald. *The Triumph of the Moon: A History of Modern Pagan Witchcraft*. Oxford: Oxford University Press, 2001.

Isay, Richard. *Being Homosexual: Gay Men and Their Development*. New York: Vintage, 2010.

"Islamic Penal Code of the Islamic Republic of Iran: Book One & Book Two." Iran Human Rights: Documentation Center, April 4, 2013. http://www.iranhrdc. org/english/human-rights-documents/iranian-codes/3200-islamic-penal-code-of-the-islamic-republic-of-iran-book-one-and-book-two.html.

Izard, Carroll E. *Human Emotions*. New York: Plenum, 1977.

Jane Doe, et al & U. S. v Anoka-Hennepin Consent Decree. US District Court for the District of Minnesota, 2012.

"Jamie Nabozny." Speak Truth to Power, April 5, 2011. http://blogs.nysut.org/sttp/defenders/jamie-nabozny/.

Janik, Rachel. "From 'No Homo Promo' to 'Model for the Nation.'" Medill Equal Media Project, October 2, 2012. http://www.equalmediaproject.com/features/no-homo-promo-model-nation.

Johns, Emily. "In Gay Slur Settlement, All Are Paying a Price." *Star Tribune/St. Paul*. August 13, 2009, Local ed. http://www.startribune.com/local/stpaul/53189752.html.

Johnson, David T. "The Homicide Drop in Postwar Japan." *Homicide Studies* 12, no. 1 (February 1, 2008): 146–160.

Johnson, Sally C. "Forensic Evaluation of Theodor Kaczynski." Ninth Circuit Court of Appeals, January 16, 1998. http://www.paulcooijmans.com/psychology/una-bombreport.html.

Johnstone, William W. *Border War (Invasion USA)*. New York: Pinnacle, 2006.

Jonnes, Jill. *Hep-Cats, Narcs, and Pipe Dreams: A History of America's Romance with Illegal Drugs*. Baltimore: Johns Hopkins University Press, 1996.

Jordan, David Starr. *The Blood of the Nation: A Study of the Decay of Races Through Survival of the Unfit*. Boston: American Unitarian Association, 1902.

"Jordanian Kills Sister to 'Cleanse Family Honor.'" *Al Arabia News*, April 30, 2013. http://english.alarabiya.net/en/News/middle-east/2013/04/30/Jordanian-kills-sister-to-cleanse-family-honor-.html.

"J.T. Ready." Southern Poverty Law Center." Accessed October 13, 2014. http://www.splcenter.org/get-informed/intelligence-files/profiles/jt-ready.

Kaczynski, Theodore. *The Unabomber Manifesto: Industrial Society and Its Future*. Filiquarian Publishing, 2005.

Kalat, James W. *Introduction to Psychology*, 10th ed. Belmont, CA: Cengage Learning, 2013.

Kanner, L. "Autistic Disturbances of Affective Contact." *Acta Paedopsychiatrica* 35, no. 4 (1968): 100–136.

Kaphle, Anup. "Pakistani Woman Stoned to Death Because She Married the Man She Loved." *The Washington Post*, May 27, 2014. http://www.washingtonpost.com/blogs/worldviews/wp/2014/05/27/photo-pakistani-woman-stoned-to-death-because-she-married-the-man-she-loved/.

Karen, Robert. *Becoming Attached: First Relationships and How They Shape Our Capacity to Love*. New York: Oxford University Press, 1998.

Karim, Kaleef K. "Quran 4:34, 'Beat Them' (Wife Abuse)?" Discover the Truth, December 4, 2013. http://discover-the-truth.com/2013/12/04/quran-434-beat-them-wife-abuse/.

Kaufman, Gershen. *Shame: The Power of Caring*. 3rd ed., rev. and exp. Rochester, VT: Schenkman Books, 1992.

Kaufman, Michael T. "Mad Bomber,' Now 70, Goes Free Today; Mad Bomber,' Now 70, Goes Free Today 37 Blasts Set Initials 'F.P.' Explained Institute Assailed." *The New York Times*, December 13, 1973. http://query.nytimes.com/gst/abstract.html?res=9B02E4DE1339E73ABC4B52DFB4678388669EDE.

Kawachi, I., and B. P. Kennedy. "Income Inequality and Health: Pathways and Mechanisms." *Health Services Research* 34, no. 1 Pt 2 (April 1999): 215–227.

Kerlik, Bobby. "Pitt Says 'No' to LA Fitness Killer's Bequest of $225,000." *Pittsburg Tribune-Review*. August 18, 2009. http://triblive.com/x/pittsburghtrib/news/tribpm/s_638749.html.

Kernberg, Otto F. "Factors in the Psychoanalytic Treatment of Narcissistic Personalities." *Journal of the American Psychoanalytic Association* 18 (1970): 51–85.

Kinnamon, Keneth, and Michel Fabre. *Conversations with Richard Wright*. Jackson: University Press of Mississippi, 1993.

Kinsey, Alfred C. *Sexual Behavior in the Human Male*. 1st ed. Bloomington: Indiana University Press, 1948.

Knoll, James L. IV. "The 'Pseudocommando' Mass Murderer: Part I, the Psychology of Revenge and Obliteration." *The Journal of the American Academy of Psychiatry and the Law* 38, no. 1 (2010): 87–94.

Kohut, Heinz. *The Analysis of the Self: A Systematic Approach to the Psychoanalytic Treatment of Narcissistic Personality Disorders*. Madison, CT: International Universities Press, 1971.

"'Kramer's' Racist Tirade—Caught on Tape." TMZ Sports, November 20, 2006. http://www.tmz.com/2006/11/20/kramers-racist-tirade-caught-on-tape/.

"Kyle Doss Wants Reparations for Kramer Calling Him a Nigger." 2006. https://www.youtube.com/watch?v=2VFGv0mdckM&feature=youtube_gdata_player.

Lansky, M. "Shame and Domestic Violence." In *The Many Faces of Shame*, edited by Donald L. Nathanson, 335–362. New York: Guilford Press, 1987.

Lapchick, Richard. *The 2013 Racial and Gender Report Card: National Basketball Association*. Executive Summary. Orlando, FL: Institute for Diversity and Ethics in Sport, June 25, 2013.

Lee, Cynthia. *Murder and the Reasonable Man: Passion and Fear in the Criminal Courtroom*. New York: New York University Press, 2003.

Lee, Martin A. *Smoke Signals: A Social History of Marijuana—Medical, Recreational and Scientific*. New York: Simon & Schuster, 2013.

Lee, Matthew R., and William B. Bankston. "Political Structure, Economic Inequality, and Homicide: A Cross-National Analysis." *Deviant Behavior* 20, no. 1 (January 1999): 27–55.

Lemons, Stephen. "Chris Simcox Worked for iMemories, Duties Didn't Include Viewing Kid Pics, Says Company, Arizona Treasurer Doug Ducey Recently Company's Board Chair (w/Update)." Feathered Bastard, June 25, 2013. http://blogs.phoenixnewtimes.com/bastard/2013/06/chris_simcox_worked_for_imemor.php.

Lepore, Jill. "The Last Amazon: Wonder Woman Returns." *The New Yorker*, September 22, 2014.

Levenkron, Steven. *Cutting: Understanding and Overcoming Self-Mutilation.* Rev. ed. New York: W. W. Norton, 1998.

Levy, David. "Primary Affect Hunger." *The American Journal of Psychiatry* 94 (1937): 643–652.

Levy, Paul. "Anoka County Expects $2.5 Million Grant for Foreclosure Aid." *Star Tribune*, February 25, 2009, http://www.startribune.com/local/north/40266167.html.

Levy, Paul. "Homelessness Rising Dramatically in Twin Cities Suburbs." *Star Tribune*, April 29, 2012, http://www.startribune.com/local/149442415.html.

Lewis, Helen B. *Shame and Guilt in Neurosis.* Madison, CT: International Universities Press, 1971.

Lewis, Helen B. "Shame and the Narcissistic Personality." In *The Many Faces of Shame*, edited by D. L. Nathanson. New York: Guilford Press, 1987.

Lewis, Jone Johnson, Sue Bennett, and Dan Hotchkiss. "American Politics: Who Were Some Famous Unitarian Universalists?" Famous Uus.com, n.d. http://www.famousuus.com/american.htm.

Linehan, Marsha. *Cognitive-Behavioral Treatment of Borderline Personality Disorder.* New York: Guilford Press, 1993.

Lombardo, Paul A. "Nazi Eugenics and the Origins of the Pioneer Fund." *Albany Law Review* 65, no. 3 (n.d.): 822.

Lucas, David. "World Population Growth and Theories." In *An Introduction to Global Studies*, edited by Patricia J. Campbell, Aran MacKinnon, and Christy R. Stevens. Hoboken, NJ: Wiley, 2011.

Luno, Nathan. "Prohibition in America: A Brief History." TheDEA.org, June 12, 2003. http://thedea.org/prohibhistory.html.

Maimonides. *Mishneh Torah Hilchot Teshuvah: The Laws of Repentance.* Translated by Rabbi Eliyahu Touger. New York: Moznaim, 1990.

Males, Mike A. *The Scapegoat Generation: America's War on Adolescents.* Monroe, ME: Common Courage Press, 1996.

Mallon, Gerald P. *We Don't Exactly Get the Welcome Wagon: The Experiences of Gay and Lesbian Adolescents in Child Welfare Systems.* New York: Columbia University Press, 1998.

March, William. *The Bad Seed.* Reissue ed. New York: Harper Perennial, 1954.

"Mark Yantzi Talks About First Case Where Offenders Met Victims." Restorative Works Learning Network, 2012. http://restorativeworks.net/2012/03/mark-yantzi-talks-about-first-case-where-offenders-met-victims/.

Martin, Del. *Battered Wives.* San Francisco, CA: Volcano Press, 1981.

Marx, Karl. "Wage Labour and Capital." Translated by Frederick Engels. *Neue Rheinische Zeitung*, 1849. https://www.marxists.org/archive/marx/works/1847/wage-labour/.

McDonald, Patrick Range. "Donald T. Sterling Fakes His Philanthropy in a New Los Angeles Times Ad." *LA Weekly*, August 20, 2008. http://www.laweekly.com/2008-08-21/news/donald-t-sterling-fakes-his-philanthropy-in-a-new-los-angeles-times-ad/.

McFadden, Robert D. "Prisoner of Rage—A Special Report; From a Child of Promise to the Unabom Suspect." *The New York Times*, May 26, 1996, http://www.nytimes.com/1996/05/26/us/prisoner-of-rage-a-special-report-from-a-child-of-promise-to-the-unabom-suspect.html.

McKinley, Jesse. "Suicides Put Light on Pressures of Gay Teenagers." *The New York Times*, October 3, 2010, http://www.nytimes.com/2010/10/04/us/04suicide.html.

McNulty, Faith. *The Burning Bed.* 1st ed. New York: Harcourt, 1980.

Meyer, Ilan H. "Prejudice, Social Stress, and Mental Health in Lesbian, Gay, and Bisexual Populations: Conceptual Issues and Research Evidence." *Psychological Bulletin* 129, no. 5 (2003): 674–697.

Meyer, Shannon, and Randall H. Carroll. "When Officers Die: Understanding Deadly Domestic Violence Calls for Service." *The Police Chief: The Professional Voice of Law Enforcement* (July 2014).

Minnesota Department of Health. "Adolescent Health: A View from the Minnesota Student Survey." Presented at the MDH Maternal and Child Health Advisory Task Force, June 10, 2011.

Minnesota Department of Health. "Injury and Violence Prevention Home/Leading Causes of Death." n.d. http://www.health.state.mn.us/injury/.

Mirsky, Laura. "SaferSanerSchools: Transforming School Cultures with Restorative Practices." *Reclaiming Children and Youth* 16, no. 2 (2007): 5–12.

Moran, Lisa. "Shame and Violence." Letter to *Psychiatric News*, June 15, 2001.

Morgan, Lewis Henry. *Ancient Society.* New Brunswick, NJ: Transaction, 1877.

Munnell, Alicia H., Lynn E. Browne, James McEneaney, and Geoffrey M. B. Tootell3. "Mortgage Lending in Boston: Interpreting HMDA Data." *The American Economic Review* 86, no. 1 (1996): 25–53.

Murphy, Tim. "The Meltdown of the Anti-Immigration Minuteman Militia." *Mother Jones.* Accessed August 28, 2014. http://www.motherjones.com/politics/2014/08/minuteman-movement-border-crisis-simcox.

Nabozny v. Podlesny. Lambda Legal. Accessed December 6, 2013. http://www.lambdalegal.org.

Nathanson, Donald L. "Affect and Hypnosis: On Paying Friendly Attention to Disturbing Thoughts." *International Journal of Clinical and Experimental Hypnosis* 57, no. 4 (August 31, 2009): 319–342.

"National Evaluation of the Restorative Justice in Schools Programme." London: Youth Justice Board of England and Wales, 2004.

Neisser, Ulric, Gwyneth Boodoo, Thomas J. Bouchard Jr., A. Wade Boykin, Nathan Brody, Stephen J. Ceci, Diane F. Halpern, et al. "Intelligence: Knowns and Unknowns." *American Psychologist* 51, no. 2 (1996): 77–101.

"New York Domestic Violence Laws." Findlaw. Accessed August 8, 2014. http://statelaws.findlaw.com/new-york-law/new-york-domestic-violence-laws.html.

New York City Independent Budget Office. "New York City by the Numbers." August 22, 2013. http://ibo.nyc.ny.us/cgi-park2/?p=516.

Nordland, Rod. "In Spite of the Law, Afghan 'Honor Killings' of Women Continue." *The New York Times*, May 3, 2014.

O'Carroll, Patrick W., James A. Mercy, and John A. Steward. *CDC Recommendations for a Community Plan for the Prevention and Containment of Suicide Clusters.* Atlanta: Centers for Disease Control, Center for Environmental Health and Injury Control, Division of Injury Epidemiology and Control, 1988. https://www.ncjrs.gov/App/abstractdb/AbstractDBDetails.aspx?id=122038.

Ogbu, John U. "From Cultural Differences to Differences in Cultural Frame of Reference." In *Cross-Cultural Roots of Minority Child Development*, edited by P. M. Greenfield and R. R. Cocking, 365–391. Hillsdale, NJ: Lawrence Erlbaum Associates, 1994.

Oksanen, Atte. "Drinking to Death: Traditional Masculinity, Alcohol and Shame in Finnish Metal Lyrics." *Nordic Studies on Alcohol and Drugs* 28, no. 4 (January 1, 2011): 357–372.

Olson, Mary, and Brett Johnson. "Support, Not Litigation, Is the Best Path to Aiding GLBT Students in Anoka-Hennepin." Press Release. Educational Service Center, July 20, 2011. http://i.cdn.turner.com/cnn/2011/images/07/20/a.h.response.splc.nclr.pdf.

Olweus, Dan. *Bullying at School*. Oxford: Blackwell, 1993.

Olweus, Dan. "Bully/Victim Problems in School: Facts and Intervention." *European Journal of Psychology of Education* 12, no. 4 (1997): 495–510.

Onions, C. T., ed. *The Oxford Dictionary of English Etymology*. Oxford: Oxford University Press, 1966.

Pager, Devah, and Hana Shepherd. "The Sociology of Discrimination: Racial Discrimination in Employment, Housing, Credit, and Consumer Markets." *Annual Review of Sociology* 34, no. 1 (January 1, 2008): 181–209.

Palisades School District. "School Profiles 2014–2015: Palisades High School." Kintnersville, PA: Palisades School District, 2014. http://www.palisadessd.org/cms/lib03/PA01000106/Centricity/Domain/167/2014-2015%20school%20profile.pdf.

Parent Action League. "Email to Rolling Stone: Discussion of Homosexuality Leading to Suicide." Quoted by Erdeley, 2012.

Parker-Pope, Tara. "Suicide Rate Rises Sharply in U.S." *The New York Times*, May 2, 2013, http://www.nytimes.com/2013/05/03/health/suicide-rate-rises-sharply-in-us.html.

Paroski, Paul A. "Health Care Delivery and the Concerns of Gay and Lesbian Adolescents." *Journal of Adolescent Health Care* 8, no. 2 (March 1987): 188–192.

Pearson, Roger. *Race, Intelligence and Bias in Academe*. 2nd ed. Washington, DC: Scott Townsend, 1997.

Perlmutter, Emanuel. "Kennedy Orders Wide Manhunt For Movie Bombing Perpetrator." *The New York Times*, December 4, 1956. http://query.nytimes.com/gst/abstract.html?res=9F02EEDE163AE23ABC4C53DFB467838D649EDE.

Petrosino, Anthony, Carolyn Turpin-Petrosino, and John Buehler. "Scared Straight and Other Juvenile Awareness Programs for Preventing Juvenile Delinquency: A Systematic Review of the Randomized Experimental Evidence." *The Annals of the American Academy of Political and Social Science* 589, no. 1 (September 1, 2003): 41–62.

Pew Research Center for the People and the Press. "Columbine Shooting Biggest News Draw of 1999," May 1, 2000. www.people-press.org/yearendrpt.htm.

Pew Research: Hispanic Trends Project. *2011 Hispanic Origin Profiles*. Pew Research, July 22, 2014. http://www.pewhispanic.org/.

Phillips, David P. "The Influence of Suggestion on Suicide: Substantive and Theoretical Implications of the Werther Effect." *American Sociological Review* 39 (1974): 340–354.

Pickett, Kate, and Richard Wilkinson. *The Spirit Level: Why Greater Equality Makes Societies Stronger*. Reprint ed. New York: Bloomsbury, 2011.

Plotnik, Rod, and Haig Kouyoumdjian. *Introduction to Psychology*, 9th ed. Belmont, CA: Cengage Learning, 2010.

Plutarch, and William Watson Goodwin. *Plutarch's Lives*. Boston: Little, Brown, 1874.

Pokin, Steve. "'My Space' Hoax Ends with Suicide of Dardenne Prairie Teen." *St. Charles County Suburban Journal*, November 11, 2007. http://www.stltoday.com/suburban-journals/stcharles/news/stevepokin/my-space-hoax-ends-with-suicide-of-dardenne-prairie-teen/article_0304c09a-ab32-5931-9bb3-210a5d5dbd58.html.

"Police Witness Ends Life by Shot; P.B.A. Treasurer Dies in Bronx Park—Testified at Jury Inquiry into Funds." *The New York Times*, April 20, 1951, sec. A.

Potter-Efron, R. T. *Shame, Guilt and Alcoholism: Treatment Issues in Clinical Practice.* New York: Haworth Press, 1989.

Potter-Efron, Ronald T., and Donald E. Efron. "Three Models of Shame and Their Relation to the Addictive Process." *Alcoholism Treatment Quarterly* 10, no. 1–2 (August 6, 1993): 23–48.

Poulson, C. "Shame: The Master Emotion?" University of Tasmania, School of Management Working Paper Series. Hobart: University of Tasmania, 2000.

Prichard, Tom. "Gay Activists Manipulate Suicide Tragedy for Ideological Purposes." Minnesota Family Council, September 28, 2010. http://mnfamilycouncil. blogspot.com/2010/09/gay-activists-manipulate-suicide.html.

"Programs: Names Can Really Hurt Us." Anti-Defamation League, n.d. http:// regions.adl.org/connecticut/programs/names-can-really-hurt-us.html.

Pulkkinen, L. "Proactive and Reactive Aggression in Early Adolescence as Precursors to Anti and Prosocial Behavior in Young Adults." *Aggressive Behavior* 22, no. 4 (1996): 241–257.

Quillian, Lincoln. "New Approaches to Understanding Racial Prejudice and Discrimination." *Annual Review of Sociology* 32 (2006): 299–328.

Ransford, H. Edward. "Isolation, Powerlessness, and Violence: A Study of Attitudes and Participation in the Watts Riot." *American Journal of Sociology* 73, no. 5 (March 1, 1968): 581–591.

Ravilious, Kate. "Humans 80,000 Years Older than Previously Thought?" *National Geographic News*, December 3, 2008. http://news.nationalgeographic.com/new s/2008/12/081203-homo-sapien-missions.html.

Rea, Steven. "'55 School Killer: A Life Taken, Lived Film Spotlights Swarthmore, Forgiveness." *Philadelphia Inquirer*, April 13, 2007. http://articles.philly. com/2007-04-13/news/25241455_1_forgiveness-daughters-psychology.

Reeve, Arthur B. "Fortune Hunters (A Serialized Novel): Chapter IV, The Weed of Madness." *The San Francisco Chronicle*. January 17, 1923.

Reinhold, Robert. "After Shooting, Horror But Few Answers." *The New York Times*, January 19, 1989, http://www.nytimes.com/1989/01/19/us/ after-shooting-horror-but-few-answers.html.

Reinhold, Robert. "Killer Depicted as Loner Full of Hate." *The New York Times*, January 20, 1989, http://www.nytimes.com/1989/01/20/us/killer-depicted-as-loner-full-of-hate.html.

Rhee, Soo Hyun, and Irwin D. Waldman. "Genetic and Environmental Influences on Antisocial Behavior: A Meta-Analysis of Twin and Adoption Studies." *Psychological Bulletin* 128, no. 3 (May 2002): 490–529.

"Right-Wing Hysterical Over Hate Crimes Bill." US House, C-Span, 2009. http:// www.youtube.com/watch?v=7jgYFIG7BRg&feature=youtube_gdata_player.

Roth, Ariel A. "The Dishonor of Dueling." *Origins* 16, no. 1 (1989): 3–7.

Rousseau, Jean-Jacques. *Émile, Or, Treatise on Education.* Translated by William Harold Payne. New York: D. Appleton, 1892.

Rush, Benjamin. *An Inquiry into the Effects of Public Punishment Upon Criminals and Upon Society.* Philadelphia, PA: Joseph James, 1787.

"SaferSanerSchools: Transforming School Culture with Restorative Practices." Bethlehem, PA: International Institute for Restorative Practices.

"SaferSanerSchools: Whole-School Change Through Restorative Practices." Bethlehem, PA: International Institute of Restorative Practices, 2011. http://www.iirp.edu/pdf/WSC-Overview.pdf.

Scheff, Thomas J. *Emotions, the Social Bond, and Human Reality: Part/Whole Analysis.* Cambridge, UK: Cambridge University Press, 1997.

Scheff, Thomas. *Bloody Revenge: Emotions, Nationalism and War.* Lincoln, NE: iUniverse, 2000.

Scheff, Thomas J. "Social-Emotional Origins of Violence: A Theory of Multiple Killing." Unpublished manuscript, 2012.

Scheff, Thomas J., and Suzanne M. Retzinger. *Emotions and Violence.* Lincoln, NE: iUniverse, 2002.

Schlesinger, Louis B. "The Catathymic Crisis, 1912–Present: A Review and Clinical Study." *Aggression and Violent Behavior* 1, no. 4 (1996): 307–316.

Schott, Paul. "Names Day Program Targets Bullying." GreenwichTime.com, November 22, 2013. http://www.greenwichtime.com/news/article/Names-Day-program-targets-bullying-5003120.php.

Schott, Webster. "Civil Rights and the Homosexual: A 4-Million Minority Asks for Equal Rights." *New York Times Magazine*, November 12, 1967. http://query.nytimes.com/mem/archive/pdf?res=F30A11FB395B107B93C0A8178AD95F438685F9.

"Senator, Arrested at Airport, Pleads Guilty." *The New York Times*, August 28, 2007, http://www.nytimes.com/2007/08/28/washington/28craig.html.

"Senior Ends Life as Class Dances." *The New York Times*, May 23, 1936.

Shapiro, Thomas M., and Melvin L. Oliver. *Black Wealth/White Wealth: A New Perspective on Racial Inequality.* 1st ed. New York: Routledge, 1997.

Shaw, Gillian. "Amanda Todd's Mother Speaks Out About Daughter's Suicide." *Vancouver Sun*, October 14, 2012.

Shaw, Mary, Helena Tunstall, and Danny Dorling. "Increasing Inequalities in Risk of Murder in Britain: Trends in the Demographic and Spatial Distribution of Murder, 1981–2000." *Health & Place* 11, no. 1 (2005): 45–54.

Sheehan, Tim. *Shame.* Center City, MN: Hazelden, 2002.

Sinoski, Kelly. "Extraditing Dutch Man for Amanda Todd Case Could Take Years: Expert." *The Vancouver Sun*, April 19, 2014.

Smith, Cary Stacy. *The Patriot Act: Issues and Controversies.* Springfield, IL: Charles C Thomas, 2009.

Solomon, Robert C. *The Passions: Emotions and the Meaning of Life.* Indianapolis: Hackett, 1976.

Sourander, A. et al. "Childhood Bullying Behavior and Later Psychiatric Hospital and Psychopharmacologic Treatment: Findings from the Finnish 1981 Birth Cohort Study." *Archives of General Psychiatry* 66, no. 9 (September 1, 2009): 1005–1012.

Sourander, Andre, Peter Jensen, John A. Rönning, Solja Niemelä, Hans Helenius, Lauri Sillanmäki, Kirsti Kumpulainen, et al. "What Is the Early Adulthood Outcome of Boys Who Bully or Are Bullied in Childhood? The Finnish 'From a Boy to a Man' Study." *Pediatrics* 120, no. 2 (2007): 397–404.

Southern Poverty Law Center. *Jane Doe et al v. Anoka-Hennepin* (Complaint). US District Court: Court of Minnesota, 2011.

Stamp, Gavin. "Counting the Cost of the Slave Trade." BBC News, March 20, 2007, http://news.bbc.co.uk/2/hi/business/6422721.stm.

Stana, Richard M. *Secure Border Initiative Fence Construction Costs.* Darby, PA: Diane Publishing, 2009.

Stanton, Elizabeth Cady. "The Matriarchate Or Mother-Age: An Address of Mrs. Stanton Before the National Council of Women, February 1891. Voluntary Motherhood : Address of Mrs. Stanton Blatch Before the National Council of Women." Washington, DC: National Bulletin, 1891.

Starr, K., M. Hobart, and J. Fawcett. *Every Life Lost Is a Call for Change: Findings and Recommendations From the Washington State Domestic Violence Fatality Review.* Seattle: Washington State Coalition Against Domestic Violence, December 2004. http://www.wscadv.org.

"Statistics & Data." Honour Based Violence Awareness Network, n.d. http://hbv-awareness.com/.

Steinberg, Laurence. "Commentary: A Behavioral Scientist Looks at the Science of Adolescent Brain Development." *Brain and Cognition* 72, no. 1 (February 2010): 160–164.

Stout, David. "House Votes to Expand Hate-Crime Protection." *The New York Times,* May 4, 2007. http://www.nytimes.com/2007/05/04/washington/04hate.html.

Strauss, Valerie. "19 States Still Allow Corporal Punishment in School." *The Washington Post,* September 18, 2014. http://www.washingtonpost.com/blogs/answer-sheet/wp/2014/09/18/19-states-still-allow-corporal-punishment-in-school/.

Strommen, Erik F. "Family Member Reactions to the Disclosure of Homosexuality." *Journal of Homosexuality* 18, no. 1–2 (1989): 37–58.

Stubbs, J. "Beyond Apology? Domestic Violence and Critical Questions for Restorative Justice." *Criminology and Criminal Justice* 7, no. 2 (May 1, 2007): 169–187.

Sue, Derald Wing. *Microaggressions in Everyday Life: Race, Gender, and Sexual Orientation.* Hoboken, NJ: Wiley, 2010.

"Swarthmore Man Slain as a Hazer; Proctor, Infuriated by Pranks, Shoots Sleeping Student in Dormitory Rampage." *The New York Times.* January 12, 1955.

Tangney, J. P, and Ronda L. Dearing. "Working with Shame in the Therapy Hour: Summary and Integration." In *Shame in the Therapy Hour,* 1st ed., edited by Ronda L. Dearing and June Price Tangney. Washington, DC: American Psychological Association, 2011.

Taylor, Jeanette, Bryan R. Loney, Leonardo Bobadilla, William G. Iacono, and Matt McGue. "Genetic and Environmental Influences on Psychopathy Trait Dimensions in a Community Sample of Male Twins." *Journal of Abnormal Child Psychology* 31, no. 6 (2003): 633–645.

Teoh, Jin-Inn. "The Changing Psychopathology of Amok." *Psychiatry* 35, no. 4 (1972): 345–351.

Thandeka. *Learning to Be White: Money, Race and God in America.* New York: Continuum, 2000.

"The Bomber's Grievances Came to Light in a Series of Letters; Paper Received Notes; Text of His Correspondence to Journal-American Tells of Bitterness Over Injury Suspect's First Letter Sent From Westchester Final Communications." *The New York Times,* January 23, 1957. http://select.nytimes.com/gst/abstract.html?res=F60A11F63C5F147B93C1AB178AD85F438585F9.

The KJV Study Bible. Nashville: Barbour, 2011.

"The Rule of Thumb." *Woman's Hour.* London: BBC Radio, October 15, 2001. http://www.bbc.co.uk/radio4/womanshour/15_10_01/monday/info3.shtml

The Sentencing Project. "The Federal Prison Population: A Statistical Analysis." Washington, DC: The Sentencing Project, 2004. http://www.sentencingproject.org/doc/publications/inc_federalprisonpop.pdf.

Thurston, Robert. *The Witch Hunts: A History of the Witch Persecutions in Europe and North America.* 2nd ed. New York: Routledge, 2006.

Tobin, Kay, and Randy Wicker. *The Gay Crusaders.* New York: Arno Press, 1975.

Trent, Dolores J. "Wife Beating: A Psycho-Legal Analysis." *Women Lawyers Journal* 65 (1979): 9.

"Trillions Demanded in Slavery Reparations." BBC News, August 20, 1999, http://news.bbc.co.uk/2/hi/africa/424984.stm.

Truth and Reconciliation Commission. *Promotion of National Unity and Reconciliation Act 34 of 1995,* 1995. http://www.justice.gov.za/legislation/acts/1995-034.pdf.

Turner, Margery Austin, Michael Fix, and Raymond J. Struyk. *Opportunities Denied, Opportunities Diminished: Racial Discrimination in Hiring.* Washington, DC: Urban Institute Press, 1991.

Turner, Margery A., Stephen Ross, George C. Galster, and John Yinger. *Discrimination in Metropolitan Housing Markets: National Results from Phase 1 of the Housing Discrimination Study (HDS).* Working paper. Storrs: University of Connecticut, Department of Economics, 2002. http://ideas.repec.org/p/uct/uconnp/2002-16.html.

"UCLA Rejects Donald Sterling Gift." UCLA University News, April 29, 2014. http://newsroom.ucla.edu/releases/ucla-rejects-donald-sterling-gift.

"UCLA to Donald Sterling: We Don't Want Your Money!" TMZ Sports, April 29, 2014. http://www.tmz.com/2014/04/29/donald-sterling-ucla-gift-money-racist/.

US Bureau of Labor Statistics. *Labor Force Characteristics by Race and Ethnicity, 2012.* Washington, DC: US Bureau of Labor Statistics, October 2013. http://www.bls.gov/cps/cpsrace2012.pdf.

US Census Bureau. "U.S. and World Population Clock." US Census Bureau, n.d. http://www.census.gov/popclock/.

US Census Bureau. "USA Quick Facts from the US Census Bureau." *State & County Quick Facts,* 2014. http://quickfacts.census.gov/qfd/states/00000.html.

Venkatesh, Sudhir Alladi. *Off the Books: The Underground Economy of the Urban Poor.* Cambridge, MA: Harvard University Press, 2006.

Vera's Center on Sentencing, and Public Safety Performance Project of the Pew Center on the States. *The Price of Prisons: What Incarceration Costs Tax Payers.* New York: Vera Institute of Justice, January 2012. http://www.vera.org/sites/default/files/resources/downloads/the-price-of-prisons-40-fact-sheets-updated-072012.pdf.

Violence Policy Center. *When Men Murder Women: An Analysis of 2009 Homicide Data.* Washington, DC: Violence Policy Center, September 2011. http://www.vpc.org/studies/wmmw2011.pdf.

Von Kraft-Ebbing, Richard. *Psychopathia Sexualis.* Translated by Victor Robinson. Rochester, NY: Pioneer Publications, 1953.

Wachtel, Ted. "Defining Restorative." Bethlehem, PA: International Institute for Restorative Practices, 2013. http://djci4vzeaw44g.cloudfront.net/wp-content/uploads/sites/13/2014/04/A4_IIRP_Europe_Defining_Restorative.pdf.

Wagner, Dennis. "Minuteman's Goal: To Shame Feds into Action." *USA Today,* May 25, 2006. http://usatoday30.usatoday.com/news/nation/2006-05-24-minuteman-goals_x.htm.

Walker, Hunter. "Minuteman Founder Doesn't Want To Be Confused With Alleged Murderer." *New York Observer.* Accessed October 17, 2014. http://observer.com/2012/05/minuteman-founder-doesnt-want-to-be-confused-with-alleged-murderer/.

Wang, Jack. "Inside the Clippers." *Anderson Cooper 360°*. CNN, May 13, 2014. http://www. insidesocal.com/clippers/2014/05/13/full-transcript-donald-sterlings-interview-with-cnns-anderson-cooper/.

Watson, Angus. "Why I Used to Be a Bully." *The Telegraph*, June 7, 2004, http://www. telegraph.co.uk/education/educationnews/3340735/Why-I-used-to-be-a-bully.html.

Watson, Angus. "Experience: I Was a Bully." *The Guardian*, March 19, 2010, http:// www.guardian.co.uk/lifeandstyle/2010/mar/20/i-was-a-bully.

Weavil, Bambi. "Rare Interview with Sarah Lindstrom: 'We Gave Them Confidence to Come out & Be Themselves.'" *Out Impact*, February 17, 2011.

Webb, Kelly R. "Flogging." In *Encyclopedia of Prisons and Correctional Facilities*, edited by Mary Bosworth, 326–328. Thousand Oaks, CA: SAGE, 2004.

Wertham, F. "The Catathymic Crises." In *Violence: Perspectives on Murder and Aggression*, edited by I. L. Kutash, S. B. Kutash, and Louis B. Schlesinger, 165–70. San Francisco, CA: Jossey-Bass, 1978.

Widom, C. S. "Does Violence Beget Violence? A Critical Examination of the Literature." *Psychological Bulletin* 106, no. 1 (1989): 3–28.

Widom, C. S. "The Cycle of Violence." *Science* 244, no. 4901 (1989): 160–166.

Williams, Chris. "Sarah Lindstrom And Desiree Shelton, Lesbian Couple, Cheered By School After Winning Rights." *Huffington Post*, January 31, 2011. http://www.huffingtonpost. com/2011/02/01/sarah-lindstrom-desiree-shelton-lesbian-students_n_817057. html.

Williams, Edward Huntington. "Negro Cocaine 'Fiends' Are a New Southern Menace; Murder and Insanity Increasing Among Lower Class Blacks Because They Have Taken to 'Sniffing' Since Deprived of Whisky by Prohibition." *The New York Times*, February 8, 1914. http://query.nytimes.com/mem/archive-free/pdf?re s=9901E5D61F3BE633A2575BC0A9649C946596D6CF.

Wolfe, Samuel, and Shannon Minter. "Proposed Meeting to Resolve Claims." May 24, 2011. http://www.splcenter.org/sites/default/files/downloads/case/ Anoka-Hennepin-Letter.pdf.

Wolfe, Samuel, Shannon Minter, and Michael A. Ponto. "Letter from Southern Poverty Law Center Regarding Injunction on Behalf of Desiree Shelton and Sarah Lindstrom," January 28, 2011.

"Women CEOs of the Fortune 1000." Catalyst, July 14, 2014. http://www.catalyst. org/knowledge/women-ceos-fortune-1000.

Wood, David. "Bobby Henline, U.S. Soldier Saved From the Brink of Death, Pursues His Stand-Up Comedy Dreams (Video)." *Huffington Post*, October 21, 2011. http://www.huffingtonpost.com/2011/10/21/bobby-hemline-us-soldier-_n_1023916.html.

Wooldridge, Frosty. *Immigration's Unarmed Invasion: Deadly Consequences*. 1st edition. Bloomington, IN: AuthorHouse, 2004.

World Health Organization. "Understanding and Addressing Violence Against Women: Femicide." Geneva: World Health Organization, 2012. http://apps. who.int/iris/handle/10665/77421.

World Health Organization. "Understanding and Addressing Violence Against Women: Intimate Partner Violence." Geneva: World Health Organization, 2012. http://apps.who.int/iris/handle/10665/77432.

World Health Organization. *Preventing Suicide, a Global Imperative*. Geneva: World Health Organization, 2014.

Wrong, Dennis H. "The Oversocialized Conception of Man in Modern Sociology." *American Sociological Review* 26, no. 2 (1961): 183–193.

Wurmser, L. "Shame: The Veiled Companion of Narcissism." In *The Many Faces of Shame*, edited by D. L. Nathanson. New York: Guilford Press, 1987.

Yap, Pow Meng. "Classification of the Culture-Bound Reactive Syndromes." *Australasian Psychiatry* 1, no. 4 (1967): 172–179.

Zehr, Howard. *The Little Book of Restorative Justice*. Intercourse, PA: Good Books, 2002.

"Zillow Metrics (Counties): Homes Foreclosed (Out of 10k)—Anoka, MN." Accessed June 5, 2014. http://www.quandl.com/ZILLOW/MCOUNTY_ HOMESSOLDASFORECLOSURESRATIO_ALLHOMES_ANOKAMN- Zillow-Metrics-Counties-Homes-Foreclosed- Out-of-10k-Anoka-MN.

INDEX

Page numbers in italics indicate figures and tables.